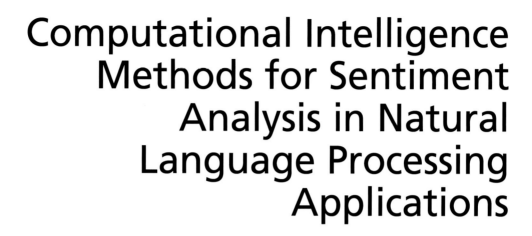

Computational Intelligence Methods for Sentiment Analysis in Natural Language Processing Applications

Computational Intelligence Methods for Sentiment Analysis in Natural Language Processing Applications

Edited by

D. Jude Hemanth

Department of ECE, Karunya Institute of Technology and Sciences, Coimbatore, Tamil Nadu, India

ISBN: 978-0-443-22009-8

For Information on all Morgan Kaufmann publications
visit our website at https://www.elsevier.com/books-and-journals

Publisher: Mara Conner
Acquisitions Editor: Chris Katsaropoulos
Editorial Project Manager: Tom Mearns
Production Project Manager: Neena S. Maheen
Cover Designer: Christian J. Bilbow

Typeset by MPS Limited, Chennai, India

Working together
to grow libraries in
developing countries

www.elsevier.com • www.bookaid.org

Contents

List of contributors

S. Balamurugan   School of Computers, Madanapalle Institute of Technology and Science, Madanapalle, Andhra Pradesh, India

Theresa V. Cherian   Computer Science and Engineering, Karunya Institute of Technology and Sciences, Coimbatore, Tamil Nadu, India

Sebastian Cippitelli   CI2S Labs, Buenos Aires, Argentina

Saroj S. Date   Department of Computer Science and IT, Dr. Babasaheb Ambedkar Marathwada University, Aurangabad, Maharashtra, India

Daniela López De Luise   CI2S Labs, Buenos Aires, Argentina

Sachin N. Deshmukh   Department of Computer Science and IT, Dr. Babasaheb Ambedkar Marathwada University, Aurangabad, Maharashtra, India

Mohammad Faiz   School of Computer Science & Engineering, Lovely Professional University, Phagwara, Punjab, India

Muskan Garg   Mayo Clinic, Rochester, MN, United States

Deepika Ghai   School of Electronics & Electrical Engineering, Lovely Professional University, Phagwara, Punjab, India

Vedika Gupta   Jindal Global Business School, O.P. Jindal Global University, Sonipat, Haryana, India

E. Gurumoorthi   Department of IT, CMR College of Engineering and Technology, Hyderabad, Telangana, India

S. Haseena   Department of Information Technology, Mepco Schlenk Engineering College, Sivakasi, Tamil Nadu, India

Immanuel Johnraja Jebadurai   Computer Science and Engineering, Karunya Institute of Technology and Sciences, Coimbatore, Tamil Nadu, India

Ranjit Kaur   School of Computer Applications, Lovely Professional University, Phagwara, Punjab, India

S. Lakshmi   SRM Institute of Science and Technology, Kattankulathur, Chennai, Tamil Nadu, India

P.M. Lavanya   Department of Computer Science & Engineering, SRM Institute of Science & Technology, Kattankulathur, Chennai, Tamil Nadu, India; Department of Information Technology, Easwari Engineering College, Ramapuram, Chennai, Tamil Nadu, India

R. Maruthamuthu   Department of Computer Applications, Madanapalle Institute of Technology and Science, Madanapalle, Andhra Pradesh, India

N. Naveenkumar   Department of Computer Applications, Madanapalle Institute of Technology and Science, Madanapalle, Andhra Pradesh, India

Getzi Jeba Leelipushpam Paulraj   Computer Science and Engineering, Karunya Institute of Technology and Sciences, Coimbatore, Tamil Nadu, India

Joyce Beryl Princess   Computer Science and Engineering, Karunya Institute of Technology and Sciences, Coimbatore, Tamil Nadu, India

Ramandeep Sandhu   School of Computer Science & Engineering, Lovely Professional University, Phagwara, Punjab, India

S. Saroja   Department of Computer Applications, National Institute of Technology, Trichy, Tamil Nadu, India

E. Sasikala   Department of Data Science & Business Systems, SRM Institute of Science & Technology Kattankulathur, Chennai, Tamil Nadu, India

Chandni Saxena   The Chinese University of Hong Kong, Ma Liu Shui, Hong Kong

Deepawali Sharma   Department of Computer Science, Banaras Hindu University, Varanasi, Uttar Pradesh, India

Shabari Shedthi B   Department of Computer Science and Engineering, NMAM Institute of Technology (Nitte Deemed to be University), Nitte, Karnataka, India

Mahesh B. Shelke   Bosch Global Software Technologies Pvt. Ltd., Pune, Maharashtra, India

Vidyasagar Shetty   Department of Mechanical Engineering, NMAM Institute of Technology (Nitte Deemed to be University), Nitte, Karnataka, India

Vivek Kumar Singh   Department of Computer Science, Banaras Hindu University, Varanasi, Uttar Pradesh, India

Kiran V. Sonkamble   Department of Computer Science and IT, Dr. Babasaheb Ambedkar Marathwada University, Aurangabad, Maharashtra, India

Ravi Shekhar Tiwari   École Centrale School of Engineering, Computer Science and Engineering, Mahindra University, Hyderabad, Telangana, India

Suman Lata Tripathi   School of Electronics & Electrical Engineering, Lovely Professional University, Phagwara, Punjab, India

V. Vijayalakshmi   Department of DSBS, Faculty of Engineering and Technology, SRM Institute of Science and Technology, Kattankulathur, Tamil Nadu, India

Gurleen Kaur Walia   School of Electronics & Electrical Engineering, Lovely Professional University, Phagwara, Punjab, India

Preface

Social media analytics has become superimportant in today's scenario with the rise in Internet technology. The impact of social media on day-to-day life is enormous with applications ranging from new connections formation to restaurant selection. Sentiment analysis is one of the application areas where a complete opinion on a specific entity is generated by artificial intelligence (AI) techniques. Sentiments which can be termed "opinions" may be positive or negative or neutral. The opinions are normally given in the form of text data which are a part of natural language processing (NLP). The opinions registered by the users on a specific subject is collectively analyzed to provide a final comment on the subject. Analyzing these data is a tedious task that can be solved by machine learning (ML) techniques. Hence, the combination of sentiments and ML techniques is extremely important to derive any information from the huge social media data. In this book, different types of ML and deep learning methods are explored in the context of different dimensions of sentiment analysis.

Chapter 1 provides an in-depth information on the basic concepts of ML and sentiment analysis. Different types of ML models are suitable for different sentiment analysis applications. These aspects are highlighted in this chapter along with the challenges and future scope of these methods. Deep learning is the advanced version of ML which is discussed in Chapter 2. The advantages of deep learning are explored in the context of aspect-based sentiment analysis. A complete package of text-based sentiment analysis is provided in Chapter 3. The merits and demerits of the different techniques are analyzed in detail. A different dimension of natural linguistic reasoning is discussed in Chapter 4. The concepts of rule-based systems in NLP are dealt in detail in this chapter.

Chapter 5 deals with the deep learning models for detecting the hate speeches in social media such as Twitter. Specifically, long-short-term memory methods are used in this work. Drug review classification from social data is the focal point of Chapter 6. Different NLP-based methodologies are used in this work to classify the input data. Chapter 7 discusses about the concepts of human behavior analysis. Emotion detection with text data is the main application area of this chapter. Different ML techniques are tested in this work and a detailed evaluation on these methods is provided in terms of the performance measures. Analyzing the opinions about movies is the base of the research works in Chapter 8. Different ML and optimization techniques are used in this work for the sentiment analysis. Since the rise of online platforms for movies, this type of analysis has gained high significance in the entertainment industry.

Customer feedback analysis on different products is discussed in Chapter 9. This type of sentiment analysis is very important for e-commerce-based applications. The ML methods concentrate on double negative sentence detection in this work. Sarcastic words/sentences are heavily used in all modes of communication, specifically in the social media. Deep learning—based methods are used to detect sarcasm in Chapter 10. Abusive comments are another unwanted concept in any language. The deep learning—based methods discussed in Chapter 11 are used to detect these comments in Tamil language. Stock market data-based sentiment analysis is elaborated in Chapter 12. Hateful and offensive contents on social media are detected using several AI-based approaches in Chapter 13.

I am thankful to the contributors and reviewers for their excellent contributions in this book. My special thanks to Elsevier, especially to Mr. Chris Katsaropoulos (Senior Acquisitions Editor) for the excellent collaboration. Finally, I would like to thank Mr. Tom Mearns who coordinated the entire proceedings. This edited book covers the fundamental concepts and application areas in detail. Being an interdisciplinary book, I hope it will be useful for both health professionals and computer scientists.

D. Jude Hemanth

Role of machine learning in sentiment analysis: trends, challenges, and future directions

Shabari Shedthi B[1], Vidyasagar Shetty[2]

[1]DEPARTMENT OF COMPUTER SCIENCE AND ENGINEERING, NMAM INSTITUTE OF TECHNOLOGY (NITTE DEEMED TO BE UNIVERSITY), NITTE, KARNATAKA, INDIA
[2]DEPARTMENT OF MECHANICAL ENGINEERING, NMAM INSTITUTE OF TECHNOLOGY (NITTE DEEMED TO BE UNIVERSITY), NITTE, KARNATAKA, INDIA

1.1 Introduction

Researchers are increasingly interested in analyzing and mining user sentiments due to the rapid expansion of the internet and the use of a variety of data-mining techniques. Sentiment analysis (SA) is one of the main study areas at present that combines data mining and natural language processing (NLP). The sentiments of users are mined using a variety of algorithms and opinion-mining techniques. The main contributions of this chapter give a detailed overview of SA, the various steps involved in it, the level of analysis, background information, and related work. It also provides studies of SA review, information about tools used, application challenges, and future directions for SA.

The structure of this chapter is as follows: the basics of SA and the level of analysis are covered in this section. The background research for SA is covered in the next section, i.e., Section 1.2. Performance metrics are discussed in Section 1.3, while Section 1.4 lists the tools available for SA. In Section 1.5, the main thrust areas of SA are discussed, and challenges are discussed in Section 1.6. We discuss conclusions in Section 1.7 and address the field's future directions in Section 1.8.

1.1.1 Fundamentals of sentiment analysis

The analytical study of people's ideas, emotions, sentiments, and attitudes is called SA [1]. Opinion mining or SA is used to study human emotions, and from that, we can derive insight. The term "sentiment analysis" perhaps first occurred in the study by Yi et al. [2], while the term "opinion mining" first appeared in the study by Dave et al. [3]. When making decisions—people, governments, companies, and social networks can all greatly benefit from and be

Computational Intelligence Methods for Sentiment Analysis in Natural Language Processing Applications
DOI: https://doi.org/10.1016/B978-0-443-22009-8.00011-2

influenced by the viewpoints of others. Opinions or sentiments associated with terms such as "evaluation," "appraisal," "attitude," "emotion," and "mood" that are related to them are all about our subjective thoughts and feelings. They both convey the same meaning. However, according to some experts, "opinion mining" and "SA" have slightly distinct ideas [4]. Sentiment is the key influencers of our behaviors. SA is a topic of study that uses various computer techniques to mine the opinions and attitudes of people from natural language text.

People express their feelings toward specific brands, products, services, people, companies, and organizations when talking about certain topics, societal issues, and several other topics. People use emojis on social media sites in addition to conventional texts to convey their emotions. Therefore, there are various methods of SA that are used to examine people's feelings. There are various methods for identifying sentiments, and the goal is to discover hidden sentiments in documents rather than texts [5]. Mainly, sentiments are categorized into "very positive," "positive," "neutral," "negative," and "very negative." That is shown in Fig. 1−1, and all the sentiments express human feelings toward the intended target.

SA primarily concentrates on beliefs that explicitly or implicitly convey positive or negative feelings, often known as "positive" or "negative" sentiments in ordinary language. Utilizing client comments to improve a product, service, or brand is possible through SA. When we mine user opinions about a specific product, for example, keywords such as "excellent," "amazing," or "good" indicate the users' positive feelings about the product, which helps build a favorable brand reputation. Customer opinion about a specific product, such as "very bad," "bad," or "worst," is indicated by keywords that indicate the user's negative feelings about the product, resulting in an unfavorable brand reputation. Neutral opinions are neither good nor bad, and neutral posts do not benefit or harm a brand's reputation. However, neutral training examples help learners

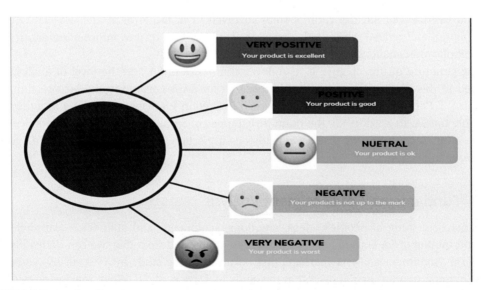

FIGURE 1–1 Types of sentiments.

to distinguish between positive and negative examples more effectively. Some sentiments are easiest to identify, and some are difficult to identify especially surprising sentiments.

The fast expansion of discussion forums, e-commerce platforms, product review sites, and social media channels has enabled a never-ending flow of ideas and viewpoints. Due to these numerous channels, companies find it difficult to compile opinions and attitudes about items. The growth of user-generated material on the internet and tools such as SA gives marketers the chance to learn more about how customers feel about their goods [6]. SA is essential for the business world since it helps companies refine their strategies and learn more about what their customers are saying about their products. Customer sentiment understanding is becoming more and more important in today's customer-focused company culture. SA can be used effectively used for understanding the entire attitude of the customer toward your company, its goods, or its services. Every customer displays his/her feelings in a unique way and different contexts, whether directly or indirectly.

Using three ways to keep track of or monitor customer sentiments, i.e.,

1. Reviews
2. Social media
3. Direct feedback.

Customers' ratings and reviews of products, services, and organizations are referred to as "customer review data." Marketing professionals can reach out to customers who need special attention by extracting emotions from product reviews, increasing customer satisfaction and sales, and ultimately benefiting the company [7]. Beyond only evaluating star ratings, modern technology enables the sentiment classification of reviews. In essence, opinion mining enables firms to comprehend a customer's attitude by analyzing the actual opinion within a review. SA provides information that allows you to customize your response rather than responding the same way to each review. Inferred from user reviews, sentiment trends could be revealed or extracted by algorithms. Extracting actionable insights from reviews helps the company grow in a positive direction by building a strong bond with customers.

Social media refers to a collection of online communication platforms that promote user-generated content, participation, and community involvement. People can use this social media to connect with one another, join a community of like-minded people, and then participate in the conversion. From a business perspective, if we think, we can listen and understand what is happening in the marketing place by analyzing the fact. Due to the high usage of social media among all age groups, much real-time data are generated, and using this, we can effectively mine the sentiments of people toward anything that is discussed through social media.

Direct feedback is acquired from customers by asking them about a company, a product, a customer service experience, or other touchpoints in the customer journey. Because consumers are brand ambassadors, it is a good idea to directly ask them about their experience with the business or the product. This helps the company to better understand its customers' needs. It gives clients a sense of value while also accurately portraying how they feel about the business. Social analytics should enable understanding of customer essentials in order to target or aim for new offers and products in a cost-effective manner via various social media channels. To enhance the brand, react more quickly with precise, timely, and pertinent insight into customer requests. It should also be highly scalable and be able to perform a robust search that can pull information from multiple social media channels, such as blogs, Twitter, Facebook, LinkedIn, and many others. This provides a stage for connecting and interacting with customers, promoting companies, and increasing website traffic. This helps grow business, and by analyzing data, the customer experience can be improved, which helps improve brand reputation among our competitors. Key performance indicator measures can be used ultimately make the business stronger. Social media experts have proposed some insights to improve the impact of social media on business, such as establishing precise objectives for each social media campaign and creating metrics based on those objectives to increase brand reputation. Using intelligent technologies [8], we can effectively get insight from acquired data, and we can compare performance by using different performance metrics (Fig. 1−2).

What are the five main steps of SA?

1. **Data gathering:** This is the first step of machine learning (ML). Data from various sources are collected and analyzed in order to extract the required insight. Data in plain text, JSON, XML, HTML, .xls, or .csv formats can be considered. Like data from various social media platforms, collected or already stored data can be used. The most popular social media SA platform is Twitter. This, in our opinion, is due to Twitter's well-organized application programming interfaces (APIs) and the abundance of R and Python packages that are readily available and facilitate data collection. Facebook limits data

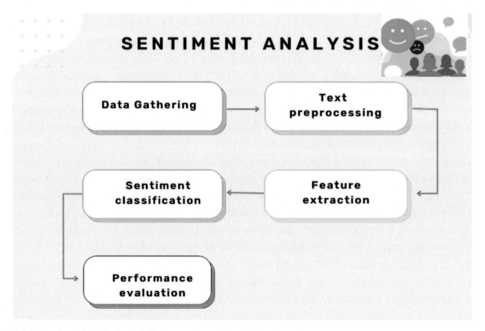

FIGURE 1–2 Sentiment analysis workflow.

imports, which makes it challenging to collect messages, feedback, and user engagement statistics.

2. **Text preprocessing:** In this step, data are preprocessed and made ready for further processing. The processing of the data will depend on the kind of information it has. This step is very important because the correctness of this step clearly implies the accuracy of the model. Stemming, lemmatization, tokenization, online text cleaning, spell correction, removing stop words, removing repeated words, etc. are done according to the requirement. We will be able to process the data and get it ready for analysis using text-cleaning techniques.

3. **Feature extraction:** Depending on the requirement, required features need to be extracted from the preprocessed data.

4. **Sentiment classification:** It is an automated approach to locating and classifying opinions in text. Various algorithms are used for the classification of various sentiments. For SA, lexicon-based, ML, and hybrid algorithmic approaches are used.

5. **Performance evaluation:** However, evaluating sentiments is a significant challenge, and getting good results is considerably harder than what people typically believe. An important part of accuracy measurement using SA is played by performance evaluation. SA employs evaluation metrics such as "accuracy, precision, recall, and F-score." Suitable performance metrics should be selected based on the dataset and algorithm used.

The selection of the optimal algorithm is still challenging because each technique has pros and cons, although numerous classifiers have been examined for SA purposes.

1.1.2 Level of analysis

SA can occur at one of the three levels, i.e., "document level, sentence level, or aspect level."

1.1.2.1 Document level

The objective of this level is to identify the document's general viewpoint. SA at the document level makes the assumption that each document contains opinions about a single subject. This type of SA is not commonly used. It can be applied to categorize a book's chapters or pages as good, negative, or neutral [9]. The feature vector in these tasks is a collection of words that must be constrained to the given domain (Fig. 1−3).

1.1.2.2 Sentence level

At this level, the challenge is to identify whether each sentence expresses an opinion or not. In this, actual facts are expressed in objective sentences, while opinions are expressed in subjective sentences. Solutions in this situation consist of two steps: first, determining whether or not the sentence communicated an opinion, and second, determining the polarity of that opinion. The major problem, however, is that objective statements might include subjective language. It is not enough to just understand that statements might be interpreted positively or negatively. This is a middle phase that assists in removing statements that lack opinion and, to a certain extent, assists in determining if opinions about things and their

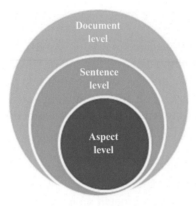

FIGURE 1–3 Level of analysis.

features are positive or negative. Although SA at the document and sentence levels is helpful, it does not reveal what people like or dislike nor identify opinion targets [10].

1.1.2.3 Aspect-level analysis

This level uses NLP and does a finer analysis. At this level, polarity and a target of thought define an opinion. In this situation, the solutions consist of two steps: first, identifying the item and its relevant elements, and second, evaluating the viewpoint on each aspect. Find out if an opinion is either "positive, negative, or neutral" by identifying and extracting object features that the opinion holder has focused on.

There are four separate tasks that consist of finding sentiments for aspects:

1. Text extraction: Extract words and sentences from reviews.
2. Sentiment classification: Use a sentiment classifier to identify extracted data that contain a positive, negative, or neutral sentiment.
3. Aspect extractor: Determine the polarity of each detected aspect and perform aspect term extraction for the ones that express a sentiment.
4. Aspect polarity aggregation: Combine the opinions expressed about the aspects to create a final summary.

1.2 Related background

SA is becoming very popular because of the rapid growth of internet-based applications and the extensive usage of social media and other sites. This huge amount of data cannot be controlled and analyzed effectively using the traditional way, so many researchers have developed efficient techniques to deal with it. Several recent surveys [9,11−14] addressed SA methods, applications, and challenges. The authors have outlined the issue of SA and suggested potential directions. Huge efforts are being made in the field of SA to address real-time commercial challenges. Existing SA methods are divided into four

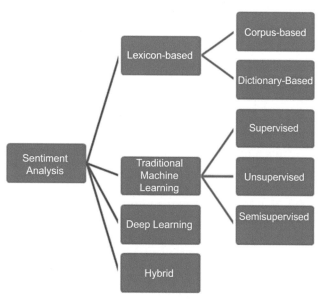

FIGURE 1–4 Approaches used for sentiment analysis.

primary classes: lexicon-based, traditional ML, deep learning (DL), and hybrid methods. (Fig. 1−4).

1.2.1 Lexicon-based approach

This approach aggregates the sentiment scores of all the terms in the document to assess a document using a pre-prepared sentiment lexicon [15,16]. Concerning the *lexicon-based approaches*, the first work was presented by Turney and Littman [17]. Dictionary- and corpus-based approaches are the two major methods used to tag subjective words with a semantic orientation.

1.2.1.1 Dictionary-based approach

The dictionary includes sentiments that have been expressed through words, phrases, or concepts. This method has the advantages of being straightforward and providing rich lexical relationships between words. The dictionary-based approach has a significant drawback in that it cannot identify opinion words with domain- and context-specific orientations and produces a huge number of false positives as a result of the dictionary's short entries.

1.2.1.2 Corpus-based approach

The challenge of discovering opinions with context-specific orientations is overcome by the corpus-based approach. When domains are distinct, the results are better. The main benefit of a corpus-based approach is this. They cannot be employed separately in this strategy due to the challenges of delivering substantial texts while still being able to cover all of the text terms.

To identify the semantic orientation of the text, lexicon-based approaches use adjectives and adverbs. In order to calculate any text orientation, adjective and adverb combination words are retrieved along with their "sentiment orientation value" [18]. For a particular review or text, the lexicon-based approach performs the score aggregation for each token, i.e., "positive," "negative," and "neutral" values are summed independently. The text is given an overall polarity in the final stage based on the maximum value of the individual scores. As a result, the text or document is first broken into single-word tokens; after that, each token's polarity is determined and then totaled. Domain dependence is a drawback of this approach [19].

Extracting sentiment from text using a lexicon-based method was presented by Taboada et al. in their paper [20]. The Semantic Orientation CALculator is used for the polarity classification task, which involves labeling texts positively or negatively based on how they feel about their major subject matter. This research has led us to the conclusion that lexicon-based SA techniques are reliable, produce good cross-domain results, and are simple to improve. However, their technique cannot analyze sarcasm.

The Serendio taxonomy was used by Palanisamy et al. [21] to create a lexicon-based technique for identifying feelings. "Positive, negative, negation, stop words, and phrases" make up the Serendio taxonomy. The lexicon-based approach for students' comments was implemented by Aung and Myo [22]. Positivity, negativity, and neutrality were successfully detected; the restriction was the inability to evaluate sarcasm. For the study of sentiment in news items, Taj et al. [23] offer a lexicon-based method. The trials were carried out using the BBC News dataset from 2004 to 2005, and it was discovered that the categories of business and sports had more positive items, while entertainment and tech had a preponderance of negative stories. Kundi et al. [24] used lexicons and dictionaries to create a framework for sentiment classification. Obtained an accuracy of 92% in binary classification and 87% accuracy in multi-class classification. However, lexicon-based approaches have the disadvantage of requiring human intervention during text analysis [25].

1.2.2 Machine learning

ML techniques have already been used to perform a major amount of research in the field of SA. In most cases, the ML approach outperforms the lexicon-based approach [26]. ML and NLP methods can be used for SA. ML techniques have previously been used extensively in the subject of SA, and it is now one of many computational study areas in NLP. There are three categories of ML techniques: unsupervised, supervised, and semi-supervised.

1.2.2.1 Unsupervised
Unsupervised learning techniques group related unlabeled data together. Unsupervised SA is crucial for many applications in social media since it is simple to gather enormous amounts of unlabeled data but very difficult and expensive to obtain labels of sentiment [27]. When

we do not have well-labeled datasets, the unsupervised learning technique can be used. Unsupervised dependency parsing was used by Fernández-Gavilanes et al. [28] to propose a strategy to predict sentiment in unstructured texts, and it demonstrated competitive performance. The "fuzzy rule-based" unsupervised technique for social media posts was used by Vashishtha and Susan [29]. When compared to the state of the art, they produced better results.

In order to assess Twitter feeds on the sentiments of a specific brand using the real dataset gathered over the course of a year, Hima and Gladston [30] suggested a novel fuzzy clustering approach. Then, using the metrics of accuracy, precision, recall, and execution time, a comparison is done with the currently used partitioning clustering approaches, K-means, and expectation maximization algorithms. The proposed method is tested to see if it can produce high-quality results for Twitter SA, according to the experimental analysis. In comparison of the two methods for extracting sentiment from tweets, Rout et al. [31] discovered that the proposed method was more precise than the lexicon-based method. For the SA of financial news, Yadav et al. [32] developed hybrid and noun−verb techniques and obtained good results.

1.2.2.2 Supervised

Its use of labeled datasets to train data classification algorithms defines it. When the output variable is categorical, that is, has two or more classes, classification is used. ML algorithms such as "Support Vector Machine (SVM)," "Naive Bayes (NB)," "Logistic Regression," "Random Forest," "Decision Tree," and "Artificial Neural Networks (ANN)" are extensively used for SA. Unlike topic-based categorization, which has an accuracy of 90% or higher, the paper [33] used ML classifiers such as "NB, maximum entropy, and SVM" to classify sentiment and achieved accuracy ranges of 75% to 83%. An extensive literature on algorithms used for analysis of Twitter and other social media has been produced by Ramesh and Weber [34]. When examining their studies, it became clear that the most popular algorithm used was SVM, which was followed by NB. Additionally, it has been noted that numerous studies compare accuracy levels using multiple algorithms. Li et al.'s [35] linear SVM model performed admirably, with an "F1 score of 83.4% and a mean AUC of 0.896." In addition, their algorithm revealed a pattern in email exchanges that was predicted from the emotion of unseen emails. SVM was also used by Ali et al. [36] to analyze Twitter tweet data for the experiment. They discovered that compiling opinions for microblogs was beneficial. For SA, Srivastava et al. [37] contrasted the lexicon and ML approaches. The SVM model outperforms when compared to supervised and unsupervised lexicon techniques, with an accuracy of 96.3% and lexicon accuracy of 88.7%.

When combined with other methods, the decision tree is employed in the work of Jain et al. [38] to identify genuine reviews from fake ones. One of the most popular computer intelligence methods for recognizing human emotion is ANN. Hemanth et al. performed human emotion analysis based on brain signals using neural networks. The shortcomings of conventional neural networks in terms of computational complexity and accuracy are addressed in this work by the "Circular Back Propagation Neural Network and Deep

Kohonen Neural Network." Future research will discuss the use of DL for recognizing human emotions. [39]. A model was put up by Yenkikar et al. [40] to use a unique feature extraction method to assess feelings in order to know consumer expectations, purchasing patterns, and product improvements. This work offers significant insights into developing a general expert system for SA can be used across industries and be extended to all social media platforms.

1.2.2.3 Semi-supervised

This learning method uses both unlabeled and labeled data during the training process. In comparison to supervised learning, this method can produce satisfactory accuracy while requiring less human input. In cross-domain and cross-language classification, unlabeled data can be used to extract domain or language-invariant characteristics, and labeled target data can be used to fine-tune the classifier. A semi-supervised strategy for POS tagging has been put forth by Rani et al. [41] that combines untagged text data with part-of-speech (POS) tagged corpora to create a classifier model using association rules. A paradigm for "semi-supervised learning" includes "pre-processing and classification" methods for unlabeled datasets [42]. Semi-supervised learning for sentiment classification was proposed by Lee et al. [43]. The unlabeled data are helpful in enhancing the data's performances, according to the results. It is not a guarantee, however, and unlabeled data must be handled carefully to avoid negatively affecting the model's performance. Sentiment prediction from this representation also appears to be consistently superior to other representations in both the Amazon and Yelp datasets, according to Park et al.'s semi-supervised distributed representation learning method [44].

SA using semi-supervised learning was introduced by Han et al. [45]. They provide a unique semi-supervised approach based on dynamic thresholds and multi-classifiers, and it works well to address the situation of insufficient initial labeled data. It was found that the unsupervised and supervised procedures combined outperformed the other approaches.

1.2.3 Deep learning

DL is a branch of ML that uses "ANN" to replicate how the human brain calculates data. It is a hierarchical ML system that combines numerous algorithms in a sequential chain of actions to solve complex issues, enabling you to process vast volumes of data accurately and with a minimum of human input. The DL algorithms all automatically achieve feature extraction. This motivates researchers to extract distinguishing features with the least amount of effort and knowledge possible [46]. DL can be used in situations where the amount of data is enormous and our limited reasoning power is needed [47]. SA is one such technique that falls under such techniques. SA now uses DL methods such as long-short-term memory (LSTM), bidirectional LSTM, and convolutional neural networks (CNN). Fig. 1−5 displays the differences between DL and traditional ML for categorizing sentiment polarity. ANN and DL now give the best answers to many problems in the fields of audio and image identification, as well as NLP [48].

While DL techniques such as CNN require fine tuning of initial parameters as a starting point, the training time will be large [49]. DL algorithms have shown excellent results and significant evolution in SA, but they need large data and a black box method. For sentiment

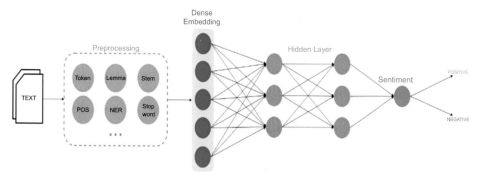

FIGURE 1–5 Two classification approaches of sentiment polarity, machine learning (*top*) and deep learning (*bottom*) [48].

classification, researchers are also combining different DL techniques. The LSTM and CNN DL networks were merged by Huang et al. [50]. For classifying short texts on top of word2-vec, Hassan and Mahmood [51] suggested an architecture dubbed ConvLstm that once again integrated CNN and LSTM. Dynamic memory networks were suggested by Zhang et al. [52] as a method for modeling target sentiment classification into Q&A systems. Deep belief networks (DBNs) with the delta rule were used by Jin et al. [53] for SA.

A review by Habimana et al. [54] was provided; it identifies current problems and suggests potential fixes for future research. Bidirectional encoder representations from transformers (BERT), cognition-based attention models, sentiment-specific word embedding models, commonsense knowledge, reinforcement learning, and generative adversarial networks are a few suggestions. To locate COVID-19-infected areas, Hasni and Faiz [55] suggested a DL model and found that employing bidirectional LSTM improved accuracy. Alsayat [25] constructed an LSTM network and presented a tailored DL model using an enhanced word embedding technique. Additionally, they put out an ensemble model for SA, which combines the basic classifier with additional cutting-edge classifiers.

The most significant work of SA using DL architectures has been done, according to the literature. SA uses the most successful and well-known DL models, including "CNNs, Rec NNs, recurrent neural networks (RNNs), LSTM, gated recurrent units (GRU), and DBN," among others. We may claim that SA using DL algorithms is a potential research area based on the thorough reviews of several DL-based systems and their good performances.

1.2.4 Hybrid approach

This strategy combines lexicon-based techniques with ML. A hybrid approach for SA of Twitter data was presented by Pandey et al. [56]. The random initialization issue in "cuckoo search" is addressed by a hybrid cuckoo search approach, which uses K-means to solve the random initialization of the population problem. The suggested algorithm outperformed five well-known algorithms, and it is also more accurate.

Combining lexicon-based and ML approaches, Mahmood et al. [57] trained two classifiers (NB and SVM classifiers) using the output from the lexicon-based approach as training data. Good accuracy was obtained for the hybrid strategy, which can significantly lower the cost of gathering exhaustive training data for use in the ML approach. A ML-based hybrid strategy incorporating random forest (RF) and SVM was suggested by Al Amrani et al. [58]. They demonstrated that the separate models of SVM and RF had accuracy of 81.01% and 82.03%, respectively, in the product review dataset provided by Amazon.com, while the hybrid model had an accuracy of 84%. A hybrid ML strategy using SVM and two feature selection strategies utilizing the multi-verse optimizer was developed by Hassonah et al. in their work [59]. A hybrid model (BERT−BiLSTM−TextCNN) was proposed by Jiang et al. [60] to improve the accuracy of text-based behavioral analysis of online comments.

1.3 Performance metrics

Metrics for evaluation are used to gauge the model's quality. For the performance assessment of SA systems based on unbalanced datasets, it would be wise to use information retrieval evaluation metrics such as precision, recall, and the F1-score. Another parameter that could be used to assess the effectiveness of systems trained on balanced datasets is accuracy. Other metrics that can be used to assess the degree of correlation between the output of SA systems and data labeled as ground truth include statistical measurements such as the Kappa statistic and Pearson correlation. The best metric should be selected based on how evenly the classes are distributed across the dataset [61].

The most common evaluation metrics used for SA are "precision, recall, F-score, and accuracy," which are described below:

- **Accuracy:** It is the degree of closeness between a measurement and its true value and it tells the fraction of predictions our model makes in the right way.

    Accuracy = Number of right predictions/total number of predictions.
- **Precision:** It describes the relationship between measurements of the same item. Precision gauges the model's correctness and is unrelated to accuracy. Lower false positives are indicated by higher precision.

    Precision = Number of true positives/all positives.

- **Recall:** It measures positive examples that the model accurately recognizes as positive; it is also known as sensitivity. A high recall value indicates that few positive cases were incorrectly classified as positives.

    Recall = True_positives/(true_positives + false_negatives).
- **F-Score or F1-measure:** It represents the harmonic mean of recall and precision.

    F1 Score = 2 × (Precision × Recall)/(Precision + Recall).

1.4 Tools for sentiment analysis

At present, industries are offering widespread tools for opinion mining for the purposes of data preprocessing, classification, clustering, SA, etc. SA tools offer a way to determine the mood of a team based on textual communication. There are a number of different SA tools that have been developed and applied in various contexts. An overview of the state of research on SA in software engineering is presented in a paper [62,63]. SentiStrength, Senti4SD, SentiStrength-SE, NLTK, SentiCR, CoreNLP, Vader, EmoTxt, Alchemy, BERT, DEVA, Syuzhet R, WNLU, and WordNet are some of the tools that are used for SA. Out of many tools, some of the most popular tools that use ML approaches are discussed below:

- **Senti4SD:** It is a classifier for emotion polarity that uses supervised learning developed to analyze sentiments in developers' communication channels. A gold standard of Stack Overflow questions, answers, and comments that have been carefully annotated for sentiment polarity is used to train and validate Senti4SD [64]. Also included in the toolbox is a training technique that allows the classifier to be customized using a gold standard as input. Any word entered into the tool yields a predicted label in the categories of "positive, neutral, or negative." According to the authors, the tool performed well with a small number of training documents (F1 = 0.84).
- **SentiCR:** It is a SA tool that makes use of a feature vector produced by computing the "bag of words" retrieved from the input text using the tf-idf algorithm. SentiCR is a program created especially for code reviews. SentiCR uses simple preprocessing to extend contractions, handle negations and emoticons, remove stop words, extract word stems, and remove code snippets from the raw input text. It employs a gradient boosting tree training methodology and reports that the tool has a mean accuracy of 0.83 [65].
- **CoreNLP:** Stanford CoreNLP is simple and straightforward. With the help of CoreNLP, users can generate linguistic annotations for text, such as "token and sentence borders, parts of speech, named entities, numerical and time values, dependency and constituency parses, coreference, sentiment, quote attributions, and relations." The models for ML components and several other data files are kept by Stanford CoreNLP in a separate models jar file [66].
- **EmoTxt:** It was specifically created to identify emotions rather than polarities, such as fear or joy. Stack Overflow and Jira were used to extract two large gold standard datasets

from text, which were then trained and tested. EmoTxt is an open-source toolkit that supports the training of individual emotion categorization models as well as emotion detection from text [67]. EmoTxt's classification model is trained with an SVM-supervised algorithm, and it achieves comparable performance with different datasets.

- **BERT:** BERT is a language representation model. By cooperatively conditioning on both left and right contexts in all layers, it is intended to pretrain deep bidirectional representations from unlabeled text [68]. By facilitating transfer learning with huge language models that can capture complicated textual patterns, BERT has advanced the state of the art for a wide range of NLP applications. In a survey paper [62], it was noted that neural network-based approaches, such as BERT, should be used because they outperform all other tools and approaches we looked into in terms of accuracy and F1 score. A huge improvement in model performance over older techniques. Senti4SD, SentiStrength, and SentiStrength-SE, the three most popular tools, all perform noticeably worse than BERT. BERT is conceptually simple and empirically powerful.

1.5 Trends of sentiment analysis

1.5.1 Social media monitoring

This involves keeping track of hashtags, keywords, and mentions that are pertinent to your company in order to learn more about your target market and sector. It is the process of identifying and determining what is being said about a brand, individual, or product through different social and online channels. Social media offers an opportunity to connect and inter-act with customers, promote brands, and drive traffic to the site. It creates collaboration among people, helps become an expert, and helps you stay relevant.

1.5.2 E-commerce

One of the most essential applications for analysis is the rating system of online stores where each product is rated and reviewed by the buyers. Depending on the kind of rating given by the buyers, the online stores suggest a list of recommended items for buyers so that they can increase the sales and revenue of the company. Knowing the sentiment of users toward a company's new products or services and that of their competitors guides better decision-making.

1.5.3 Voice of customer

This is used by businesses to describe the needs and requirements of their customers. The customer shares his/her experience with a product and communicates his/her opinion and attitude about it using natural language comments. This provides us with crucial insight into whether the consumer is satisfied and, if necessary, how we can improve the product. Listening and analysis of the voice or opinion of the customer helps improve the business.

1.5.4 Health care

SA can be applied in the medical domain in multiple ways. It allows health-care service providers to understand patients' opinions about their services and helps gauge patient satisfaction with the health services they have received. Through analysis, we can segment information based on various factors, such as departments or clinicians, to identify areas for patient care improvement. SA can improve health-care services in different ways, through higher patient satisfaction, better patient care, and more patient referrals.

1.5.5 Financial services

The analysis of financial news, particularly news referring to predicting the behavior and potential trend of stock markets, is the most typical use of SA in the financial industry. This assists people in making financial decisions.

1.5.6 Political elections

The concept of SA is widely used for predicting election results. By listening rather than asking, opinion mining makes sure that reality is accurately reflected. There are many voting guidance applications on the market that assist voters in researching the political landscape and other voters' perspectives.

1.5.7 Recommendation system

The customer uses comments in natural language to share his experience with a product and express his/her thoughts and attitudes toward it. This gives us vital information about whether the customer is happy and, if not, how we can enhance the product. The detailed method of catching a customer's expectations, preferences, and aversions is described by voice of the customer (VOC). It benefits the firm to pay attention to consumer feedback or opinions.

1.5.8 Employee retention

Determine the level of employee happiness by analyzing a lot of employee feedback data. The SA tool makes use of the insights to raise staff morale and efficiency while also letting you know how they are feeling. The SA of the employee helps keep talented and productive workers, and this promotes a positive work atmosphere. Through SA, we can reduce employee turnover.

1.6 Challenges
1.6.1 Data gathering

The unwillingness of some social media sites to make their data available to the public is the main obstacle to data collection for SA. Because Twitter is the only platform with available APIs for more extensive data collection, 80% of SA is performed on tweets.

1.6.2 Sarcasm text

One of the trickier NLP tasks is still detecting sarcasm in text. Human judgment is still far more accurate as a gauge in SA. Text may contain sarcastic sentences or hidden emotions. These emotions are hard to identify and may lead to erroneous opinion mining. Automated systems cannot differentiate sarcasm from sincere text, nor can they always correctly analyze the specific contextual meaning of a word.

1.6.3 Emojis

Emojis are commonly used on social media platforms in addition to standard text to express emotions. Emojis, however, are difficult to classify using SA methods that are written for textual phrases. The accuracy of our analysis will increase if we identify the emoji tags and include them in our SA system.

1.6.4 Polarity

Identifying the midpolarity words in text is a challenging task in SA. Words with strong positive $(+1)$ and negative (-1) polarity scores include "Good" and "Bad." These are simple concepts to comprehend. However, there are words that fall in the middle of the polarity spectrum, such as "Not bad" which can also indicate an average feeling. We need to handle such words carefully.

1.6.5 Incomplete information

A model for SA works well only when we provide it with complete and accurate data to work with. If information is missing, the built model may fail to complete the intended task, resulting in an incorrect result. Handling incomplete data is challenging, and this is a very important step in the SA phases.

1.6.6 Multimodal sentiment analysis

Different people have different ways of expressing their feelings or ideas. Earlier, the text was considered as the primary medium to express an opinion. This is known as a unimodal approach. With the advancement of technology and science, people are now shifting toward visual (videos, images, or clips) and audio (speech) modalities to express their sentiments. "Multimodal SA" refers to the process of combining or fusing more than one modality to detect an opinion. Hence, researchers are now focusing on this direction for improving the sentiment classification process.

1.6.7 Multilingual sentiment analysis

The vast majority of SA research has utilized datasets in English, but in social media, multilanguage data are available. NLP packages get help from built-in word lists in order to remove words that do not have a significant meaning. Built-in are available for other languages, but this is not expanded. Some sentiments, however, might be lost in translation because SA technologies are generally trained to classify words in a single language. When conducting SA on reviews or feedback in languages other than English, this creates a significant problem.

If we handle these challenges effectively, intelligent SA systems will be capable of handling semantic knowledge, making analogies, engaging in continuous learning, and detecting emotions, leading to highly efficient SA.

1.7 Conclusion

This chapter mainly gives a detailed idea of SA and its trends, challenges, and future directions with respect to ML. SA can be used effectively for brand building by effectively using social media, and this helps spur innovation in business. Today's technology allows for sentiment classification of reviews beyond just analyzing star ratings, and many algorithms have been effectively proven to handle complex sentiments. SA is not a single activity; it is a process, meaning that it contains a series of activities. Effective handling of each activity makes a serious impact on the overall performance of the SA. Data gathering is the first and foremost step of this analysis process, and it is an important step because data empower machines to make informed decisions. For SA, social media is the main source, so here we need to address the nature of social media data, i.e., that it is huge, noisy, and dynamic. Without solid data, algorithms are more likely to make mistakes and reach incorrect conclusions. In terms of sentiment, we can see it from two perspectives, i.e., who posts the opinion and who sees the opinion. In SA, conveyed information should be perceived in the same manner, and that decides the accuracy of the developed analysis. Till now, lots of ML algorithms have been applied to SA, as shown in most of the review papers published in this regard. Algorithms such as Logistic Regression, SVM, NB, Random Forest, K-Nearest Neighbor, Decision Trees, Maximum Entropy, Fuzzy Algorithms, CNN, RNNs, DBNs, and LSTM are some of the traditional ML and DL algorithms that are applied for SA.

According to the literature, the hybrid model sometimes outperforms traditional ML algorithms. DL is now spreading its wings to all fields, and it is also emerging in SA fields due to its added benefits. The SA established trends in brand monitoring, sales improvement, customer experience enhancements, decision-making, policy formulation, political analysis, and many other areas.

1.8 Future direction

SA is not a simple process to do manually. The ability to recognize the feelings of the text or find the hidden emotions behind the text is very important. DL is the current generation of technology, and this can be used for various tasks of SA. There has been very little work done in this technique with respect to SA; in the future, more work needs to be done on word embeddings, i.e., how sentiment information can be incorporated into its embeddings.

The majority of SA research has relied solely on textual modalities. Multimodal information fusion is a core component of multimodal SA. The selection of reliable fusion remains a significant future work. Fine-grained annotation can also open the door to novel multimodal fusion approaches because fine-grained annotations should better guide multimodal fusion methods. Thus, apart from incorporating star rating and user rating in the form of text, one can opt for an exhaustive rating of products with the help of multimodal data, where the reviews of a product can be incorporated using various modalities such as voice, image, or emoticon.

A little research has been carried out on handling code-mixed data in SA. Future directions can be taken to develop language models for code-mixed data. In the context of SA, utilizing commonsense for associating aspects with their sentiments can be highly beneficial for this task. There will be a new wave of research focusing on the role of commonsense knowledge in SA in the near future. One of the major areas that researchers can look into in the future is multilingual SA. Promoting NLP research on languages other than English helps many people.

References

[1] B. Liu, Sentiment analysis and opinion mining, Synth. Lect. Hum. Lang. Technol. 5 (1) (2012) 1−167.

[2] J. Yi et al., Sentiment analyzer: Extracting sentiments about a given topic using natural language processing techniques, in: Third IEEE International Conference on Data Mining, IEEE, 2003.

[3] K. Dave, S. Lawrence, D.M. Pennock, Mining the peanut gallery: Opinion extraction and semantic classification of product reviews, Proc. 12th Int. Conf. World Wide Web (2003).

[4] M. Tsytsarau, T. Palpanas, Survey on mining subjective data on the web, Data Min. Knowl. Discov. 24 (3) (2012) 478−514.

[5] M. Thelwall, K. Buckley, G. Paltoglou, D. Cai, A. Kappas, Sentiment strength detection in short informal text, J. Am. Soc. Inf. Sci. Technol. 61 (12) (2010) 2544−2558.

[6] M. Rambocas, B.G. Pacheco, Online sentiment analysis in marketing research: a review, J. Res. Interact. Mark. (2018) 146−163.

[7] V. Vyas, V. Uma, Approaches to sentiment analysis on product reviews, Sentiment Analysis and Knowledge Discovery in Contemporary Business, IGI Global, 2019, pp. 15−30.

[8] D.Jude Hemanth (Ed.), Human Behaviour Analysis Using Intelligent Systems, Springer International Publishing, 2020.

[9] M. Wankhade, A.C.S. Rao, C. Kulkarni, A survey on sentiment analysis methods, applications, and challenges, Artif. Intell. Rev. (2022) 1−50.

[10] A. Katrekar, A.V.P. Big Data Analytics, An Introduction to Sentiment Analysis, *GlobalLogic Inc.*, 2005.

[11] A.A.Q. Aqlan, B. Manjula, R. Lakshman Nail, A study of sentiment analysis: concepts, techniques, and challenges, Proceedings of International Conference on Computational Intelligence and Data Engineering, Springer, Singapore, 2019.

[12] A. Yousif, et al., A survey on sentiment analysis of scientific citations, Artif. Intell. Rev. 52 (3) (2019) 1805−1838.

[13] M. Birjali, M. Kasri, A. Beni-Hssane, A comprehensive survey on sentiment analysis: approaches, challenges and trends, Knowl. Syst. 226 (2021) 107134.

[14]   A. Ligthart, C. Catal, B. Tekinerdogan, Systematic reviews in sentiment analysis: a tertiary study, Artif. Intell. Rev. 54 (7) (2021) 4997–5053.

[15]   C.M. Whissell, The dictionary of affect in language, The Measurement of Emotions, Academic Press, 1989, pp. 113–131.

[16]   V. Hatzivassiloglou, K. McKeown, Predicting the semantic orientation of adjectives," in: 35th Annual Meeting of the Association for Computational Linguistics and 8th Conference of the European Chapter of the Association for Computational Linguistics, 1997.

[17]   P.D. Turney, M.L. Littman, Measuring praise and criticism: Inference of semantic orientation from association, ACM Trans. Inf. Syst. (TOIS) 21 (4) (2003) 315–346.

[18]   N. Gupta, R. Agrawal, Chapter 1: application and techniques of opinion mining, Hybrid Comput. Intell. (2020) 1–23.

[19]   A. Moreo, et al., Lexicon-based comments-oriented news sentiment analyzer system, Expert. Syst. Appl. 39 (10) (2012) 9166–9180.

[20]   M. Taboada, J. Brooke, M. Tofiloski, K. Voll, M. Stede, "Lexicon-based methods for sentiment analysis, Comput. Linguist. 37 (2) (2011) 267–307.

[21]   P. Palanisamy, V. Yadav, H. Elchuri, Serendio: simple and practical lexicon based approach to sentiment analysis, in: Second Joint Conference on Lexical and Computational Semantics (*SEM), Volume 2: Proceedings of the Seventh International Workshop on Semantic Evaluation (SemEval 2013), 2013.

[22]   K.Z. Aung, N.N. Myo, Sentiment analysis of students' comment using lexicon based approach, in: 2017 IEEE/ACIS 16th International Conference on Computer and Information Science (ICIS), IEEE, 2017.

[23]   S. Taj, B.B. Shaikh, A.F. Meghji, Sentiment analysis of news articles: a lexicon based approach, in: 2019 2nd International Conference on Computing, Mathematics and Engineering Technologies (iCoMET), IEEE, 2019.

[24]   F.M. Kundi, et al., Lexicon-based sentiment analysis in the social web, J. Basic. Appl. Sci. Res. 4 (6) (2014) 238–248.

[25]   A. Alsayat, Improving sentiment analysis for social media applications using an ensemble deep learning language model, Arab. J. Sci. Eng. 47 (2) (2022) 2499–2511.

[26]   A. Patil, G. Shiwani, A review on sentiment analysis approaches, Int. Conf. Workshop Commun. Comput. Virtualiz. (2015).

[27]   X. Hu, et al., Unsupervised sentiment analysis with emotional signals, Proc. 22nd Int. Conf. World Wide Web (2013).

[28]   M. Fernández-Gavilanes, T. Álvarez-López, J. Juncal-Martínez, E. Costa-Montenegro, F.J. González-Castaño, Unsupervised method for sentiment analysis in online texts, Expert. Syst. Appl. 58 (2016) 57–75.

[29]   S. Vashishtha, S. Susan, Fuzzy rule based unsupervised sentiment analysis from social media posts, Expert. Syst. Appl. 138 (2019) 112834.

[30]   H. Suresh, An unsupervised fuzzy clustering method for twitter sentiment analysis, in: 2016 International Conference on Computation System and Information Technology for Sustainable Solutions (CSITSS), IEEE, 2016, pp. 80–85.

[31]   J.K. Rout, K.-K.R. Choo, A.K. Dash, S. Bakshi, S.K. Jena, K.L. Williams, A model for sentiment and emotion analysis of unstructured social media text, Electron. Commer. Res. 18 (1) (2018) 181–199.

[32]   A. Yadav, C.K. Jha, A. Sharan, V. Vaish, Sentiment analysis of financial news using unsupervised approach, Procedia Comput. Sci. 167 (2020) 589–598.

[33]   B. Pang, L. Lee, S. Vaithyanathan, Thumbs up? sentiment classification using machine learning techniques, in: Proceedings of the 2002 Conference on Empirical Methods in Natural Language Processing (EMNLP), 2002.

[34]   B. Ramesh, C.M. Weber, State-of-art methods used in sentiment analysis: a literature review, in: 2022 Portland International Conference on Management of Engineering and Technology (PICMET), IEEE, 2022.

[35] F. Li, et al., Comparative study on vulnerability assessment for urban buried gas pipeline network based on SVM and ANN methods, Process. Saf. Environ. Prot. 122 (2019) 23−32.

[36] S.M. Ali, et al., Topic and sentiment aware microblog summarization for twitter, J. Intell. Inf. Syst. 54 (1) (2020) 129−156.

[37] R. Srivastava, P.K. Bharti, P. Verma, Comparative analysis of lexicon and machine learning approach for sentiment analysis, Int. J. Adv. Comp. Sci. Appl. 13 (3) (2022).

[38] P.K. Jain, R. Pamula, S. Ansari, A supervised machine learning approach for the credibility assessment of user-generated content, Wirel. Personal. Commun. 118 (4) (2021) 2469−2485.

[39] D. Hemanth, Jude, J. Anitha, Brain signal based human emotion analysis by circular back propagation and deep Kohonen neural networks, Comp. Electr. Eng. 68 (2018) 170−180.

[40] A. Yenkikar, C.N. Babu, D.J. Hemanth, Semantic relational machine learning model for sentiment analysis using cascade feature selection and heterogeneous classifier ensemble, PeerJ Comput. Sci. (2022) 2022.

[41] P. Rani, V. Pudi, D.M. Sharma, A semi-supervised associative classification method for POS tagging, Int. J. Data Sci. Anal. 1 (2) (2016) 123−136.

[42] F. Janjua, et al., Textual analysis of traitor-based dataset through semi supervised machine learning, Future Gener. Comput. Syst. 125 (2021) 652−660.

[43] V.L.S. Lee, K.H. Gan, T.P. Tan, R. Abdullah, Semi-supervised learning for sentiment classification using small number of labeled data, Procedia Comput. Sci. 161 (2019) 577−584.

[44] S. Park, J. Lee, K. Kim, Semi-supervised distributed representations of documents for sentiment analysis, Neural Netw. 119 (2019) 139−150.

[45] Y. Han, Y. Liu, Z. Jin, Sentiment analysis via semi-supervised learning: a model based on dynamic threshold and multi-classifiers, Neural Comput. Appl. 32 (9) (2020) 5117−5129.

[46] Y. LeCun, Y. Bengio, G. Hinton, Deep learning, Nature 521 (7553) (2015) 436−444.

[47] L. Alzubaidi, J. Zhang, A.J. Humaidi, A. Al-Dujaili, Y. Duan, O. Al-Shamma, et al., Review of deep learning: concepts, CNN architectures, challenges, applications, future directions, J. Big Data 8 (1) (2021) 1−74.

[48] N.C. Dang, M.N. Moreno-García, F.Dla Prieta, Sentiment analysis based on deep learning: a comparative study, Electronics 9 (3) (2020) 483.

[49] A. Yadav, D.K. Vishwakarma, Sentiment analysis using deep learning architectures: a review, Artif. Intell. Rev. 53 (6) (2020) 4335−4385.

[50] Q. Huang et al. Deep sentiment representation based on CNN and LSTM, in: 2017 International Conference on Green Informatics (ICGI), IEEE, 2017.

[51] A. Hassan, A. Mahmood Deep learning approach for sentiment analysis of short texts, in: 2017 3rd International Conference on Control, Automation and Robotics (ICCAR), IEEE, 2017.

[52] Z. Zhang, et al., The optimally designed dynamic memory networks for targeted sentiment classification, Neurocomputing 309 (2018) 36−45.

[53] Y. Jin, H. Zhang, D. Du Improving deep belief networks via delta rule for sentiment classification, in: 2016 IEEE 28th International Conference on Tools with Artificial Intelligence (ICTAI), IEEE, 2016.

[54] O. Habimana, et al., Sentiment analysis using deep learning approaches: an overview, Sci. China Inf. Sci. 63 (1) (2020) 1−36.

[55] S. Hasni, S. Faiz, Word embeddings and deep learning for location prediction: tracking Coronavirus from British and American tweets, Soc. Netw. Anal. Min. 11 (1) (2021) 1−20.

[56] A.C. Pandey, D.S. Rajpoot, M. Saraswat, Twitter sentiment analysis using hybrid cuckoo search method, Inf. Process. Manag. 53 (4) (2017) 764−779.

[57] Alaa THAMER Mahmood, Siti Sakira Kamaruddin, Naser Raed Kamil, Maslinda Mohd Nadzir, A combination of lexicon and machine learning approaches for sentiment analysis on facebook, J. Syst. Manag. Sci. 10 (3) (2020) 140−150.

[58] Y. Al Amrani, M. Lazaar, K.E.E. Kadiri, Random forest and support vector machine based hybrid approach to sentiment analysis, Procedia Comput. Sci. 127 (2018) 511−520.

[59] M.A. Hassonah, et al., An efficient hybrid filter and evolutionary wrapper approach for sentiment analysis of various topics on Twitter, Knowl. Syst. 192 (2020) 105353.

[60] X. Jiang, et al., Research on sentiment classification for netizens based on the BERT-BiLSTM-TextCNN model, PeerJ Comput. Sci. 8 (2022) e1005.

[61] Z. Kastrati, et al., Sentiment analysis of students' feedback with NLP and deep learning: a systematic mapping study, Appl. Sci. 11 (9) (2021) 3986.

[62] M. Obaidi, et al., Sentiment analysis tools in software engineering: a systematic mapping study, Inf. Softw. Technol. (2022) 107018.

[63] N. Novielli, et al., Assessment of off-the-shelf SE-specific sentiment analysis tools: an extended replication study, Empir. Softw. Eng. 26 (4) (2021) 1−29.

[64] L. Calefato, F. Calefato, F. Lanubile, F. Maiorano, N. Novielli, Sentiment polarity detection for software development, Empir. Softw. Eng. 23 (3) (2018) 1352−1382.

[65] T. Ahmed et al. SentiCR: a customized sentiment analysis tool for code review interactions, in: 2017 32nd IEEE/ACM International Conference on Automated Software Engineering (ASE). IEEE, 2017.

[66] C.D. Manning et al., The Stanford CoreNLP natural language processing toolkit, in: Proceedings of 52nd Annual Meeting of the Association for Computational Linguistics: System Demonstrations, 2014.

[67] F. Calefato, F. Lanubile, N. Novielli EmoTxt: a toolkit for emotion recognition from text, in: 2017 Seventh International Conference on Affective Computing and Intelligent Interaction Workshops and Demos (ACIIW), IEEE, 2017.

[68] J. Devlin et al. Bert: Pre-training of deep bidirectional transformers for language understanding, arXiv preprint arXiv:1810.04805 (2018).

2

A comparative analysis of machine learning and deep learning techniques for aspect-based sentiment analysis

Theresa V. Cherian, Getzi Jeba Leelipushpam Paulraj,
Joyce Beryl Princess, Immanuel Johnraja Jebadurai

COMPUTER SCIENCE AND ENGINEERING, KARUNYA INSTITUTE OF TECHNOLOGY AND
SCIENCES, COIMBATORE, TAMIL NADU, INDIA

2.1 Introduction

Natural language processing (NLP) is a branch of computer science that aims to create machines that can comprehend voice and data and educates the machine to react to voice and data. It offers a variety of applications by fusing linguistics with computer science and artificial intelligence (AI). Digital assistants, dictation software, and chatbots are a few NLP applications [1]. Tasks of NLP include speech recognition, speech tagging, named entity recognition, sentiment analysis (SA), and natural language generation. In NLP, data analysis can be performed in several ways as follows [1]. (1) Topic analysis: topic analysis, also referred to as topic identification, topic modeling, or topic extraction, is a technique for categorizing and organizing huge collections of word data by the topic or theme of each text. (2) Time series analysis: this statistical technique analyzes historical data over a predetermined period to predict the future. It consists of an evenly spaced-out ordered series of data. (3) SA: SA, generally referred to as opinion mining or emotion AI, is the systematic identification, extraction, quantification, and study of affective states and subjective data using NLP, text analysis, computational linguistics, and biometrics. (4) Network analysis: network methods including Bayesian networks, neural networks, and radial basis function networks are used to analyze data.

Customer evaluations, survey results, and user reactions in online and social media are all subjected to SA, a widely used technique that enhances corporate operations and clinical practice. SA is an NLP task that mines text to extract subjective data to assist the business in understanding the preferences of its customers. SA is widely used by companies to analyze trends, access competitors, and predict the future trending market.

Computational Intelligence Methods for Sentiment Analysis in Natural Language Processing Applications
DOI: https://doi.org/10.1016/B978-0-443-22009-8.00006-9

2.2 Steps in sentiment analysis

The following are many steps in SA [2].

2.2.1 Data collection

Using application programming interfaces, data are retrieved from various sources including product reviews, movie reviews, social media, and business industries. During the phase of data collection, NLP technologies are used to process the fetched data, which then moves on to the preprocessing stage.

2.2.2 Data preprocessing

Using application programming interfaces, data are retrieved from various sources such as blogs, websites, and social media during data collecting. The data are preprocessed to remove null values, stop words, symbols, and other outliers.

2.2.3 Sentiment detection

Different sentences are formed from the preprocessed data, which are then classified into various categories such as subjective and objective. To specifically classify the text, the objective expression must be excised.

2.2.4 Sentiment classification

The category of subjective sentences is further processed using suitable machine learning (ML) or deep learning (DL) algorithms for analyzing various sentiments, such as positive, negative, neutral, good, bad, like, and dislike.

2.2.5 Output preparation

The performed algorithms are further assessed and sharpened for better performance. Various data visualization tools will be used for representing the outputs in the form of different data visualization, such as graphs and charts.

2.3 Applications of sentiment analysis

SA has its application in various fields, viz., social media, business, pharmaceutical, and politics.

2.3.1 Social media

Users register to social media and register their views in terms of news feeds, photographs, and videos. These data are analyzed for sentiments to recommend videos and advertisements to the users.

2.3.2 Business

Businesses collect data from various levels of their customers. Product reviews, customer opinions, and surveys are analyzed to understand the trends and predict product demands. This also enables the business to make a profit and be beneficial to the targeted customers.

2.3.3 Pharmaceutical industry

Users' opinions about drug usage, side effects, and results are shared on the social media page. These data are collected through web scrapping and analyzed to understand drug usage by drug manufacturers. This enables further research and design of drugs.

2.3.4 Politics

Political campaigns are greatly driven by SA. The tweets in social media have been used for predicting the election results. It is also analyzed and even used for political decision inversion in many cases.

2.4 Types of sentiment analysis

Types of SA are sentence-based SA, document-based SA, and aspect-based SA (ABSA) [2].

- Sentence-based SA
  - In sentence-based SA, the entire sentence is analyzed and the opinion is extracted.
- Document-based SA
  - The document as a whole is analyzed for sentiments.
- ABSA
  - Sentence-level and document-level SAs do not provide accurate classification. For example, consider the following example:
    "The food is tasty, but the waiter is rude"
  - In the aforementioned example, there are two aspects: food and service. It rates the food positively and service with a negative opinion. This finer opinion can be captured only using ABSA.

2.5 Aspect-based sentiment analysis

ABSA extracts the aspects in every sentence and also predicts the sentiment associated with those aspects. Various ML and DL techniques have been deployed in analyzing sentiments.

2.5.1 Machine learning-based approaches

In ML-based approaches, ABSA involves two tasks: aspect extraction and sentiment classification. The aspects are extracted using feature extraction techniques and classified using ML approaches.

2.5.1.1 Simple machine learning–based aspect-based sentiment analysis

Various techniques proposed in the literature are discussed as follows. A gradual ML approach to solve the inaccuracy of manual labeling has been proposed in ref [3]. In this approach, easy instances are labeled by the machine, and using an iterative factor graph, the most challenging instances are labeled. Lexical, morphological, syntactic, and semantic elements were extracted, and they were then classified using ML methods to enhance the ABSA of Arabic hotel reviews [4]. Specifically, naive Bayes, Bayes networks, decision tree, K-nearest neighbor, and support vector machine (SVM) classifiers are used to accomplish aspect category identification, opinion target expression extraction, and sentiment polarity identification. Precision, recall, F1-score, and ROC are employed as performance measurements.

2.5.1.2 Machine learning approaches using hybrid technique and support vector machine

ML-based customer analysis has been proposed in ref [5]. Data are extracted using application programming interfaces (APIs) and preprocessed. The preprocessed data are normalized and features are extracted which are then processed to predict customer behavior using a hybrid recommendation system. ML-based SA for Amazon products has been discussed in ref [6]. Amazon customer reviews are web crawled and processed for stemming, tokenization, casing, and stop word removal. The features are extracted and classified using an SVM. ABSA using a hybrid approach has been proposed in ref [7]. Manually annotated government smart apps dataset is taken and preprocessed to obtain clean data. Aspects are extracted and scored. After aspect scoring, a hybrid approach of ML classifiers has been implemented to classify the sentiments. A new, enhanced AdaBoost strategy for doing SA on US airline Twitter data was proposed [8]. An AdaBoost-based SVM is used to classify the attitudes once features are extracted. Precision, recall, and F-score are employed as performance indicators.

2.5.1.3 Machine learning approaches using naïve Bayes methods

Product reviews are categorized using different ML techniques in SA on product reviews using ML techniques [9]. After comparing the preprocessed data with the opinion lexicon and calculating the emotion score, all the extraneous characters will be removed in the preprocessing stage. The reviews are categorized using SVM and naive Bayes methods. The performance indicators examined are accuracy. In ref [10], SA in the sales review of the Indonesian market by applying an SVM has been proposed. Features are extracted using the term frequency-inverse document frequency method (TF-IDF). Using SVMs and naive Bayes, the text is classified.

There are some observed challenges in ML-based aspect-level SA by considering the works of literature are:

- Most of the techniques are domain dependent.
  Example: specific to movie reviews, product reviews, and government data.
- A huge lexicon needs a complex algorithm for accurate aspect-level detection.
- Feature extraction increases the time complexity of the process.

Several approaches have been proposed using ML techniques for ABSA. The comparative analysis of a few ML approaches has been summarized in Table 2−1. In all these approaches, the labor-intensive aspect extraction phase takes place. This two-step process makes SA time-consuming.

Table 2–1 Summary of ML-based ABSA.

Reference	Method	Dataset	Performance metrics	Future works
Simple ML-based ABSA [3]	Gradual ML for unlabeled data	SemEval 2015 Task 12 and 2016 Task 5	Accuracy	Improvise with less human intervention, can be incorporated into the classification task
Hybrid technique [5]	Hybrid recommendation system	Web crawled dataset	MAPE	To collect user preferences across multiple geographical locations
SVM method [6]	SA using SVM	Web crawled Amazon data	MSE, accuracy, precision, recall	Can be implemented on other applications
Hybrid technique [7]	Hybrid approach–based ABSA	Government data	Precision, recall, F1-score, and accuracy	
Naïve Bayes method [9]	ML-based SA	Amazon review data	Accuracy	Can be improved with ABSA
SVM method [10]	SVM-based SA	Indonesian online shop dataset	Accuracy	Can be improved with polarity-based ABSA
SVM method [8]	AdaBoost-based SA	US airline dataset	Precision, recall, F1-score, and accuracy	Can be experimented with for other models
[4]	ML sentiment classifiers	SemEval 2016 Task 5	Precision, recall, F1-score, and accuracy	Deep neural networks can be employed

2.5.2 Deep learning-based approaches

In recent years, DL-based architectures have been implemented in SA.

As shown in Fig. 2−1, classical NLP involves preprocessing and modeling handled by a series of algorithms. However, in DL, the entire process is handled by a series of input, hidden, and output layers. Hence, DL-based approaches have caught the attention in SA in recent years. The below section reviews various DL-based SAs.

2.5.2.1 Convolutional neural network—based aspect-based sentiment analysis

Convolutional neural network (CNN) has been used widely for SA [11]. CNN consists of various steps such as preprocessing text by removing unwanted characters, vectorization, defining, training, and testing the model. The first phase of SA is called data preprocessing, in which tokenization is performed using the NLTK tokenizer. During this process, collected documents or various data are pruned into words. Also, unwanted characters, symbols, notations, and punctuations will be removed from the data. In the next phase, stop words will be eliminated from the documents. A collection of stop words from the NLTK library will be downloaded to perform this task. Lemmatization is the process of detecting the context or meaning of the word and converting it into its base form which is performed in the phase of text classification. Vectorization is also an important process

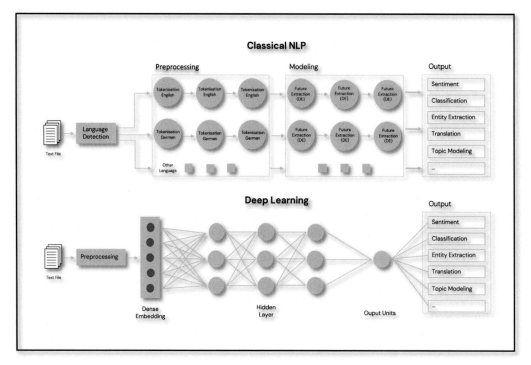

FIGURE 2–1 Comparison of classiceal and deep learning-based sentiment analysis.

performed during this phase, where words will be converted into real numbers. Various techniques are used to perform this task such as a bag of words, TF-IDF, and Google Word2vec.

They have presented a unique approach for ABSA utilizing parameterized filters and parameterized gates in parameterized CNNs for aspect-level sentiment categorization [12]. To extract aspect information, parameterized filters and parameterized gates are introduced. CNN receives the extracted data and classifies it. Accuracy is the performance metric employed in this study.

2.5.2.2 Attention-based aspect-based sentiment analysis

To create a collaborative extraction hierarchical attention network for ABSA, the approach CE-HEAT: an aspect-level sentiment classification approach with collaborative extraction hierarchical attention network [13] is proposed.

Two hierarchical attention units make up a hierarchical attention network for collaborative extraction. A single unit employs the sentiment attention layer to extract the sentiment features and the aspect attention layer to extract the specific aspect-related sentiment data. The other unit employs the aspect characteristics extracted from the aspect attention layer to obtain aspect-specific sentiment data from the sentiment attention layer. Error analysis is utilized as a performance metric. The construction of a neural attentive network for cross-domain aspect-level sentiment classification is proposed [14]. To recognize the domain information of input texts and transfer knowledge from the source domain to the target domain, a domain classifier analyzes documents in both the source and target domains. The domain classifier and an aspect-level sentiment classifier share the document modeling. Performance indicators such as accuracy and F1-score have been employed. The approach is tested using the datasets from SemEval 2015 and SemEval 2016. Convolutional multi-head self-attention on memory for aspect sentiment classification has been offered as a method by them [15].

To address the issue where the memory network overlooks the semantic information of the sequence itself, a multi-head self-attention has been implemented in this article. The network's parallelism is maintained using recurrent neural networks, long short-term memory (LSTM), and gated recurrent unit models. Accuracy and F1-score are the performance measurements employed. The suggested technique is tested using SemEval 2014 Task 4, SemEval 2015 Task 12, and SemEval 2016 Task 5. An innovative aspect-context interactive representation structure that simply uses an attention mechanism to generate sequence-to-sequence representations in both context and aspect was proposed by Zhuojia et al.[16] as a method for aspect-level sentiment classification. They have created sequence-to-sequence representations of attributes and contexts using several aspect context interactive attention (ACIA) blocks layered structures. Residual connection and standardized completely connected layers have been adopted between two ACIA blocks. Accuracy and the F1-score are employed as performance measurements.

The SemEval 2014 Task4 datasets, Restaurant and Laptop, and Twitter datasets were used. The relationship between the aspect term and the sentence it corresponds to can be strengthened by a bidirectional attention mechanism. Accuracy and the chosen SemEval 2014 Task4 and SemEval 2017 Task4 datasets are utilized as performance measures. It is suggested that educators use a multi-attention fusion modeling (Multi-AFM) for SA of educational big data [17] to perform SA, which enables educators to quickly ascertain the true feelings of students about the course and promptly adjust the lesson plan to enhance the caliber of instruction. A Multi-AFM model is mainly composed of four parts: (1) an aspect-aware sentence representation layer, (2) a memory modeling layer, (3) an attention layer, and (4) a gating layer. The suggested method uses accuracy, precision, recall, and F1-score as performance indicators. The proposed method's effectiveness is tested using the education and course datasets. Comprehensive syntactic information is proposed to be encoded for ABSA using a relational graph attention network (R-GAT) [18]. By reshaping and pruning a standard dependency parse tree, a unified aspect-oriented dependency tree structure with a target aspect as its root is offered. To encapsulate the new tree structure for sentiment prediction, an R-GAT is built. Accuracy and macro-F1 are performance metrics that are used to evaluate the approach.

Performance analysis of the approach is conducted using the SemEval 2014 and Twitter datasets. To efficiently extract the plethora of data available in sentences and perform aspect-level sentiment classification using mutual attention neural networks, researchers developed the MAN: mutual attention neural networks model for aspect-level sentiment classification in SIoT [19].

Bidirectional LSTM (Bi-LSTM) networks to obtain semantic dependence of sentences and their respective aspect terms. While learning the sentiment polarities of aspect terms in sentences by proposing the mutual attention mechanism. Accuracy and macro-F1 are the performance metrics used. The laptop and restaurant datasets from SemEval 2014 are used as a dataset in the testing phase. Transformer-based multi-grained attention network (T-MGAN) for ABSA [20] is a T-MGAN, which utilizes the transformer module to learn the word-level representations of aspects and context. The transformer encoder and tree transformer encoder are combined with specific subtasks and utilize T-MGAN to model the word-level and phrase-level features of aspects and contexts. The dual-pooling method is used to extract the key features in the hidden layer features of aspect and context. The attention mechanism is used multiple times to effectively obtain the fine-grained associated emotional features between the specific aspect and the context. Accuracy and macro-F1 are the performance matrices used and the datasets are laptop, restaurant, and Twitter datasets. The first two datasets are from SemEval 2014. Enhancing attention-based LSTM with position context for aspect-level sentiment classification [21] is proposed to devise position-aware attention-based LSTM. PosATT-LSTM, a novel attentive LSTM model, not only incorporates the position-aware vectors but also considers the significance of each context word. It illustrates the clear relationship between the aspect's context words and its location context. Accuracy is the performance metric here. Used as datasets are the SemEval 2014 laptop and restaurant datasets. For ABSA, attention and lexicon-regularized LSTM [22] are proposed to take advantage of lexical information and make the model more adaptable and reliable.

To merge lexicon information with an attention LSTM model for ABSA to leverage both the power of deep neural networks and existing linguistic resources so that the framework becomes more flexible and robust without requiring additional labeled data. Mean accuracy is the performance metric used and the datasets are SemEval 2014 Task4, restaurant domain dataset. R-transformer network based on position and self-attention mechanism for aspect-level sentiment classification [23] proposed a PSRTN model for aspect-level sentiment classification. For extracting the position-aware influence propagation between words and aspects using the Gaussian kernel and creating the impact vector for each context word, the PSRTN model for aspect-level sentiment classification is applied. Using the R-transformer to capture both global and local context information, and the self-attention mechanism to get the keyword in the aspect. For classification, context representation of a specific aspect is generated. The datasets utilized are SemEval 2014 and the Twitter dataset, and accuracy is the chosen performance metric. A target-dependent graph attention neural network for aspect-level sentiment classification was proposed by Syntax-aware aspect-level sentiment classification with graph attention networks [24]. It is a unique target-dependent graph attention network that propagates emotional features directly from the syntactic context of an aspect target while explicitly utilizing the dependency relationship between words. Accuracy is the performance metric used and the datasets are SemEval 2014 and Twitter dataset. A comparative analysis of the DL-based technique has been summarized in Table 2−2.

2.5.2.3 Long short-term memory -based aspect-based sentiment analysis

Feature-enhanced attention and aspect-based sentiment classification suggested using CNN-Bi-LSTM [27] to extract a higher-level phrase representation sequence from the embedding layer, which effectively supports subsequent coding tasks. Bi-LSTM has been proposed to capture both local aspects of phrases and global and temporal sentence semantics to enhance the quality of context encoding and maintain semantic information. To concentrate on those keywords of targets and learn more effective context representation, an attention mechanism has been developed to describe interaction links between aspect words and phrases. The dataset used to evaluate the algorithm is SemEval 2014 Task4, which includes the restaurant and laptop and Twitter dataset. The performance indicator utilized is accuracy.

A proposed lexicon-enhanced attention network for aspect-level SA [25] uses lexicons to improve its attentional capabilities. A Bi-LSTM-based lexicon-enhanced attention network model that makes use of a high-quality sentiment lexicon to determine the emotional polarity of a statement in a particular context. Performance analysis of the approach is conducted using the SemEval 2014 and Twitter datasets. Dynamically selecting the context memory is a deep selective memory network with selective attention and inter-aspect modeling for aspect-level sentiment categorization [28]. The distance information between an aspect and its context is used to propose a selective attention mechanism. To gather a wealth of aspect-aware context information, deep selective memory network (DSMN) concentrates on various context memory regions in various memory network levels. The performance measurements are accuracy and macro-F1. The approach is tested on the laptop, Twitter, and restaurant datasets.

Table 2-2 Summary of DL-based ABSA.

Reference	Method	Dataset	Performance metrics	Future work
Attention-based ABSA [14]	Cross-domain aspect-based sentiment classification	Both English (SemEval 2014, SemEval 2015, and SemEval 2016 data) and Chinese datasets (Dianping data)	Error analysis	To boost the performance of cross-domain aspect-level SA by simulating the human reading cognitive process
Attention-based ABSA [15]	Convolutional multi-head self-attention memory network	SemEval 2014s laptop and restaurant review dataset and SemEval 2016s tweets dataset	Accuracy	Memory modules in semantic information representation, and synthetically analyze their aspects according to the scores outputted by different memory modules
LSTM-based ABSA [25]	A lexicon-enhanced attention network for aspect-level SA	SemEval 2014 Task 4 (restaurant and laptop datasets)	Accuracy	—
Attention-based ABSA [18]	R-GAT for ABSA	SemEval 2014 and Twitter datasets	Error analysis	—
Attention-based ABSA [20]	T-MGAN for ABSA	Laptop, restaurant (SemEval 2014), and Twitter	Accuracy	More colloquial texts on social platforms such as Twitter, and propose a more suitable model structure for this type of text
[26]	A survey on ABSA: tasks, methods, and challenges	SemEval 2014, SemEval 2015, and SemEval 2016 (laptops and restaurants datasets)	Accuracy, F1-scores	Advances in cross-domain and cross-lingual ABSA can lead to more practical ABSA systems

2.6 Performance metrics

The following performance indicators are used to compare the enhanced classification methods utilizing the feature selection method:

1. Accuracy: The ratio of cases that were correctly categorized to all occurrences is known as accuracy. Equation contains the accuracy formula $(2-1)$:

$$\text{Accuracy} = \frac{TP + TN}{TP + FP + FN + TN} \qquad (2-1)$$

The following terms are used concerning the metrics:
When an actual true situation is accurately predicted as true, this is known as a true positive (TP). When actual false situations are correctly identified as false, this is known as a true negative (TN). False-positive (FP) situations occur when actual false cases are incorrectly identified as true cases. False negatives (FN) are situations in which actual true cases are incorrectly predicted as false.

2. Precision: The accuracy is calculated as the ratio of positive samples that were correctly classified to all samples that were classified as positive (either correctly or incorrectly). The precision measures how effectively the model aims to classify a sample as positive. The number of accurate predictions that are positive. The ratio of successfully predicted positive examples to the total number of correctly predicted positive examples is used to calculate the precision. Precision $= TP/(TP + FP)$, where TP is the true positive and FP is the false positive.

3. Recall: Recall is a metric that determines the ratio of accurate positive predictions among all possible positive predictions. Recall gives an indicator of missed positive predictions, unlike precision, which only comments on the accurate positive predictions out of all positive predictions. The percentage of observed positive cases is known as recall. It is calculated by dividing TPs by the total number of TPs and FN. Recall $= TP/(TP + FN)$, where TP is the true positives, and FN is the false negatives.

4. F-measure: It can be derived from the values of precision and recall. The equation used for calculating-measure is given below: F-measure $= (2 \times \text{Precision} \times \text{Recall})/(\text{Precision} + \text{Recall})$.

2.7 Datasets

The dataset is a crucial component of DL-based ABSA. Traditional datasets such as SemEval 2014, 2015, and 2016 have been available for analyzing the performance metrics of algorithms, or domain-specific datasets can be scrapped for analysis.

2.7.1 Domain-specific dataset

Data from news feeds of social media, blogs, chats, and other websites are scrapped using APIs and web scrapping tools such as big data query language [29–32]. The collected data are cleaned and processed for further analysis. The data have to be manually or programmatically annotated for usage.

2.7.2 Language-specific datasets

Few research papers have worked on ABSA in specific languages and domains. This enables us to analyze the culture and needs and understand the behavior of people living in those regions. ABSA in this domain has also enabled to enhance the tourism and business in specific locations [4,10,33,34].

2.7.3 SemEval datasets

SemEval 2014 consists of over 6000 sentences having reviews about laptops and restaurants. They have polarity as positive, negative, neutral, and conflicts. SemEval 2015 is a continuation of the previous version. They have a continuous sentence of review rather than individual sentences. SemEval 2016 is the latest dataset with five domains and eight languages. The English language is present in the Restaurant16 section of the dataset.

2.8 Future research challenges

2.8.1 Domain adaptation

In general, handling unlabeled datasets affects the efficiency of the aspect extraction process, and extending it to a new domain may lead to error. However, if an establishment mechanism is used to carry out cross-domain transfer learning, model interpretations could be improved through pretraining and fine-tuning. Because self-attention networks may combine input words in conjunction with their context and positional information, they are capable of handling complex information [35]. Advancements in text representation, such as linguistic and statistical characteristics, label propagation, and efficient semisupervised learning, are required to tackle this challenge [29,30].

2.8.2 Multilingual application

To improve cross-lingual alignment on the target data which are not labeled to confirm the significance of language-specific information for the ABSA problem [26,31,34]. The limitations of multilingual SA include word sense ambiguity, language-specific structure, and translation errors.

2.8.3 Unified model for multiple tasks

ABSA is focused on directions that are expressed in natural language and sometimes necessitate a significant amount of human effort. To this objective, fuzzy suggestions or directives may be thought of as a replacement for automated prompt design, which may be discovered from data collected during downstream task training [26,32]. It is necessary to create an integrated model that can handle several ABSA tasks at once.

2.8.4 Syntax-aware and position-aware model

Numerous tests have shown that a model that is both syntax- and position-aware can efficiently condense the useful word dependency paths to extract the relevant syntax- and position-related concepts separately [33]. Future studies should also be mindful of adopting transformer-based related models and utilizing multi-class SA [31] to my fine-grained sentiment polarity, such as happy, joy, rage, and disgust [36]. Building a fusion model which allows the combination of Syntax and position-aware model is needed.

2.9 Conclusion

DL is an advanced branch of ML that excels in SA in terms of performance and adaptability. In several areas, including domain adaption, multilingual application, unified model for many tasks, syntax, and position awareness, DL outperforms ML. DL can be used to devise a unified aspect-level SA approach considering cross-domain. This paper describes various ML and DL algorithms and discusses significant challenges and inferences. Compared to various classical NLP techniques, ABSA greatly benefits from the use of DL. DL techniques can also be used in multilingual applications and cross-domain features. Various performance matrices are discussed in this paper based on various proposed methods. However, future research directions are also covered in this study to increase the analysis's accuracy.

References

[1] J. Zhou, J.X. Huang, Q. Chen, Q.V. Hu, T. Wang, L. He, Deep learning for aspect-level sentiment classification: survey, vision, and challenges, IEEE Access. 7 (2019) 78454−78483. Available from: https://doi.org/10.1109/ACCESS.2019.2920075.

[2] H. Liu et al., Aspect-based sentiment analysis: a survey of 7 (6) (2020) 1358−1375.

[3] Y. Wang, Q. Chen, J. Shen, B. Hou, M. Ahmed, Z. Li, Aspect-level sentiment analysis based on gradual machine learning, Knowl. Syst. 212 (2021) 106509. Available from: https://doi.org/10.1016/j.knosys.2020.106509.

[4] M. Al-Smadi, M. Al-Ayyoub, Y. Jararweh, O. Qawasmeh, Enhancing aspect-based sentiment analysis of Arabic hotels' reviews using morphological, syntactic and semantic features, Inf. Process. Manag. 56 (2) (2019) 308−319. Available from: https://doi.org/10.1016/j.ipm.2018.01.006.

[5] S. Yi, X. Liu, Machine learning based customer sentiment analysis for recommending shoppers, shops based on customers' review, Complex. Intell. Syst. 6 (3) (2020) 621−634. Available from: https://doi.org/10.1007/s40747-020-00155-2.

[6] N. Nandal, R. Tanwar, J. Pruthi, Machine learning based aspect level sentiment analysis for Amazon products, Spat. Inf. Res. 28 (5) (2020) 601−607. Available from: https://doi.org/10.1007/s41324-020-00320-2.

[7] O. Alqaryouti, N. Siyam, A.A. Monem, K. Shaalan, Aspect-based sentiment analysis using smart government review data, Appl. Comput. Inform. (2019). Available from: https://doi.org/10.1016/j.aci.2019.11.003.

[8] E. Prabhakar, M. Santhosh, A.H. Krishnan, T. Kumar, R. Sudhakar B B Student, Sentiment analysis of US Airline Twitter data using new Adaboost approach, Int. J. Eng. Res. Technol. 7 (01) (2019) 1−3. Available from: http://www.ijert.org.

[9] R.S. Jagdale, V.S. Shirsat, S.N. Deshmukh, Sentiment analysis on product reviews using machine learning techniquesno. January 768, Springer Singapore, 2019.

[10] A.A. Lutfi, A.E. Permanasari, S. Fauziati, Sentiment analysis in the sales review of Indonesian marketplace by utilizing support vector machine, J. Inf. Syst. Eng. Bus. Intell. 4 (1) (2018) 57. Available from: https://doi.org/10.20473/jisebi.4.1.57-64.

[11] H.T. Phan, N.T. Nguyen, D. Hwang, Convolutional attention neural network over graph structures for improving the performance of aspect-level sentiment analysis, Inf. Sci. (Ny). 589 (2022) 416−439. Available from: https://doi.org/10.1016/j.ins.2021.12.127.

[12] H. Binxuan, K.M. Carley, Parameterized convolutional neural networks for aspect level sentiment classification, arXiv Prepr. arXiv 1909 (2019) 06276.

[13] G. Yang, et al., CE-HEAT: an aspect-level sentiment classification approach with collaborative extraction hierarchical attention network, IEEE Access. 7 (2019) 168548−168556.

[14] Y. Min, et al., Neural attentive network for cross-domain aspect-level sentiment classification, IEEE Trans. Affect. Comput. 12 (3) (2019) 761−775.

[15] Z. Yaojie, B. Xu, T. Zhao, Convolutional multi-head self-attention on memory for aspect sentiment classification, IEEE/CAA J. Autom. Sin. 7 (4) (2020) 1038−1044.

[16] W. Zhuojia, et al., Aspect-context interactive attention representation for aspect-level sentiment classification, IEEE Access. 8 (2020) 29238−29248.

[17] Z. Guanlin, et al., Multi-attention fusion modeling for sentiment analysis of educational big data, Big Data Min. Anal. 3 (4) (2020) 311−319.

[18] W. Kai, et al., Relational graph attention network for aspect-based sentiment analysis, arXiv Prepr. arXiv 2004 (12362) (2020).

[19] J. Nan, et al., MAN: mutual attention neural networks model for aspect-level sentiment classification in SIoT, IEEE Internet of Things J. 7 (4) (2020) 2901−2913.

[20] S. Jiahui, et al., Transformer based multi-grained attention network for aspect-based sentiment analysis, IEEE Access. 8 (2020) 211152−211163.

[21] Z. Jiangfeng, X. Ma, K. Zhou, Enhancing attention-based LSTM with position context for aspect-level sentiment classification, IEEE Access. 7 (2019) 20462−20471.

[22] B. Lingxian, P. Lambert, T. Badia, Attention and lexicon regularized LSTM for aspect-based sentiment analysis, in: Proceedings of the 57th Annual Meeting of the Association for Computational Linguistics: Student Research Workshop, 2019.

[23] Z. Ziyu, Q. Wang, R-transformer network based on position and self-attention mechanism for aspect-level sentiment classification, IEEE Access. 7 (2019) 127754−127764.

[24] H. Binxuan, K.M. Carley., Syntax-aware aspect level sentiment classification with graph attention networks, arXiv Prepr. arXiv 1909 (2019) 02606.

[25] R. Zhiying, et al., A lexicon-enhanced attention network for aspect-level sentiment analysis, IEEE Access. 8 (2020) 93464−93471.

[26] W. Zhang, X. Li, Y. Deng, L. Bing, W. Lam, A survey on aspect-based sentiment analysis: tasks, methods, and challenges, arXiv:2203.01054v2 [cs.CL] 6 Nov 2022.

[27] M. Wei, et al., Aspect based sentiment analysis with feature enhanced attention CNN-BiLSTM, IEEE Access. 7 (2019) 167240−167249.

[28] L. Peiqin, M. Yang, J. Lai, Deep selective memory network with selective attention and inter-aspect modeling for aspect level sentiment classification, IEEE/ACM Trans. Audio, Speech, Lang. Process. 29 (2021) 1093−1106.

[29] M.K. Das, D. Singh, S. Sharma, Media news on vaccines and vaccination: the content profile, sentiment, and trend of the online mass media during 2015−2020 in India, Clin. Epidemiol. Glob. Heal. 10 (January) (2021) 100691. Available from: https://doi.org/10.1016/j.cegh.2020.100691.

[30] Neha, H. Gupta, S. Pande, A. Khamparia, V. Bhagat, N. Karale, Twitter sentiment analysis using deep learning, IOP Conf. Ser. Mater. Sci. Eng. 1022 (1) (2021). Available from: https://doi.org/10.1088/1757-899X/1022/1/012114.

[31] S. Cunningham-Nelson, M. Baktashmotlagh, W. Boles, Visualizing student opinion through text analysis, IEEE Trans. Educ. 62 (4) (2019) 305−311. Available from: https://doi.org/10.1109/TE.2019.2924385.

[32] Q. Hou, M. Han, Z. Cai, Survey on data analysis in social media: a practical application aspect, Big Data Min. Anal. 3 (4) (2020) 259−279. Available from: https://doi.org/10.26599/BDMA.2020.9020006.

[33] M. AL-Smadi, M.M. Hammad, S.A. Al-Zboon, S. AL-Tawalbeh, E. Cambria, Gated recurrent unit with multilingual universal sentence encoder for Arabic aspect-based sentiment analysis, Knowl. Syst. (2021) 107540. Available from: https://doi.org/10.1016/j.knosys.2021.107540.

[34] J. Zhang, X. Lu, D. Liu, Deriving customer preferences for hotels based on aspect-level sentiment analysis of online reviews, Electron. Commer. Res. Appl. 49 (September) (2021). Available from: https://doi.org/10.1016/j.elerap.2021.101094.

[35] N. Singha, U.C. Jaiswalb, Cross domain sentiment analysis techniques and challenges: a survey, in: India 4th International Conference on Communication and Information Processing, (ICCIP-2022). Available on: SSRN.

[36] G. Zhai, Y. Yang, H. Wang, S. Du, Multi-attention fusion modeling for sentiment analysis of educational big data, Big Data Mining Anal. 3(4) (2020) 311−319. Available from: https://doi.org/10.26599/BDMA.2020.9020024. ISSN 2096-0654 06/06.

A systematic survey on text-based dimensional sentiment analysis: advancements, challenges, and future directions

Saroj S. Date[1], Mahesh B. Shelke[2], Kiran V. Sonkamble[1], Sachin N. Deshmukh[1]

[1]DEPARTMENT OF COMPUTER SCIENCE AND IT, DR. BABASAHEB AMBEDKAR MARATHWADA UNIVERSITY, AURANGABAD, MAHARASHTRA, INDIA [2]BOSCH GLOBAL SOFTWARE TECHNOLOGIES PVT. LTD., PUNE, MAHARASHTRA, INDIA

3.1 Introduction

Sentiment analysis has been one of the most significant as well as the most appealing research topics for the last two decades. There are numerous research studies that have analyzed sentiments. Their primary goal is to identify if the statement(s) is(are) positive, negative, or neutral. This aids in assessing people's views through their words and writing. People's everyday language use may reveal a wealth of information about their thought processes, beliefs, anxieties, social interactions, and personalities. Researchers in this domain are increasingly demonstrating the significant linguistic and psychological importance of human language. Pang and Lee pioneered the usage of machine learning (ML) approaches for sentiment analysis. Maximum entropy, support vector machines (SVMs), and naive Bayes (NB) classifiers were used to categorize the movie reviews. With the SVM classifier and unigram features, they were 82.9% accurate [1]. Automatically recognizing affective information from texts is the purpose of sentiment analysis. In a broad sense, dimensional approach and categorical approach are the two primary ways used to depict affective states of information [2].

The dimensional approach toward sentiment analysis specifies affective states using continuous numerical values on several dimensions such as the valence-arousal (VA) space, whereas the categorical method denotes affective states as discrete classes such as positive, negative, or neutral [3]. The level of pleasant (positive) and unpleasant (negative) feelings is known as valence. The extent of excitement and calmness is measured by arousal. Any emotional state, such as valence and arousal, can be represented as a point in the VA coordinate

Computational Intelligence Methods for Sentiment Analysis in Natural Language Processing Applications
DOI: https://doi.org/10.1016/B978-0-443-22009-8.00014-8

plane using two-dimensional (2-D) representation. Sentiment analysis has a subcategory called dimensional sentiment classification. The aim of sentiment classification has traditionally been binary, mainly represented as positive or negative value, or categorical, such as happy, angry, and sad. The dimensional approach, rather than classifying various emotions into a defined number of classes, maps each emotion to VA space.

3.1.1 Basic types of sentiment analysis tasks

Sentiment analysis is classified into two types: *categorical sentiment analysis and dimensional sentiment analysis (DSA)*. Table 3−1 shows comparison for the same.

3.1.2 Need for multidimensional sentiment analysis

- The use of computers in every field has increased, which is helping the decision makers to make decisions based on various reviews, comments, or posts. These textual data can be spontaneous or entered after a thought. However, for such analysis, there is a need for various repositories. If repositories are created, the analysis of text data will be increased. Furthermore, data available on social media platforms and websites, which are in bulk amount, can be analyzed to make a decision using an automated process. As of date, there is a dearth of such rrepositories; this will be a step toward linguistic resource development.
- It is increasingly customary to check a product's rating as rated by other users before purchasing it. The data demonstrate that online advice and suggestions are not the sole reasons for the buzz in this area. There are further factors from the company's perspective, such as the company's desire to know. How successful was their most recent campaign or product launch based on consumer reviews on websites such as Amazon, Yelp, and others?
- Nowadays, many Android and IOS applications, social network platforms, data search engines, and government websites are using regional languages of India. This generates a massive volume of data on the Internet. It gives a motivation to develop resources for Indian languages and to do research in the domain of natural language processing considering Indian languages.
- It can be stated from the preceding that on the social media platform, people express themselves by using regional languages, so much user-generated content written in regional languages is available. These data can be analyzed to get meaningful insights for various applications, such as advertisements, surveys, predictions, and government uses. Hence, it is appropriate to go for the development of resources for regional languages to effectively analyze the available data.
- Generally, the categorical sentiment classification task identifies the polarity of the given text as positive, neutral, or negative. The dimensional technique, rather than that of dividing various emotions into a predetermined number of classes, projects each emotion to VA space.

Table 3–1 Categorical versus Dimensional Sentiment Analysis.

Categorical sentiment analysis	Dimensional sentiment analysis
Categorical sentiment analysis approach represents the affective states with the help of discrete classes such as positive, negative, and neutral. For example, it is a one-dimensional way to represent affect states, such as happiness, fear, anger, disgust, surprise, and sadness.	Dimensional sentiment analysis approach represents the affective states using continuous numeric values for multiple dimensions. For example, VA space is the most widely used dimensional space. It is a 2-D way to represent the affect states.

Negative Neutral Positive

High

Negative ← Arousal → Positive

Neutral

Valence

Low

- Multidimensional sentiment analysis (MDSA) can be used in various domains. Depending on the domain, we need to decide the various aspects/features to be considered. These aspects/features will act as dimensions.
- The outline of this chapter is as follows. Relevant research and advancements in the field of DSA are covered in Section 3.2. Section 3.3 contains an in-depth analysis of the existing literature. Section 3.4 discusses various open issues and challenges in the DSA process. Section 3.5 gives future directions for DSA. Section 3.6 brings the paper to a conclusion.

3.2 Literature survey

This section discusses advancements of DSA by researchers in this field. The evolution of DSA is examined in relation to diverse types of sentiment analysis and framing survey queries (SQs) for systematic literature reviews.

3.2.1 Types of sentiment analysis

Researchers have studied sentiment analysis over the years. Apart from traditional sentiment analysis, various modified versions are being explored. Some of these are as mentioned here:

3.2.1.1 Multi-aspect sentiment analysis
It is among the emerging fields of sentiment analysis. It makes an attempt to analyze a variety of presumably related aspects that are usually discussed in a single review [4].

3.2.1.2 Multiclass sentiment analysis
Sentiment analysis and opinion mining for social media networking are the currently emerging research topics. The majority of research studies on automatic sentiment classification of text data gathered from microblogging websites and social media networks are directed to either be classified as binary (positive or negative) or ternary (positive, negative, or neutral). A revolutionary technique called multiclass sentiment analysis performs text categorization into several sentiment classes, rather than binary and ternary classification [5].

3.2.1.3 Multidimensional sentiment analysis
The two basic techniques for describing affect states are (1) categorical approach and (2) dimensional approach. The first depicts affect states using distinct binary classifications such as positive and negative. The second approach, in comparison to the category approach, portrays affective process states by using a continuous numerical value. VA space is largely explored in DSA. The valence shows the level of positive and negative sentiment, and the arousal reveals the level of calmness and excitement. [6].

3.2.1.4 Multidomain sentiment analysis

The task of sentiment analysis for multiple domains determines the polarity of any text/document by utilizing domain-specific characteristics. One of the primary issues, in this case, is determining the polarity of text data belonging to domains other than those utilized to create the opinion model [7].

3.2.1.5 Multi-lingual sentiment analysis

Most modern sentiment analysis techniques are confined to only English language. However, as the Internet spreads around the world, individuals are leaving comments in a diverse range of languages, mainly in regional languages. Sentiment analysis, particularly for a language, raises the possibility of ignoring valuable textual information written in plenty of other languages. These approaches have been designed to assess data in multiple languages [8].

3.2.1.6 Multi-modal sentiment analysis

Basic multi-modal sentiment analysis is formed through the combinations of three different modalities, i.e., audio, image/video, and text, for analyzing sentiments [9].

3.2.1.7 Multiscale sentiment analysis

Multiscale sentiment analysis technique shows how positive or negative a given text is. It provides more insight into sentiment analysis tasks. Humans may find it difficult to comprehend opinions since a binary categorization of opinions as positive or negative would not be adequate. The degree of positivity or negativity in text data (called rank) is represented by scale values. It is helpful for numerous practical applications, such as analyzing many opinions and assigning rankings to various opinions [10].

3.2.1.8 Multi-source sentiment analysis

Generally, sentiment analysis has been conducted on a single data source, such as news articles, tweets, blogs, and product reviews. The requirement to generate a more exact and thorough result has led to the tendency toward executing sentiment analysis on numerous data sources. These analyses include features from various data sources, such as e-commerce reviews, online news, tweets, blogs, and social media data. The incorporation of multi-source data might provide ample datasets that may be needed during sentiment classifier training [11].

This review paper mainly focuses on "dimensional sentiment analysis."

3.2.2 Framing survey queries for systematic literature review

This review paper concentrates on recognizing and analyzing the existing research work that outlines various methodologies and approaches applied to MDSA. This study is carried out by collecting similar research publications published in reputed journals, conferences, and workshops from 2010 to 2022. This paper includes reviews of about 50 research papers and is based on the formulation of a series of *SQs*. These queries are shown in Table 3–2. Following a detailed analysis, the results of these queries are collated.

Table 3–2   List of Survey Queries.

S. no.	Query
SQ(1)	What has been the year-by-year advancement of the multidimensional sentiment analysis (MDSA) task during previous decade?
SQ(2)	What is the relevance of published studies considered?
SQ(3)	For MDSA, which languages are widely used so far?
SQ(4)	Which multidimensional model (2D or 3D) is being widely used for MDSA?
SQ(5)	What online datasets and lexical aids are known for MDSA?
SQ(6)	What are the mostly used approaches for MDSA?
SQ(7)	What are different performance evaluation metrics considered while performing MDSA?
SQ(8)	What are the open issues and challenges identified from the literature review?

3.2.3 Advancements of dimensional sentiment analysis

The advancements of DSA cover methodologies and datasets used for sentiment classification. Hsu et al. classified data obtained from YouTube streaming service. For sentiment analysis, the authors used multidimensional sentiment measures such as video preferences, YouTuber preference, and excitement level. They tested the model using ML, deep learning (DL), and bidirectional encoder representations from transformers (BERT) to recognize three sentiment indicators of an audience's remarks in order to evaluate their performance [12]. Yu et al. aimed to find a real value sentiment score of educational text submitted by Chinese students. These comments are written in both valence and arousal dimensions [13]. Yen et al. developed a unique prediction approach for organizations' future financial performance. This method is based on the 2-D VA sentiment analysis [14]. Wang et al. designed a regional convolutional neural network (CNN) long short-term memory (LSTM) model. It is used for the prediction of text data ratings/scores by using valence and arousal values [15]. Wu et al. used variational autoencoder to construct a semi-supervised DSA method. The experimental findings showed that the technique may successfully minimize reliance on labeled data while also improving DSA task performance [16].

Chauhan and Sutaria discussed the significance of semiotics while performing sentiment analysis. They presented a method for determining a tweet's sentiment value using semiotics and MDSA [17] Yu et al. discovered a real-valued rating for Chinese words. They considered phrases of single words and multiple words for valence and arousal dimensions [18]. Wu et al. used a densely linked LSTM network with word characteristics for Chinese language words and phrases, in order to perform DSA task. To complete this objective, they utilized word characteristics and deep networks such as part-of-speech (POS) and word cluster. In addition, for boosting the performance of their technique, they adopted a random model ensemble strategy [19]. Zhong and Wang demonstrated an ML regression model. It is used for prediction of valence and arousal scores of Chinese language words and phrases. They created word vector for the lexical vocabulary via word embedding. As per the experimental works, the authors revealed that the suggested strategy produces accurate predictions. Other regression methods were outperformed by the support vector regression (SVR) approach [20].

Zhou et al. used boosted neural network (NN). This was being used for DSA in relation to Chinese words and phrases [21]. To perform DSA, Chen et al. suggested a unique technique that incorporates information from images. According to the authors, it is a resource that had not before been utilized in this domain [22]. Yeh et al. used vector representation for DSA. They discovered that the proposed strategy is successful based on the experimental findings and is applicable to Chinese phrases [23]. Yu et al. calculated real-valued sentiment scores for Chinese words using a DSA approach [24]. Hsieh et al. combined support vector regression and a word embedding-based model with K-nearest neighbor for prediction of valence and arousal of Chinese words [25]. Using sentiment word vectors and pretrained semantics, Wang et al. suggested supervised ensemble learning models. This is used to find valence and arousal rating of Chinese words [26].

Cheng et al. generated the VA of given Chinese emotive words in two ways. The first way is by using synonym lexicons. The second way is by using word embeddings [27]. Li extended a seed traditional Chinese emotive lexicon with a combination of SVR and word embedding [28]. Yeh et al. adopted linear regression to accomplish DSA work. It was used for Chinese language words and phrases [29]. As per the research from Lin and Chang, information from semantic resources is used to predict sentiment feature values. For this, the weighted average of similar words in CiLin or WordNet is used [30].

Wang et al. developed a system that is regional CNN-LSTM. It is used to predict VA ratings of the given text. This technique outperforms regression and traditional NN-based methods by considering local information inside sentences as well as long-distance dependence across phrases [31]. Yamamoto et al. proposed a method for assessing multidimensional sentiments. These sentiments were extracted from a microblogging system. They estimated tweet sentiment values using emoticon roles. To test the hypothesis, Qiwei and Yu employed MDSA and text-mining techniques to examine restaurant reviews [32]. Using Thayer's model, Tejwani devised a novel approach to classify text content in two dimensions and map emotions [33].

Zheng et al. established a framework for the domain of e-commerce surveys. They introduced a novel framework and recommended several new methods to address the sentiment word disambiguation and sentiment polarity annotation problems. Furthermore, they built dimensional sentiment lexicon using the technique as sentiment lexicon expansion and presented a mechanism for sentiment analysis that is rule-based [34]. Harris et al. suggested a novel MDSA agent which was used for online learning [35].

Honkela et al. performed sentiment analysis on the gathered texts using a five-dimensional PERMA framework and related vocabulary. They developed a method that combined this model, self-organizing map, and statistical analysis [36]. Maas et al. created a vector-space approach that learns from distributions across emotional categories while still collecting fundamental semantic information by using an unsupervised approach [37]. Xie et al. introduced a multidimensional connection model with three methodologies. These are internal method, external method, and combination modes. They additionally designed a Chinese VAI sentiment corpus. It is the first multidimensional corpus to account for sarcasm on a continuous scale. Experiment findings suggest that adding dimension relationships into the prediction process can outperform standard approaches that address each variable individually [6].

By placing them in the context of textual analysis, Fahim et al. introduced a fresh challenge of automatically categorizing social media communications into three categories based on the conventional paradigm of informational, persuasive, and transformational advertising [38]. Thanangthanakij et al. used sentiment classification techniques and natural language processing techniques for online reviews of many dimensions. The purpose of this study was to determine the most important part of speech in emotional analysis and the performance of multidimensional classification algorithms. According to research on restaurant reviews, the most significant part of speech for emotional analysis is the adjective [39]. He investigated a Bayesian modeling method toward multiclass sentiment classification and prediction of multidimensional sentiment distributions. He introduced successful strategies that incorporate supervised information into model learning, such as labeled feature restrictions [40]. Gupta and Baghel suggested a strategy for feature selection that is based on particle swarm optimization. It can create high-quality features out of a huge range of characteristics [41].

Kim and Calvo presented innovative strategies for automatically determining the polarity of sentiments, that is, positive/negative. For the study, the authors considered student replies. The study performs a comparison of the categorical model versus the dimensional model [42]. Wu et al. utilized the idea of dimensional VA for sentiment analysis of stock market data. They predicted the degrees of these data by using a DL model [43]. Cheng et al. investigated company public perception by examining content on fan pages on Facebook. The aim of this investigation is to check the massive volume of public opinion data provided by social media in an efficient manner. The researchers presented a bidirectional LSTM (BiLSTM). It is used to encode comprehensive sentiment information which is hidden in the data [44]. Vorakitphan et al. adopted a three-dimensional affect model based on dimensions such as valence, arousal, and dominance in the domain of politics-related data [45].

The emotional states of Chinese instructional texts were predicted by Yiwei et al. The authors proposed a realistic framework that makes use of pretrained language models such as BERT and MacBERT. According to the results, MacBERT-based approaches outperform pretrained MacBERT [46]. Using Chinese valence-arousal sentences (CVAS) and Chinese Valence-Arousal Texts datasets, Hung et al. applied the MacBERT transformers. The authors compare MacBERT's performance in the valence and arousal aspects to those of the other two converters, BERT and RoBERTa. As an assessment metrics, the MAE and correlation coefficient (r) were employed [47]. Lin and Yu developed an adaptive method to expand the sentiment dictionary. In order to make it expandable and adaptable to different fields, this study used the embedding technology of DL [48]. Chen et al. suggested an expansion approach that incorporated a part-of-speech filter with a word2vec-like word finder. The results of the experiments revealed that using expansion samples as training data in a prediction model outperformed using only original training data [49].

Yen et al. predicted the financial future performance of companies that are publicly traded. The authors collected text data from online news and stock forums. To calculate the valence and arousal ratings of all web content, they used the Chinese Valence-Arousal Words (CVAW) lexicon [14]. Liu et al. applied sentiment analysis techniques on online restaurant reviews. The authors used restaurant data, Shanghai, in this example, to assess using a multidimensional model [50]. To compute the VA ratings for the given emotional words automatically, Li et al. proposed a weighted graph model. It includes the relationships of the various nodes as well as their similarities as nodes [51]. When examining the impact of attitudes and review qualities on star ratings of restaurant, Gan et al. revealed the structure of online reviews of restaurants [52]. Semiotics' significance in sentiment analysis was highlighted by Chauhan et al. The authors have employed a variety of techniques for calculating a statement's sentiment score using semiotics [53]. Cheng et al. suggested a BiLSTM-based neural network with emotional information. To analyze the sentiment, the dependence link between texts was added to the DL model in addition to taking valence and arousal. Experimental findings demonstrated that the research performed well in terms of predicting language terms for valence and arousal [54].

3.3 Observations drawn from the literature survey

This chapter is written by keeping the aim in mind to undertake an organized literature review in the domain of MDSA. This will make it easier to conduct a detailed analysis to respond to the survey questionnaires listed in Table 3−1.

3.3.1 Responses to survey queries

In response to **SQ(1)**, it has been investigated how MDSA publications have changed over time. This includes the publications in this field from 2010 to 2022. Year-wise advancement of publication over the last decade is depicted in Fig. 3−1. As seen in the figure, it has been determined that research in this field has increased over the past few years.

Scopus, Web of Science, Google Scholar, etc., are literature databases. These are used to identify published materials from various books, journals, conferences, etc. The databases

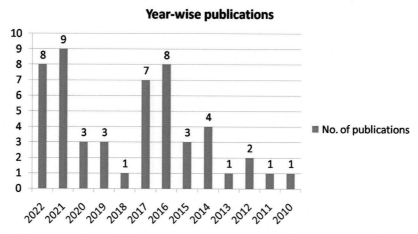

FIGURE 3−1 Advancement of the multidimensional sentiment analysis task during the previous decade.

also provide citation analysis of authors. To address the **SQ(2)**, citation data from Scopus and Google Scholar databases have been analyzed and recorded in Table 3−3. It should be noticed from this table that, according to the Google Scholar database, 60% of the published studies taken into account for this survey have fewer than five citations (as of December 2022). Moreover, it is 32% as per the Scopus database. The work by Wang et al., which has more than 400 citations as of December 2022, is the most referenced research study. In order to forecast the valence and arousal ratings of text data, authors constructed a tree structure-based CNN-LSTM model. This work established the standard in this field; therefore, subsequent researchers replicated their methods for doing DSA.

The data in Fig. 3−2 aid in obtaining the response to SQ(3). This highlights that 49% of the research papers considered were written in Chinese, while 40% were written in English. These are the two mostly explored languages till now for performing MDSA. As far as the locality of researchers is considered, around 72% of the researchers belong to the country Taiwan and China. The remaining 28% of research papers are written by researchers from Australia, Belgium, Finland, India, Japan, Thailand, the United Kingdom, and the United States.

DSA is used for finding real-valued sentiment scores of text data in multiple dimensions. Commonly used models for characterizing sentiment dimensions include VA and VA dominance. Fig. 3−3 shows that 60% of the considered research papers adopted VA model. This addresses **SQ(4)** of Table 3−1.

Table 3–3 Count of publications based on citations.

Citations count	< = 5	6 to 20	21 to 50	> = 50
Publications count as per the Scopus database	15	4	1	1
Publications count as per the Google Scholar database	28	11	4	4

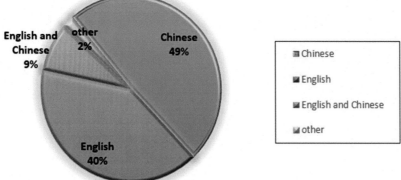

FIGURE 3–2 Dimensional sentiment analysis work done for languages.

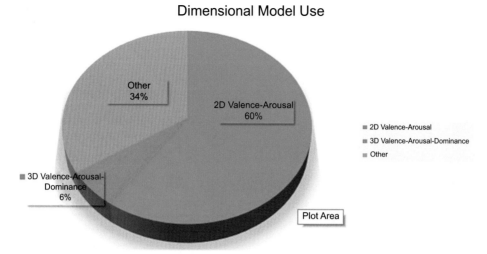

Dimensional Model Use

FIGURE 3–3 Representation of dimensional models used by researchers.

MDSA techniques can be used in various areas of interest such as service reviews, product reviews, and social media data analytics. As per the literature survey, there are some publicly available datasets and resources for DSA in texts. As a part to discuss **SQ(5)**, these are shown in Table 3–4. One of the significant problems with resources is that the majority of them are only available in English and Chinese. Because of this, sentiment analysis and emotion identification from languages other than these, particularly regional languages, present both a significant challenge and a great potential for researchers. Datasets that have already been gathered and labeled, however, can assist and accelerate further study in this field.

There are currently two techniques being applied for optimizing multiple DSA tasks: (1) lexicon-based and (2) algorithm-based. Lexicon-based approaches use predefined words and rules to orient the sentence toward an emotion or sentiment. ML, DL, and transfer learning (TL) are three categories into which algorithm-based approaches may be subdivided. **SQ(6)** intends to categorize the various approaches used for DSA. This categorization is displayed in Fig. 3–4.

Based on the applications to be used and the type of data we need to work with, there are two main approaches for MDSA.

- **Lexicon-based techniques:** For every dimension, it has a predefined list of words. This wordlist is the main entity for sentiment analysis task. The input text is matched or compared with the wordlist. The algorithm then identifies which kind of phrases or sentiments are more prominent in it. This form of lexicon-based sentiment analysis is simple to build, but it lacks flexibility and does not take into consideration context.
- **Algorithm-based techniques:** Algorithm-based techniques are mostly based on ML, DL, and TL approaches. All of these are quite useful for analysis of complex texts. SVM, linear regression, NB, and random forest are some types of ML approaches. DL techniques include CNN, LSTM, Bi-LSTM, etc.

Table 3–4 Publicly available lexical resources and datasets for dimensional sentiment analysis.

Sr. no.	Particular	Description
Lexical resources		
1	"EmoBank" [55]	A resource for Chinese valence-arousal is the EmoBank repository. The resource is the first of its kind in Chinese. It includes a sizable corpus of literature that has been carefully tagged with emotion in accordance with the psychological valence-arousal-dominance concept.
2	CVAW—Chinese Valence Arousal Words [48]	Chinese Valence Arousal Words (CVAW) vocabulary consists of affective processes words with valence-arousal rating.
3	CVAP—Chinese Valence Arousal Phrases [13]	Chinese multiword phrases are included in Chinese Valence-Arousal Words (CVAP)
4	CVAT—Chinese Valence Arousal Texts [31]	Chinese Valence-Arousal Texts (CVAT) contain Chinese phrases. Essentially, it comprises texts that have been carefully graded as valence-arousal dimensions ranging from 1 to 9.
5	Valence arousal irony and valence arousal dominance (3-dimensional) [6]	A three-dimensional corpus is the Chinese valence arousal irony corpus. It includes positive terms with contradictory meanings that were taken from social media and the Chinese ironic corpus.
Datasets		
6	Facebook-valence arousal dataset [56]	It is a collection of Facebook posts that have been graded by two annotators. On a nine-point scale, these scales depict the emotions of valence and arousal.
7	Stanford sentiment treebank dataset [57]	There are 8544 training text data, 2210 test text data, and 1101 validation text data in Stanford Sentiment Treebank. Each text was evaluated on just one valence metric, which ranged from (0, 1).

To test the developed model, researchers used statistical measures such as accuracy, precision, recall, F1-score, mean absolute error, Pearson correlation coefficient, root mean square error, and standard deviation. This addresses the **SQ(7)**. Performance measures of DSA task can be selected as per the domain. For example, the performance metrics such as return on assets, return on equity, and Tobin's Q are suitable for the financial domain.

3.3.2 Levels of sentiment analysis

There are four levels at which MDSA techniques are applied: aspect level, phrase level, sentence level, and document level.

3.3.2.1 Aspect-level sentiment analysis

It is executed at an aspect level of the given input sentences/texts. There may be several aspects in each sentence. All aspects are considered from a sentence are considered to assign dimensional values, which are continuous in nature. For the complete sentence, finally, an aggregate sentiment is found out.

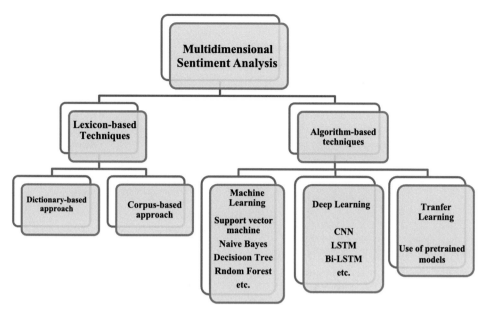

FIGURE 3–4 Approaches for multidimensional sentiment analysis.

3.3.2.2 Phrase-level sentiment analysis

It is carried out on phrases of the given text. Each phrase can have single or multiple aspects. Every phrase is analyzed to determine its dimension value (such as valence and arousal) using some approaches.

3.3.2.3 Sentence-level sentiment analysis

It is executed at the sentence level of the given text. To determine the dimensional values, each sentence is independently analyzed using some methodologies.

3.3.2.4 Document-level sentiment analysis

This type of analysis is carried out on a complete document. Finally, dimension scores for valence/arousal are assigned to the whole document.

3.3.3 Steps to perform dimensional sentiment analysis

To perform the DSA tasks, fundamental steps are followed as shown in Fig. 3−5.

DSA steps

1. Data collection: To perform the DSA task, it is one of the most important key steps. The subsequent steps will be dependent on the quality of the data that has been gathered as well as how it has been annotated or labeled.

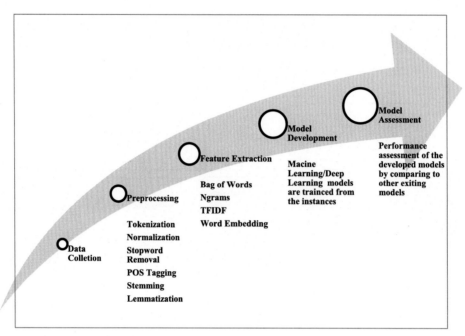

FIGURE 3–5 Basic steps to perform dimensional sentiment analysis.

2. Data processing: The processing of the data in sentiment analysis consists of a series of tasks such as normalization, removal of stop words, parts of speech tagging, stemming, and lemmatization.

3. Feature extraction: Feature extraction is the process of converting raw data into numerical features that may be processed while preserving the information in the original dataset. It yields better results than simply applying ML to raw data. Various techniques for feature extraction are Bag of Words, Word Embedding, term frequency-inverse document frequency (TF-IDF), etc.

4. Model development: In this step, various ML models are tested. This iterative process will be carried out until a model fitting the required criteria is built. Various approaches for model development are lexicon-based, ML algorithms, DL algorithms, or transfer-based learning algorithms.

5. Model assessment: Model assessment is a process of evaluating the performance of developed models by comparing to other existing models.

3.4 Open issues and challenges in dimensional sentiment analysis

This section, which highlights various challenges associated with implementing DSA, provides the response to **SQ(8)**. An affective lexicon set properly annotated with dimensional sentiment values is a prime and essential resource in DSA. Some open issues and challenges in performing DSA are presented in this section.

- The majority of dimensional approaches now in use rely upon built-in dictionaries or lexicon sets. These are collection of words that correlate to various emotion dimensions in order to map text into a multidimensional emotion space. These types of approaches are obviously lacking when analyzing text that includes unusual and new words. In addition, they are ineffective in languages with limited lexical resources.
- As mentioned in Section 3.3, there exist a few datasets and resources for English and Chinese languages. In order to balance the amount of work done in various languages, the availability of rich resources in other languages would considerably promote study in the area.
- To build dimensional sentiment applications, sentiment lexicon sets having VA ratings are beneficial resources. The majority of resources are available in English and Chinese, which is one of the challenges with resources. Sentiment analysis and emotion identification from languages other than English, particularly regional languages, is challenging for researchers. Moreover, some of the corpora and lexicons are domain-specific, which restricts their applicability to other fields.
- Social networking users frequently express a lot of comments and feedback in the form of sarcasm, irony, implication, and so on, which is extremely difficult for a machine to interpret.
- People are producing a lot of data in the Internet era in the form of informal and unofficial text. Data gathered from social networking sites present many difficulties, such as spelling errors, the use of short forms, new slang, and improper grammatical usage. It is difficult for machines to do sentiment and emotion analysis under these conditions.
- Future research in this area will concentrate on bringing the VA prediction up to the sentence and document levels from the word level.

3.5 Future directions

DSA is a technique for identifying and extracting relevant information from the source material. After performing the analysis on the data, it may help businesses to know about the sentiment about their products, brands, and services. In this way, business people may monitor the respective online conversations. Many applications are built using traditional sentiment analysis methods. Similarly, in the future, applications will be developed using existing lexical resources of DSA. Following are some of the areas where DSA techniques may be used.

1. Product recommendation systems
2. Social media monitoring
3. Speech data analysis
4. Customer feedback analysis
5. Sentiment analysis for entertainment industry
6. Market research analysis
7. Identifying emotions in text data
8. Sentiment analysis of educational text

9. Public opinion analysis
10. Sentiment analysis of restaurant reviews
11. Sentiment analysis of healthcare reviews
12. Sentiment analysis of e-commerce reviews
13. Product band monitoring and analysis
14. Movie sentiment analysis
15. Sports sentiment analysis.

3.6 Conclusion

The key motivation to exercise this literature review in the domain of DSA is the potential growth of the research work carried out over the past couple of years. This study includes a comprehensive literature review on text-based DSA, along with several publicly accessible datasets and lexical resources. In the end, open issues and challenges are discussed by researchers of the domain of text-based DSA. Lexical resources that use VA ratings are useful for developing dimensional sentiment applications. The majority of lexical resources are available in English and Chinese. Consequently, sentiment analysis and emotion identification in regional languages offer promising research opportunities.

References

[1] B. Pang, L. Lee, A sentimental education: sentiment analysis using subjectivity summarization based on minimum cuts, arXiv preprint cs/0409058 (2004).

[2] R.A. Calvo, S. Mac Kim, Emotions in text: dimensional and categorical models, Computat. Intell. 29 (3) (2013) 527−543.

[3] J.A. Russell, A circumplex model of affect, J. Person. Soc. Psychol. 39 (6) (1980) 1161.

[4] B. Lu, M. Ott, C. Cardie, B.K. Tsou, Multi-aspect sentiment analysis with topic models, 2011 IEEE 11th International Conference on Data Mining Workshops, IEEE, 2011, pp. 81−88. December.

[5] M. Bouazizi, T. Ohtsuki, A pattern-based approach for multi-class sentiment analysis in Twitter, IEEE Access. 5 (2017) 20617−20639.

[6] H. Xie, W. Lin, S. Lin, J. Wang, L.C. Yu, A multi-dimensional relation model for dimensional sentiment analysis, Inf. Sci. 579 (2021) 832−844.

[7] M. Dragoni, G. Petrucci, A fuzzy-based strategy for multi-domain sentiment analysis, Int. J. Approx. Reason. 93 (2018) 59−73.

[8] K. Dashtipour, S. Poria, A. Hussain, E. Cambria, A.Y. Hawalah, A. Gelbukh, et al., Multilingual sentiment analysis: state of the art and independent comparison of techniques, Cognit. Comput. 8 (4) (2016) 757−771.

[9] T.P. Kumar, B.V. Vardhan, A review on multi-model sentiment analysis using deep learning for text, speech, & emoji reorganization, J. Harbin Inst. Technol. 54 (4) (2022) 2022.

[10] W. Philemon, W. Mulugeta, A machine learning approach to multi-scale sentiment analysis of Amharic online posts, HiLCoE J. Comput. Sci. Technol. 2 (2) (2014) 8.

[11] N.A. Abdullah, A. Feizollah, A. Sulaiman, N.B. Anuar, Challenges and recommended solutions in multi-source and multi-domain sentiment analysis, IEEE Access. 7 (2019) 144957−144971.

[12] C.W. Hsu, C.L. Chou, H. Liu, J.L. Wu, A corpus for dimensional sentiment classification on YouTube streaming serviceOctober Proceedings of the 33rd Conference on Computational Linguistics and Speech Processing (ROCLING 2021) (2021) 286–293.

[13] L.C. Yu, J. Wang, B. Peng, C.R. Huang, ROCLING-2021 shared task: dimensional sentiment analysis for educational textsOctober Proceedings of the 33rd Conference on Computational Linguistics and Speech Processing (ROCLING 2021) (2021) 385–388.

[14] M.F. Yen, Y.P. Huang, L.C. Yu, Y.L. Chen, A two-dimensional sentiment analysis of online public opinion and future financial performance of publicly listed companies, Computat. Econ. 59 (4) (2022) 1677–1698.

[15] J. Wang, L.C. Yu, K.R. Lai, X. Zhang, Tree-structured regional CNN-LSTM model for dimensional sentiment analysis, IEEE/ACM Trans. Audio, Speech, Lang. Process. 28 (2019) 581–591.

[16] C. Wu, F. Wu, S. Wu, Z. Yuan, J. Liu, Y. Huang, Semi-supervised dimensional sentiment analysis with variational autoencoder, Knowl. Syst. 165 (2019) 30–39.

[17] D. Chauhan, K. Sutaria, Multidimensional sentiment analysis on Twitter with semiotics, Int. J. Inf. Technol. 11 (4) (2019) 677–682.

[18] L.C. Yu, L.H. Lee, J. Wang, K.F. Wong, IJCNLP-2017 task 2: dimensional sentiment analysis for Chinese phrasesDecember Proceedings of the IJCNLP 2017, Shared Tasks (2017) 9–16.

[19] C. Wu, F. Wu, Y. Huang, S. Wu, Z. Yuan, Thu_ngn at ijcnlp-2017 task 2: dimensional sentiment analysis for Chinese phrases with deep LSTMDecember Proceedings of the IJCNLP 2017, Shared Tasks (2017) 47–52.

[20] P. Zhong, J. Wang, LDCCNLP at IJCNLP-2017 Task 2: dimensional sentiment analysis for Chinese phrases using machine learningDecember Proceedings of the IJCNLP 2017, Shared Tasks (2017) 84–88.

[21] X. Zhou, J. Wang, X. Xie, C. Sun, L. Si, Alibaba at IJCNLP-2017 task 2: a boosted deep system for dimensional sentiment analysis of Chinese phrasesDecember Proceedings of the IJCNLP 2017, Shared Tasks (2017) 100–104.

[22] S.M. Chen, Z.Y. Chen, L.W. Ku, NLPSA at IJCNLP-2017 Task 2: imagine scenario: leveraging supportive images for dimensional sentiment analysisDecember Proceedings of the IJCNLP 2017, Shared Tasks (2017) 105–111.

[23] J.F. Yeh, J.C. Tsai, B.W. Wu, T.Y. Kuang, NCYU at IJCNLP-2017 task 2: dimensional sentiment analysis for Chinese phrases using vector representationsDecember Proceedings of the IJCNLP 2017, Shared Tasks (2017) 112–117.

[24] L.C. Yu, L.H. Lee, K.F. Wong, Overview of the IALP 2016 shared task on dimensional sentiment analysis for Chinese words, *2016 International Conference on Asian Language Processing (IALP 2016)*, IEEE, 2016, pp. 156–160. November.

[25] Y.L. Hsieh, C.A. Wang, Y.W. Wu, Y.C. Chang, W.L. Hsu, IASL valence-arousal analysis system at IALP 2016 shared task: dimensional sentiment analysis for Chinese words, *2016 International Conference on Asian Language Processing (IALP 2016)*, IEEE, 2016, pp. 297–299. November.

[26] F. Wang, Y. Zhou, M. Lan, Dimensional sentiment analysis of traditional Chinese words using pretrained not-quite-right sentiment word vectors and supervised ensemble models, *2016 International Conference on Asian Language Processing (IALP 2016)*, IEEE, 2016, pp. 300–303. November.

[27] W. Cheng, Y. Song, Y. Zhu, P. Jian, Dimensional sentiment analysis for Chinese words based on synonym lexicon and word embedding, *2016 International Conference on Asian Language Processing (IALP 2016)*, IEEE, 2016, pp. 312–316. November.

[28] B. Li, Learning dimensional sentiment of traditional Chinese words with word embedding and support vector regression, *2016 International Conference on Asian Language Processing (IALP 2016)*, IEEE, 2016, pp. 324–327. November.

[29] J.F. Yeh, T.Y. Kuang, Y.J. Huang, M.R. Wu, Dimensional sentiment analysis in valence-arousal for Chinese words by linear regression, *2016 International Conference on Asian Language Processing (IALP 2016)*, IEEE, 2016, pp. 328−331. November.

[30] C.J. Lin, H.T. Chang, Dimensional sentiment analysis by synsets and sense definitions, *2016 International Conference on Asian Language Processing (IALP 2016)*, IEEE, 2016, pp. 332−335. November.

[31] J. Wang, L.C. Yu, K.R. Lai, X. Zhang, Dimensional sentiment analysis using a regional CNN-LSTM modelAugust 54th Annual Meeting of the. Association for Computational Linguistics. Proceedings of the Conference, Vol. 2 (Short Papers). (2016) 225−230.

[32] Q. Gan, Y. Yu, Restaurant rating: industrial standard and word-of-mouth−a text mining and multi-dimensional sentiment analysis, *2015* 48th Hawaii International Conference *on* System *Sciences*, IEEE, 2015, pp. 1332−1340. January.

[33] R. Tejwani, Two-dimensional sentiment analysis of text, arXiv Prepr. arXiv 1406 (2014) 2022.

[34] L. Zheng, P. Jin, J. Zhao, L. Yue, Multi-dimensional sentiment analysis for large-scale e-commerce reviews, International Conference on Database and Expert Systems Applications, Springer, Cham, 2014, pp. 449−463. September.

[35] S.C. Harris, L. Zheng, V. Kumar, Multi-dimensional sentiment classification in online learning environment, 2014 IEEE Sixth International Conference *on* Technology *for* Education, IEEE, 2014, pp. 172−175. December.

[36] T. Honkela, J. Korhonen, K. Lagus, E. Saarinen, Five-dimensional sentiment analysis of corpora, documents and words, Advances in Self-Organizing Maps and Learning Vector Quantization, Springer, Cham, 2014, pp. 209−218.

[37] A.L. Maas, A.Y. Ng, C. Potts, Multi-dimensional sentiment analysis with learned representations, 9, *Stanford University, Zugriff am*, 2011, p. 2014.

[38] R. Machedon, W. Rand, Y.V. Joshi, Automatic classification of social media messaging using multi-dimensional sentiment analysis and crowdsourcing, Available SSRN (2013) 2244353.

[39] S. Thanangthanakij, E. Pacharawongsakda, N. Tongtep, P. Aimmanee, T. Theeramunkong, An empirical study on multi-dimensional sentiment analysis from user service reviews, 2012 Seventh International Conference on Knowledge, Information and Creativity Support Systems, IEEE, 2012, pp. 58−65. November.

[40] Y. He, A Bayesian modeling approach to multi-dimensional sentiment distributions predictionAugust Proceedings of the First International Workshop on Sentiment Discovery Opinion Mining (2012) 1−8.

[41] S.L. Gupta, A.S. Baghel, High dimensional sentiment classification of product reviews using evolutionary computation, Int. J. Bus. Intell. Data Min. 17 (4) (2020) 526−541.

[42] S. Mac Kim, R.A. Calvo, Sentiment analysis in student experiences of learningJune EDM (2010) 111−120.

[43] J.L. Wu, M.T. Huang, C.S. Yang, K.H. Liu, Sentiment analysis of stock markets using a novel dimensional valence−arousal approach, Soft Comput. 25 (6) (2021) 4433−4450.

[44] Y.Y. Cheng, Y.M. Chen, W.C. Yeh, Y.C. Chang, Valence and arousal-infused bi-directional LSTM for sentiment analysis of government social media management, Appl. Sci. 11 (2) (2021) 880.

[45] V. Vorakitphan, M. Guerini, E. Cabrio, S. Villata, Regrexit or not regrexit: aspect-based sentiment analysis in polarized contextsDecember Proceedings of the 28th International Conference on Computational Linguistics (2020) 219−224.

[46] Y.W. Wang, W.Z. Chang, B.H. Fang, Y.C. Chen, W.K. Huang, K.Y. Chen, NTUST-NLP-1 at ROCLING-2021 shared task: educational texts dimensional sentiment analysis using pretrained language modelsOctober Proceedings of the 33rd Conference on Computational Linguistics and Speech Processing (ROCLING 2021) (2021) 354−359.

[47] M.C. Hung, C.Y. Chen, P.J. Chen, L.H. Lee, NCU-NLP at ROCLING-2021 shared task: using macBERT transformers for dimensional sentiment AnalysisOctober Proceedings of the 33rd Conference on Computational Linguistics and Speech Processing (ROCLING 2021) (2021) 380−384.

[48] Y.L. Lin, L.C. Yu, An adaptive method for building a Chinese dimensional sentiment lexiconSeptember Proceedings of the 32nd Conference on Computational Linguistics and Speech Processing (ROCLING 2020) (2020) 223–237.

[49] H.S. Chen, P.C. Chen, S.C. Huang, Y.C. Chiu, J.L. Wu, SCUDS at ROCLING-2021 shared task: using pre-trained model for dimensional sentiment analysis based on sample expansion methodOctober 33rd Conference on Computational Linguistics and Speech Processing (ROCLING 2021) (2021) 346–353.

[50] C. Liu, L. Li, C. Shan, X. Hu, Z. Diao, M.E. He, Exploring neighborhood service and development strategies by multi-dimensional sentiment analysis of online restaurant review, 2021 3rd International Symposium on Smart and Healthy Cities (ISHC), IEEE, 2021, pp. 120–125. December.

[51] L.C. Yu, J. Wang, K.R. Lai, X.J. Zhang, Predicting valence-arousal ratings of words using a weighted graph methodJuly Proceedings of the 53rd Annual Meeting of the Association for Computational Linguistics and the 7th International Joint Conference on Natural Language Processing (Volume 2: Short Papers) (2015) 788–793.

[52] Q. Gan, B.H. Ferns, Y. Yu, L. Jin, A text mining and multidimensional sentiment analysis of online restaurant reviews, J. Qual. Assur. Hosp. Tour. 18 (4) (2017) 465–492.

[53] D. Chauhan, K. Sutaria, R. Doshi, Impact of semiotics on multidimensional sentiment analysis on Twitter: a survey, 2018 Second International Conference *on* Computing Methodologies *and* Communication *(ICCMC)*, IEEE, 2018, pp. 671–674. February.

[54] Y.Y. Cheng, W.C. Yeh, Y.M. Chen, Y.C. Chang, Using valence and arousal-infused Bi-LSTM for sentiment analysis in social media product reviewsOctober Proc. 33rd Conf. Computational Linguist. Speech Process. (ROCLING 2021) (2021) 210–217.

[55] L.H. Lee, J.H. Li, L.C. Yu, Chinese EmoBank: building valence-arousal resources for dimensional sentiment, ACM Trans. Asian Low-Resour. Lang. Inform. Process. 21 (4) (2022) 1–18.

[56] D. Preoţiuc-Pietro, H.A. Schwartz, G. Park, J. Eichstaedt, M. Kern, L. Ungar, et al., Modelling valence and arousal in Facebook posts, 7th Workshop on. Computational Approaches to Subjectivity, Sentiment and Social Media Analysis, 2016, , pp. 9–15. June.

[57] R. Socher, A. Perelygin, J. Wu, J. Chuang, C.D. Manning, A.Y. Ng, et al., Recursive deep models for semantic compositionality over a sentiment treebank, Proceedings of the 2013 Conference on Empirical Methods in Natural Language Processing (2013) 1631–1642.

4

A model of time in natural linguistic reasoning

Daniela López De Luise, Sebastian Cippitelli

CI2S LABS, BUENOS AIRES, ARGENTINA

4.1 Introduction

Many authors have studied the relationship between communication, time, and language usage, and concepts such as fractals, systems, communication effectiveness, and efficiency arise [1,2]. There are many biological clues that support the idea of timeline administration in humans. Specialists in philosophy of science, cognitive psychology, sociolinguistics, communication theory, linguistics, and several other fields have supported the same idea. For instance, Friesen explains that humans build reality from a systematic pattern of thought mainly based on space and time conceptions [3]. The two-step pattern was first introduced by Gentner: to identify cognitive modules that are adequate for current events and then articulate them with it.

The extensive number of publications presents a diversity of perspectives coverage, including mathematical models explaining the articulation of sentences [4], models for the cultural influence in natural thoughts [5], chaos [6], thermodynamics [7,8], and fractals [2,9] explanations of language in native speakers. Among the topics, there is a question of how the time conception originates and works in communication and, in general, in language. Probably, the most ancient cognitive experiment belongs to Laplace in 1814, currently known as Laplace's demon [10], that postulates time with no direction (forward or backward). In fact, it does not matter which direction could be selected since any living being with universal knowledge not only can know the present but can also imagine how the past was and infer the future. A bit more than a hundred years later in a private letter of 1934 with his opinion on quantum physics, Albert Einstein writes, "God tirelessly plays dice under laws which he has himself prescribed." With that, he understands that everything has an order in the universe, and there is no randomness in it: the universe would be an unlimited and incorruptible chain of facts. This conception known as *casual determinism* is afterward tackled by quantum mechanics, and the Heisenberg's uncertainty principle has been the most relevant argument against the deterministic conception. Language, as a production of the mind, lies under these considerations. However, it does not explain how people can select from thousands of words, combine, and transform them encoding semantics with a few grammar rules, along with a strong bias called slang and dialectics, all these in a highly successful approach in real time. How is it possible?

An explanation from Wildgen adapts the second law of thermodynamics to linguistics [11]: entropy never decreases in linguistics because the system is expanding in a kind of entropy multiplication. A sentence in t_{i+1} just extends the linguistic performance of t_i. As a consequence, the system reaches balance with the communication successful and complete but far from thermodynamic equilibrium. This happens with other biological, chemical, and physical systems in nature. Some effects that the author finds are the loss of certain syllables and lexical and grammatical innovations in living languages.

Although thermodynamics involves time-dependent explanations, it is important to note the difference between timelines and time conception within this context. Although both concepts could be easily confused, there is no yet evidence that they are identical. Thermodynamics works for a universe with timelines, with past, present, and future in a sequence valid for every element in it. However, language refers to mind productions where timelines are produced by subject consciousness under a specific communication boundary of a certain type. Furthermore, as will be precised in the following sections, the human brain conceives a time deeply related to space and feelings, biased by them at every individual in a different way. Thus, probably, there is a different timeline for every person. For that reason, a model of linguistic reasoning needs to define how this *timeline is*. This chapter is based on previous findings by the author [1,2] and describes these timelines as part of a set of rules belonging to a kind of thermodynamic linguistics explaining brain and mental performance.

Note that, as it will be presented here, while a definition of the timeline is required and underlays mind structure and performance, it is possible to eliminate the notion of time [12]. According to Prigogine, a theological analysis considering God's conception of everything given by Him implies a timeless perspective of the universe. However, communication is time dependent (as it is first produced and then transferred to a target) and makes use of a certain ordered approach or timeline.

An interesting modeling of this time dependency is the theory of synergetic dissipative structures of Evans et al. [6], with a combination of a timeline flow of energy with an immutable catalyst that mutates it in outputs competing between them in the form of modes of expression. There is a kind of evolution consideration here, where the survival mode is best suited for communication in the current context. The other modes are unnecessary and discarded.

The synergic concept is very strong in the perspective that Evans presents because language is a complex production in humans, much more than in other living beings of nature. Language expresses in different levels of abstraction adding a global dynamic that needs to be integrated to inter- and intra-individual considerations. Extra complexity is given by the diverse communication channels (written text, vocalizations, graphics, icons, music, art, etc.).

Abstraction levels have been studied by many authors. One way is to consider sayings as an aggregation of words that can be associated with a learned heuristic to a container that self-expresses context and probably other features that may help fetch them again in later uses. In this line, Wildgen proposed a delimitation in meaning that is trespassed with the linguistic pragmatics (i.e., day-by-day usage). The new frontier of the concept represents a fraction of the original scope and progresses in a cumulative way that may result in a cognitive shift or a mere expansion [11].

Zipf changes the explanation of those categories [2] when introducing a fractal function to describe word usage in texts. This type of mathematical artifact is a powerful instrument to describe nature and human expressions, such as the number of petals in a flower, or the number of persons in a city. Sometime afterward, Mandelbrot, responsible for fractals formalization, improves the model, making it evident that words are used in a critically based approach by human beings. Fractal essence relies on the concept of sequence or timeline from a starting point with an init status evolving while self-replicates.

Linguistics is an extensive field covering not only external formulation but also more subtle perspectives, such as philosophical, sociological, and historical views. From the cognitive study, the set of tasks performed naturally as part of the language praxis is the essence of linguistic reasoning analysis [1]. The main goal of thermodynamic rules for linguistic reasoning (TRLR) introduced here is to provide a reduced number of rules describing the patterns yet just tested with textual expressions [2] but intended for any type of communication.

One of the key concepts is the existence of a universe O, with an essential stage (E) where there are no messages or communications (C). When there is a C, there is a shifting from E called movement (M). During the E status, there are infinite possibilities to produce M. By definition of movement, each one has a specific usage of space (e) and time (t), being E a special case. After Rule 1 and Rule 2, any M in O is in fact a vibrational behavior [1]; therefore, any activity in O is an oscillation of some kind.

As M is a communication with a direction, the target (F) has another reference in t that takes $t = 0$ when receiving C, and the previous process exists in $t \rightarrow -\infty$. This conception is also introduced in the biological mechanism of brain nuclei for the information management in section 4.2. This idea could be applied to e. As any M (including E) is a vibration with potentially unlimited t and e, then $t \in [-\infty, +\infty]$ and $e \in [-\infty, +\infty]$.

The space e existence enables t to instantiate a communication C typically specializing it, leaving other possibilities of e not communicated. Entropy (H) flow is the metric $h(e, t)$ used here to know how is C currently, but fractal dimension $D(t)$ allows to track the quality of the process [2] of language production and interpretation. It describes the bias management in the brain by means of entropy and fractals [13].

Table 4−1 is a summary of the explained concepts. The first rule explains that a communication C is considered complete, and the concept is successfully transferred to the addressee under certain conditions: C is composed of one or more sentences c_i that holds a fraction $h(e, t)$ of H. Global entropy does not change but keeps constant obtained with a counterpart $h'(-e, -t)$ originated in destiny (F) responsible for the equilibrium. In this context, the system is considered complete and local (since e is in E).

The second rule in the table introduces E, which is a textual expression consisting mainly of nouns and verbs. Some other words labeled Appreciations make the balance between nouns and verbs not perfect. Even that, tests performed confirm the cyclical or episodic evolution of $h(e, t)$ [2]. Timing is described with a starting point in the origin of C, with its reversed progression in the target F. While there is no limit in the extension of C, it results in

Table 4–1   Main characteristics of published TRLR rules.

Rule #	Feature	Time explanation	Thesis	Property derived
1	Main behavior	Timeline balanced between M and F	Space of concepts (O) is timeless	Succeed(C) = true $<=>$ H is fully transferred
2	Dimension and rhythm	C expresses E in a behavior $h(e, t)$ with a specific rhythm and cycle	Time $t \in [-\infty, +\infty]$ determines C dynamics (h)	Elements e in E are used in a balanced H for M and F
3	Action	Here is an evolution of D in t where $D(t+1)$ depends on $D(t)$ and always $D(t+1) >= D(t)$	Language productions are movements expressed as triplet (O, E, C)	When the entropy of elements in C is expressed with a fractal dimension D
4	Duality	Hilbert fractals to model episodic memory. Organized in clouds representing temporality and content (meanings)	$H(t)$ preserves space in $R^3 h(e, t) = <x, y, z, h>$ represents both t and meaning	Message M communicates with a counterpart F. The locality of its symbolic representation in a language can be modeled by Hilbert fractals

Note that elements in E may vary. In textual processing, TRLR considers linguistic categories of words used. They are reduced specifically to one of the following three: verbs, nouns, appreciations, falling in the last category, any word that is not one of the two previous.

$t \in [-\infty, +\infty]$ for representing any complete sequence of sentences. Nevertheless, the current C exists in a lapse $[t_1; t_2]$ from M perspective, and any activity $h(e, t)$ remains in that time frame $[t_1; t_2]$ with a cyclical evolution.

Regarding the third rule, it just expresses that for C to be performed, M requires the existence of a certain combination (O, E, C). They regulate the time (t) and space (e) as a vibration movement with an origin and effect along t, by C in O. M progresses change $H(t)$ and is qualitatively evaluated using fractal dimension (D) as will be explained in section 4.4. This movement or variation (e, t) produces a fractal disposition of the variations in H, in a progressive way $D(t)$ from a starting point to its end.

The last rule associates M with a counterpart F, the target of C. It also declares that M and F happened at the same time in a sort of balance. The physical organization of (e, t) can be modeled as a Hilbert disposition of subsequent elements in the communication. The result is a structure that preserves space because it is a space-filling fractal and presents regions according to time and h evolution, as M runs under a tuple (O, E, C) with $t \rightarrow +\infty$, and e is the specific option in E at time t that makes evident in the physical world the essence of C. The model of the communication process f is here an n-dimensional parallelepiped with a Hilbert disposition of dots $h(e, t)$ for $f(x, y, z, h, t) \sim h(e, t)$ such that there is a counterpart $f(x', y'-, z'-, h'-, -t) \, t$. Note that any communication C has an f associated, and there is an infinite possibility for f derived from the infinite alternate options of e in E, since $\Sigma_{i \in [1...\infty)} \, e_i$. Thus, this rule is the first that relates current expressions in a textual interchange and the prescribed space−time approach.

As will be shown in section 4.4, to test the rules requires a corpus very special in order to preserve the proper conditions to evaluate them. The corpus used to perform this task is a number of dialogs automatically collected from a site implementing a game called 20Q.

The game will be described in that section as the properties that are accomplished by it to guarantee the correct bias.

This work aims to show the biological conception of time according to current theories on human brain functioning and to introduce its relationship with TRLR, which explains the inherent behavior of cognitive processes for making use of natural language. Time plays a vital role in any type of communication C, but specifically relevant is in any synchronous communication. The disposition of the sequence of $h(e, t)$ in H remains fractal in any case, following the statement of the fourth rule presented.

The duality expressed in it is present in the essence of many expressions of nature, starting with gender (male, female), movement (present or not), light presence (yes or not), etc. Many a times, it is presented as a range with two poles (as in white-and-black color wave frequencies).

Language can be thought of as a consequence of a biological engine called encephalon that can be placed in one of both ends of a communication, textual, or not, working in one of those poles in a virtual dialog that starts with the first intention to articulate a sentence.

The fourth rule serves to analyze the dynamics between sender and receiver; M and F are their activities and, in the current context, can also refer to the entities that perform the activity (producer and receiver, respectively). There is a dual management of time, as in the biological brain, with a timeless and a time-dependent formulation for both. Furthermore, spatial organization matches both rule and biological counterpart because Hilbert's spatial distribution assigns to every message a locus and a locus that does not diverge (just imagine a brain growing up along the entire life of an individual). As the curve is a fractal with a fixed dimension 2 that does not changes, the impact of new dots (i.e., new sentences with more information) is a density, but not an increment of the global size.

In the current context, the fractal dimension D represents a change rate in the amount of entropy encoded in the current fraction of the communication (see ref [1] for more details). Since there is a factual flow M synchronized with the one from F, both poles interact at any t balancing each other. The current flow from M could present any information, so the Hilbert model can map it but needs to be used properly settled with the smallest dimension n big enough to handle the required number of bits.

Note that t is dual in the sense that there is a process in $t \rightarrow +\infty$, concurrently with others in $t \rightarrow -\infty$. This could be analogous to what happens with tachyon particles [14] and considered as the expression of imaginary numbers in R^3 world. Nevertheless, the perspective of M and F has both individuals representing two poles acting at the same time, with a unique timeline each one but coordinated by a spot in t, which transforms both activities into an interchange.

4.2 Human biology of time

In order to determine how time works in language production, it is important to evaluate how the brain biases the time conception and the consequences of that bias. The information handled during an interchange between person's impacts somehow physically the neural

structures involved in the process. Findings in the field reveal that several brain nuclei participate in the information management when the communication inputs the individual. The
following subsections introduce several hypotheses used to lead the bibliographical research
on time perception by humans, and the explanation of how biology induces it according to
the current experts' community.

4.2.1 Working hypotheses for time management

This section describes the hypothesis considered to determine the types of previous work to
cover. Some of them are already explained in previous publications of the author:

H1. Communication C involves information [2]
H2. The biological device needs storage namely a physical space [1]
H3. There is at least one timeline in the process [2]
H4. The timeline for any communication has past, present, and future
H5. The process acquires a certain speed related to data gathering, information
processing, and reaction [2]
H6. The speed in H5 is not constant nor uniquely defined for every animal (human being
or not)
H7. Time perception is related to the speed under conditions H5 and H6.

4.2.2 Criteria for validity

In order to determine the confidence level of the findings, certain selection criteria are being
applied to the bibliographical material. Material is centered in brain nuclei covering at least
one of the following topics:

Relationship of the memories with time perception
Relationship of metabolic factors with time perception.

Any other material not raised from biological evaluations, thought potentially very solid
and aligned with the current goals, is being discarded. This is because the section intends to
gain its roots only on biological clues.

4.2.3 Materials and methods

The main contribution of this section to the rules is to provide the biological roots of some
aspects of the fourth rule. It considers time perception in humans as a general phenomenon,
specifically in the context of linguistic communication.
As a general approach, the bibliographical coverage is as follows:

— Explore animal encephalon: structures involved
— Nuclei functioning as a storage of information
— Nuclei functioning as a time device
— Metabolic rate and time perception alteration.

4.2.4 Biological foundations of time in human mind

The nervous system is responsible for encoding and managing information obtained from the environment. It gathers its input from different sources through the sensory system and internal feedback subsystems. At the retrieval moment, the biological architecture decodes it considering the temporary information encoded in its structural features. Time is expressed in parameters such as 3D disposition, strength, and associated information such as hormones and feelings [15]. The rest of this subsection explains the main gears in this biological device.

4.2.4.1 Animal encephalon structures involved

There is evidence that information is physically stored in a specific encephalon location, typically in the medial lobe temporal region [16] (see Fig. 4–1).

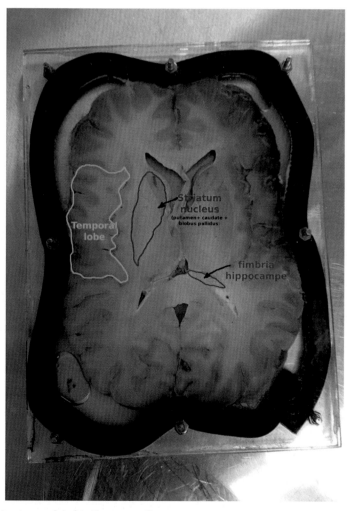

FIGURE 4–1 Brain structures related to time perception.

Experience shows that after removing this region, attention and short-term memory are preserved, but patients lose the ability to learn and remember new information in long-term periods. Note that the effect is found with the hippocampus and parahippocampal turns extirpation.

Among several documented cases of amnesia after surgical bilateral hippocampus removal,
there was a patient who was studied for 14 years starting in 1953 [17]. The man could only
learn three digits in no more than 15 min and only by repeating them constantly without los-
ing attention.

4.2.4.2 Nuclei functioning as a storage of information

According to the German biologist Richard Semon [18], memory can be thought of as a
three-part process:

Step 1: engraph, the information encoding stage.
Step 2: engram, the impact of Step 1. This is observed as a set of changes in the nervous
system, according to the inputted information.
Step 3: ecphory, the information retrieval.

Although the true conditions of the original information storage are very hardly replicated
in the real world, Semon affirms that the last step is possible only under the same conditions
as in the first step.

Poldrack and Packard performed several scans near the hippocampus and found that the
striatum activity depends on the input information status (see its location in Fig. 4−1) [19]:

a. New information: increased activity in the hippocampus and reduced activity in the striatum
b. Known information: increased activity in the striatum and reduced activity in the
hippocampus

A practical example of type b is an activity learned after several repetitions.

From the linguistic perspective, information has at least three levels of abstraction:
syntactical, semantic, and practical or contextual. The first one refers to the formal representation
of information and its expression in certain communication channels (text, sound, and image).
The second is the understanding of the information contained after individual inner and outer
context adaptations. The last one is more complex and relates to cultural and social concerns.

Linguistic levels are also studied since they involve different brain nuclei coverage.
Semantics is also a set of attributes associated with concepts being handled and affects its
storage and retrieval process during linguistic performances [20]. In fact, Poldrack found that
the left lower prefrontal region fetches attributes and handles the semantic representations
associated with any location of the brain [21] (see Fig. 4−2).

4.2.4.3 Nuclei functioning as a time device

One of the most relevant studies in the field is from Tulving, which focused on human memories [22]. He classifies storage into three systems:

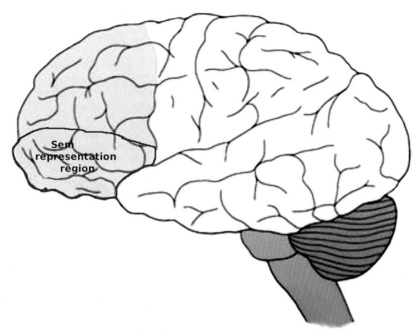

FIGURE 4–2 Semantic management according to Poldrack.

a. procedural
b. semantic
c. episodic memory.

In simple biological organisms, there is only the procedural because it allows animals to input and know how to perform a task.

Semantic memory is not involved in space−time considerations but in digits, names, and specific data as isolated and factual information available.

Conversely, episodic memory is responsible for relating space−time, sentiments, and facts in semantic memory. Therefore, any access is coupled to certain mental images built with outer and inner sensory information, timing, and factual data.

Tulving, in analogy with Semon's steps, defines for every type of memory the following three tasks: acquisition (input), representation (encoding), and expression (output). Studies in rats' brains show that episodic memory weakens over the course of time [23]. As a consequence, they can learn new tasks as a sequence of current knowledge. Based on these experiments, Roberts suggests that the time of the information added to the memories is relevant, but there are no signs revealing that animals are able to determine the specific moment where the concept is incorporated. This suggests that probably animals cannot determine temporary order and just know everything as something at present.

In contrast, Dombeck and Heys found a kind of time-ordering evidence but, in contrast with humans, associated with concrete external experiences [24]. The tests are focused on the temporal lobe, specifically in the medial entorhinal cortex (see Fig. 4−3) of mice.

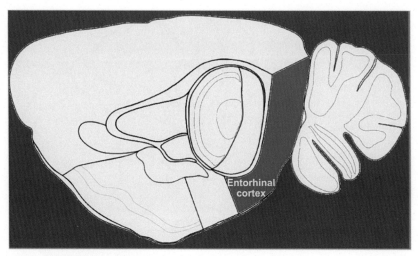

FIGURE 4–3 Entorhinal cortex in mice brain.

Dombeck identified that region as the center of episodic memory and time perception because he realized that the cells located there activate when the animal needs to wait a number of seconds for the availability of food. Episodic information entails data regarding space and points in time. In this case, data are tuple (reward, 6 s, door in the middle of the labyrinth). The tests could indicate that the entorhinal region plays a key role in the time encoding for mice.

4.2.4.4 Time perception and its alterations

Studies in animals show many interesting features of the nuclei's responsibilities. For instance, the temporal lobe shows scarce participation in the fetching process of old semantic information [25].

Another interesting aspect is the alteration of time perception according to the metabolic rhythm [26]: small animals with rapid metabolism present faster information acquisition in time, faster time perception related to critical blink fusion rate (CBFR, the maximum speed for an individual to be able to distinguish separated light spots), and slower metabolism associated to lower CBFR rates.

Hippocampus is part of the limbic system of the brain as hypothalamus, amygdala, and some other structures nearby. While the second has been found to control motivation, emotions, learning, and memory, the first one regulates body temperature, metabolic processes, and activities corresponding to the autonomic nervous system (ANS). The entire system is associated with emotions and memories [27,28].

In Fig. 4–4, there are the main structures of the limbic system. There (1) stands for hypothalamus, (2) amygdala (basic emotions), (3) fornix, (4) septum, (5) the entorhinal cortex (memory), (6) the hippocampus, (7) thalamus, (8) corpus callosum, and (9) stria terminalis.

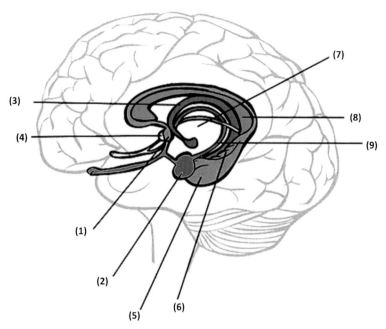

FIGURE 4–4 The limbic system.

Scientists have found that the hippocampus plays a vital role in the formation, organization, and storage of new memories, as well as in connecting some sensations and emotions to these memories.

Hypothalamus links the nervous system with the endocrine system through pituitary glands, and actually, it has a number of small nuclei with distinctive functions. The hormones released by the hypothalamus are named neurohormones, and they regulate hormones from the pituitary gland. This way, it controls feelings such as thirst, fatigue, sleepiness, certain behaviors, and circadian rhythms.

While both the hippocampus and hypothalamus control emotions and memories, hippocampus relates to motivation, emotions, learning, and memory, while the hypothalamus dominates body conditions of the ANS.

4.3 Evidence of timelines in the brain: time in linguistic reasoning

From the previous section, it is evident that memory is a complex device where different nuclei activate according to space–time requirements at the storage and retrieval moment.

The evidence shown may be summarized as follows:

1. There is a dramatic quality separation between short- and long-term memory, affecting the quality and structure of the information persisted.

2. Frontal lobe is a recent biological acquisition with the responsibility for time perception improvement.
3. Encephalon is the key organ in the process of space−time information storage and management, with certain specialized nuclei with specific duties.
4. Abstract thought in humans is affected by time consciousness.
5. Information structure and extension determine the ability to perform multiple time perspectives: past, present, and/or future.
6. Abstract information is not episodic but long term (i.e., semantic conceptions).

From the listed items, the information to provide past, present, and future perceptions coexists. The individual neuro-linguistic makes use of some kind of inborn programming to perform the shifting in time perceptions.

In this context, past and episodic information are distinct elements. While the first represents information that can be changed, the latter is handled automatically by the perception and consciousness biological engine. In fact, new episodic information may refer to past or future information.

One interesting thing here is that time perception is influenced as the information acquired increases [18]: in order to generalize and create abstractions, there is a past-information fetching and expansion (ecphory). Note that the process involves the present (the newly added information), past (the reference knowledge), and future (resulting of the process). This way, the updated status, the classification (abstraction), works in reversed time in relation to the human timeline by which data are inputted (see Fig. 4−5).

The more the information processed, the older the reference used and the more complex the feature extraction processed. The progression is centered in episodic regions. An alteration of the level of information processing impacts the time perception to more or less degree since emotions participate in the storing procedure (as expressed in the previous

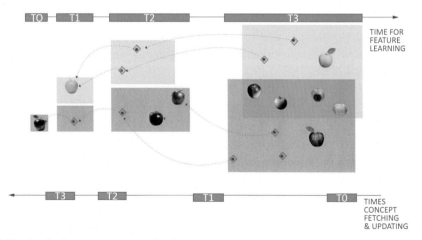

FIGURE 4–5 Timeline for input and conceptualization.

section) [15]. This has been tested using psychotropic drugs and with patients with the surgical emotion of the temporal lobe [17].

Time perceptions influence by means of the affective state of consciousness (as distinguished from the cognitive and volitional state of consciousness) [19], expressed by hormones and a complex engine that articulates feelings with neural physical disposition and functioning [29,30]. The two types of memories are declarative memory and spatial relationship memory [27,28], with two main nuclei of the limbic system involved:

— hypothalamus: participates in body homeostasis control (temperature, metabolic processes, etc.), embodies feelings, and alters time perception (with also impacts in episodic information)
— hippocampus: provides the ability to make new long-term memories and control motivation, emotions, learning, and memory.

Striatum nucleus is strongly connected with time perception [17], but declarative information such as semantics has been found to be located in the prefrontal region [21] and not related to space−time data [25] typically present in episodic memories in humans and animals [24].

Time perception is not constant nor identical for different animals or humans because it is biased by metabolic speed [26] and sensory quality (number and strength of features) [19].

As a consequence, it could be said that evidence allows us to affirm that every individual perceives a unique timeline by means of singular episodic recordings in the temporal lobe, biased by the striatum nucleus. Furthermore, time perception evolves with time and goes back in previously stored information updating it in a backward fashion from present to past.

4.4 Some clues and tests

As mentioned in section 4.1, TRLR determines a timeline for *M* and *F*, which is also compatible with the evidence presented in section 4.2, where time-related encephalon nuclei present activities showing that there is a timeline for every individual. This section shows how TRLR manages time during the evolution of a linguistic interchange where the goal is the communication (i.e., transference) of information from a source *M* represented by a human player, and *F* (the target) is an artificial intelligence (AI) artifact named 20Q. Please note that every test performed uses just Spanish as a language.

4.4.1 A device to model timelines

The timeline in TRLR and in the presented biological structures is to be considered within the time frame of a dialog, in order to delimit the time range. This section is a reduced sketch of the device described in previous publications as NNR4 [1,2]. Its architecture is a four-layer neural network with units adapted to implement the TRLR rules in Table 4−1 (see Fig. 4−6).

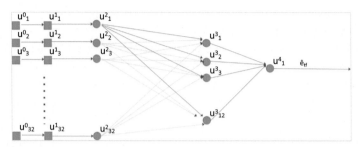

FIGURE 4–6 NNR4 architecture.

The corpus to be used is communications C consisting of dialogs. In the following sections, just one of 20 tests is studied as a use case (Test #5) since it is a typical successful communication with a size and richness that allows describing properly the key concepts. The next section explains 20Q.

NNR4 inputs every sentence word by word with metadata to denote the sequence in time and position in a sentence. The first layer has 23 Hilbert units that replace traditional sigmoid ones. They record in their structure every input as a spatial 3D location using the input sequence as a time reference. Every dot has associated the $h(e, t)$ entropy variation in H, denoted here as delta_h. All the units normalize this value in order to avoid extra bias for Layer 2.

The second layer is units that collect Layer 1 output. Every unit just connects with its predecessor in the previous layer. The unit classifies the input using expectation maximization (EM) heuristics [31]. The connection does not have just the activation function sending tuples like:

$$\left[p_t, n < x, y, z, \text{delta\_}h >\right] \tag{4-1}$$

with:

t: the ID of the test, used for statistics, validation, and future use
n: is the node sequence, from 1 to 32
x, y, z: the Hilbert coordinates assigned by the unit in Layer 1
p: cluster ID assigned by the unit in Layer 2.

The third layer has 12 traditional convolutional sigmoid units [31] fully connected with units in Layer 2.

The last layer has a unit with identity activation, and a fuzzy-c means as the transference function.

NNR4 has been implemented using Python and WEKA libraries. Every layer has a log attached to every unit for future use.

4.4.2 A use case to test timelines

The use case is an entire dialog in natural language, performed in Spanish. The entries are sentences belonging to Dialog #5, selected from a set of 20 plays. The game used here is known as 20Q, with two participants, with a clear notion of win−loss. The game goal is to guess the name of an object of any type. The condition to win is to perform proper questions to the counterpart in order to find out the word in less than 20 interactions.

The game has been selected because there is guessing of something never explicitly mentioned in the context of the test but derived from precise interactions. In addition, the interactions need to be very efficient, as the player is allowed to just perform a limited number of yes/no questions. A good thing is that the game considers any word in Spanish, so any *e* in *E* could be used here. Another proper condition is that the interaction is led by the human player while asking questions, acting as *M* but with the knowledge describing the features of the object partitioned in subsequent questions (delta_h, or *h*(*e*, *t*)) that are very clear. Note that the cultural context, which is *E* here, is the one providing the clues to the gamers.

20Q is a game created by the software specialist Robin Burgener in 1988, which implements an AI system with a neural network that learns from previous playing. The player thinks of an object, and after up to 20 questions [32], the AI performs guessing. If it is not correct, there are additional questions and the player performs a new try. The last step is the explanation of the conjectures newly learned. Knowledge in it is derived from the interpretation of previous activity, so there is not an initial knowledge base that might bias the experience. It does not develop a general taxonomy but an experimental one, so the online version may contain inaccurate information, for instance, if the user is cheating the AI. Among the limitations of the system, it cannot apply a logical linking of questions. For instance, it could ask "is it an animal?" After the question "is it a horse?" With a "no" answer.

For the sake of a controlled test framework, the protocols to perform the games are as follows:

- the player writes down a name and keeps it visible to the tester. It allowed animals, plants, prominent person names, places, or any other simple word
- the questions that AI performs can only be answered with *yes*, *no*, or *sometimes* despite there are some other options in the online application
- after up to 20 questions, the AI performs guessing and can keep making questions until a limit of 40 interactions
- the system wins if the written name matches the guessing
- every interaction (question and answer) is recorded in a log along with the name and an ID
- if the name was already used, the tester would ask the player for a new name in order to avoid duplicates.

The use case selected for the current paper is Test ID 5, which was correctly guessed after 30 interactions (compiled in the corpus as 60 sentences considering questions and answers), with a total of 232 words (21 nouns, 39 verbs, and 172 appreciations[1]). The target word in Spanish is *bolígrafo* (pen). Table 4−2 is the entire Game 5 in its original language and English.

The table has the five guessings in gray. The preprocess ends with 13,939 tuples processed by NNR4.

---

[1] The appreciation (A) is a category designed in the context of the testings and described in section **1.a**. It covers any syntagma but nouns or verbs.

Table 4–2   Sequence of questions for test ID 5.

#	Sentence (Sp)	Sentence (En)	Answer (Sp)	Answer (En)
1	Se clasifica como Otra cosa?	Can it be classified as something else?	Sí	Yes
2	Es más grande que un recipiente de mantequilla?	Is it bigger than a butter pot?	No	No
3	Tiene algo escrito?	Is there something written on it?	A veces	Sometimes
4	Se encuentra en un escritorio?	Could it be on a desk?	Sí	Yes
5	Se hace del metal?	is it made of metal?	A veces	Sometimes
6	Es crujiente?	Is it crunchy?	No	No
7	Tiene un valor en dinero?	Have monetary value?	Sí	Yes
8	Se utilizaba hace más de 100 años?	Was it used more than 100 years ago?	No	No
9	Es negro?	Is it black?	A veces	Sometimes
10	Está hecho de plástico?	It is made of plastic?	A veces	Sometimes
11	Es más pequeño que una pelota de golf?	Is it smaller than a golf ball?	Sí	Yes
12	Puede rodar?	Is that able to roll?	No	No
13	Se lleva en el bolsillo?	Can it be carried in a pocket?	A veces	Sometimes
14	Hace ruido?	Does that make noise?	No	No
15	Viene en una caja?	Is it normally found in a box?	A veces	Sometimes
16	Puedes conseguir información al usarlo?	Can you get information by using it?	No	No
17	Se puede doblar sin romperse?	Can you bend it without breaking it?	No	No
18	Puedes usarlo con tus amigos?	Can you use it with your friends?	Sí	Yes
19	Se puede oler?	Can you smell it?	No	No
20	Conjeturo que es un sacapuntas	I guess it is a pencil sharpener	A veces	Sometimes
21	Se utiliza en el trabajo?	Do you use it at work?	Sí	Yes
22	Conjeturo que es un chip	I guess it is a chip	No	No
23	Es recto?	Is it straight?	Sí	Yes
24	Conjeturo que es un puntero láser	I am guessing that is a laser pointer	A veces	Sometimes
25	Es multicolor?	Is it multicolored?	A veces	Sometimes
26	Te acercarías lo suficiente para tocarlo?	Would you get close enough to touch it?	Sí	Yes
27	Se utiliza en los viajes?	Is it used on trips?	A veces	Sometimes
28	Se quema?	Does it usually burn?	No	No
29	Conjeturo que es una pila (batería)	I guess that is a battery	A veces	Sometimes
30	Conjeturo que es un bolígrafo	I guess it is a pen	Sí	Yes

4.4.3 Modeling the use case with NNR4

NNR4 is a neural network whose architecture deploys the first four rules described in the introduction. Test 5 generates a log with the target name and mainly a set of tuples like

$$< id, Q, A > \tag{4-2}$$

with:

> *id*: the sequence number in the test (i.e., the first entry in Table 4−2), representing the identifier of a communication C between M and F. In this case, M is the player, F is the AI, and $C = \{c_1, c_2, \ldots, c_{30}\}$
> Q: the textual expression of c_i, $i \in [1, 30]$, the message originated by M
> A: the answer to c_i, the message originated by F

> From the words in c_i, there is a tagging process as follows:

> Any verb or verbal phrase receives a tag $\&V$
> Any noun or noun phrase receives a tag $\&N$
> The words not labeled with $\&V$ or $\&N$ receive the tag $\&A$. They usually are qualifications, descriptions, properties, or characteristics (expressed as adjectives, adverbs, etc.).

As explained in section 4.1, $C \sim h(e, t)$, implemented here as a Hilbert disposition of dots $h(e, t)$ by means of a function $f(x, y, z, h, t) \sim h(e, t)$ with coordinates x, y, z assigned by the Hilbert mappers in Layer 1, and h is the entropy (see [1] for details).

4.4.3.1 First rule: timelessness out of C

A communication C succeeds if the concept e is correctly received and interpreted by F (the AI). In the current context, it happens if the target word (pen) is guessed by the AI. The information transference is complete, that is, the entropy H of the process has been properly delivered in a set of $h(e, t)$ deliveries, and F is able to select current e in E since the semantic interpretation of C refers to an ontological element corresponding to the one considered by M in some way. Note that E never changes; it is timeless for both M and F and would be akin to a declarative nucleus while e is in the episodic. Note that there are several philosophical concerns about ontologies and their mental representations, such as the possibilities to consider ontologies as universal elements out of the individual. For practical reasons, the ontological element is considered as any object that may be subject of reference using language expressions.

TRLR considers only closed systems in order to cover the entire communication elements involved in the balance of the entropy in the process. As explained, every text generated by M has a virtual counterpart by F, tacit in the real world. It is expected to happen something similar in vocal and in visual communication, but this is part of future work.

Any vocal communication implies a kind of movement, just as happens with textual interactions because such a movement involves the transference of a message in (e, t). In NNR4, it generates a trace in the form of a tuple (x_t, y_t, z_t) with t evolving from a starting t_0 in which the sender performs a verbal expression until a final time t_f. From the receiver perspective, t'_0 is t_f. Then, it manages a virtual time which is a reversed (e, t), so it goes like $t': t_f \rightarrow t_0$.

Note that the constituents used in the communication of M impact the ontological space usage perspective when they become an apparent manifestation of E for a while. Then, any ontology refers to E as a manifestation in t, and the current C is just a transient association of a certain type of expression to an e. The constituents eventually used are related to a symbolic expression (for instance, a character, a symbol, or a sound) that is useful in t since they are organized, and they present an order that is effective during the valid range of t (that is the lapse of the communication). The process assigns an amount of entropy from H, which holds any E available for M. However, if there is no C, H is not being used, and the system equilibrates.

Anytime a set of constituents are organized, they can be total or partially transferred using an amount of H that moves and needs a counterpart in $-t$ (i.e., some kind of $\sim H$). Whenever the portion of H does not cover the entire possibility of e in E, then there is a gap and F does not recreate the ontological element. E is timeless, and e handles some t at a certain speed (the movement) and variation in t. H holds every and all possibilities of t management as a complete representation of E.

It is important to note that during the 20Q game, F is the one generating text, but M is generating C. Then, t_0 is determined by M not F despite the textual interchange starting with F. It can be understood considering that M is starting the process when he or she is thinking of a target name.

For practical reasons, in the successive, every id in the first column of Table 4−2 is considered as a time tic in t, despite it is not t but $-t$ in the terms described in section 4.1.

The evolution of H as a sequence of $h(e, t)$ is expressed through the entropy contained in the sentences, which is also related to the way words are used. From the linguistic perspective, words regard the linguistic categories they embody and from the communication theory to the entropy calculated from them, which relies on the relative frequencies.

Fig. 4−7 is the cumulated distribution of nouns and Fig. 4−8 are the same for verbs.

Note that distribution for nouns is typically stepped. This behavior is not present in verbs but can be observed in any of the 20 tests of the corpus (see [2] for more details).

Mining the linguistic categories raises an interesting finding: sentences present a determined structure at the beginning of the interchange and with a special evolution in t that differs in the cases of hit (AI wins) as happens in the current use case.

Table 4−3 has the five clusters found by the EM heuristic [31], each one representing a context-featured use of words in the sentence. Note that even though there are three categories, they are being (V, N, A) used in five ways.

Fig. 4−9 shows the rate of each category in every test performed in the complete dataset and highlighted in light blue Test 5 [1]. As can be seen, some of these clusters are not present in certain test cases, and they correspond to plays with difficulty in finding out the target name (for instance, Test IDs 2, 6, 13, and 18).

As can be seen, the cluster distribution (i.e., the structure of the expressions) presents Clusters 1, 2, and 4 in every case. Cluster 3 is missing in all the test cases that did not succeed or required many questions to get close to the goal.

Clusters 3 and 4 have more verbs than others, and Clusters 1 and 2 present more nouns. Cluster 1 has the highest rate of nouns. Cluster 4 contains a more diverse set of verbs than Cluster 3. Cluster 5 is not represented here and could be explained as the result of the cumulative bias in the processing.

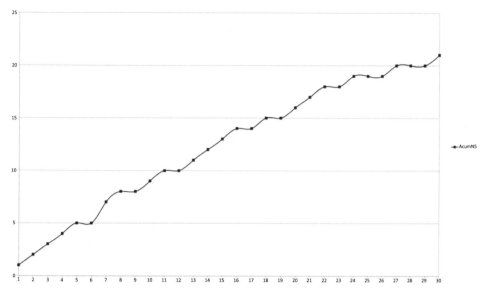

FIGURE 4–7 Cumulative distribution of nouns in Test 5.

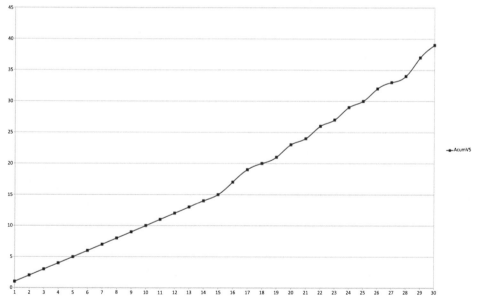

FIGURE 4–8 Cumulative distribution of verbs in Test 5.

4.4.3.2 Second rule: cycles of use case timelines

In section 4.1, it was explained that TRLR evaluates the movement produced by the existence of e in E, as a cyclical behavior whose entropy $h(e, t)$ can be modeled using fractals, specifically by assessing its dimension D at every step c_i in C.

Table 4–3   EM clustering for sentences in test ID 5.

Cluster ID	# questions	Cluster color
1	181 (35%)	Blue
2	69 (13%)	Red
3	28 (5%)	Green
4	243 (47%)	Turquoise
5	5 (1%)	Light blue

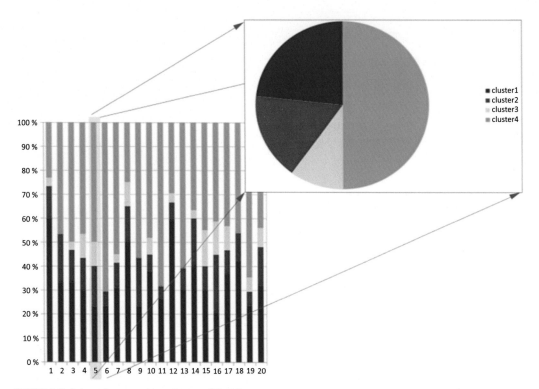

FIGURE 4–9 Categories usage in sentences of Test 5.

As nouns (N) and verbs (V) partially build the amount of H to be delivered in a sentence, this section intends to analyze how they cycle and integrate D as a whole. This is called rhythm and vibration in TRLR.

Fig. 4–10 is H in Test #5 denoted as ET. $ET(V)$, $ET(N)$, and $ET(A)$ are the corresponding entropies due to V, N, and A, respectively.

The curves do not cross (this is observed in all the tests [2]) and $ET(V) \geq ET(A) \geq ET(N)$ in all cases and all tests. The figure also shows a mark called H_s which is described in section 4.3.3.

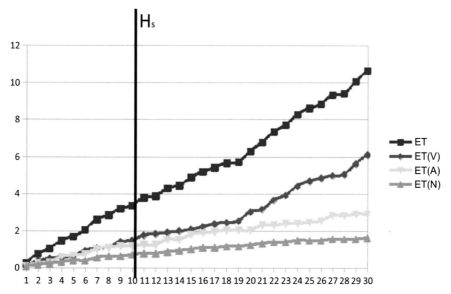

FIGURE 4–10 Entropy and corresponding values for *V*, *N*, and *A*.

$$[6.00\text{-}6.73][6.74\text{-}6.78][6.79\text{-}6.80][6.81\text{-}7.48][7.49\text{-}8.88][8.90\text{-}8.99][9.00\text{-}9.82][9.83\text{-}11.69][11.70\text{-}13.22]$$

ET

FIGURE 4–11 Hit and fail regions for *ET* values.

Being *H* the entropy explaining the information in the system, $h(e, t)$ is an excellent metric to explain the performance of the game. In fact, winner games have *ET* in [6.06−9.66] while failed games are in [9.83−10.77] (see [1,2] for more details) (Fig. 4−11).

The regions are cyclic but not with similar sizes. As the number of test cases is relatively low, it could be a sampling bias. Test case #5, the current use case, has $ET = 9.64$, a hit region. There is a dark interval that has neither a hit nor a fail. In any case, the characteristics of the regions need to be deeply studied. Entropy *ET* is calculated using the classical equation:

$$ET(\text{IDQ}) = -\,p(s).\log_2(p(s)) \quad \text{and} \quad p(s) = \frac{s}{T} \tag{4-3}$$

where

  s: number of *V*, *N*, or *A* in the sentence $c_i \in C$
  T: total words in c_i.

C is, in the use case, a dialog between the player and the 20Q system, and *e* (the hidden name) has to be described through its features expressed as instances of *E* possibilities available to describe any *e*.

Note that e could be anything, and the possibility of reaching the right answer by chance is almost none since it could be one or more combinations from about 93,000 words officially declared in the Spanish dictionary added to any name or character, or personality popular nowadays. Then, the interchange between M and F has to keep a good flow of entropy in $h(e, t)$.

Tests also show a complementary behavior between N and V. The rhythm is provided not only by the ET variation with c_i but also due to the amount of entropy due to N and V. Tests show that there is a kind of counterpart in ET between the contribution of N and V, but the balance is not perfect since there is a third type of syntagma: A. This dynamic becomes more evident in the dimensional analysis with D.

For Test ID 5, total entropy [ET, as Eq. (4−3)] is 10.63, the entropy due to N and V [EI, as Eq. (4−4)] is 13.14, and the entropy for V and A [ER, as Eq. (4−5)] is 12.99. ER and EI have no special interest in the current analysis but are used in section 4.3.3. Just ET and its relationship with the rate of V, N, and A presents a trend that can be statistically confirmed.

$$EI = - p'^{(s)}.\log_2\left(p'^{(s)}\right) \text{ and } p'(s) = \frac{s}{N_V + N_N} \qquad (4-4)$$

with

N_V: number of words labeled &V
N_N: number of words labeled &N.

$$ER = - p''(s).\log_2(p''(s)) \text{ and } p'(s) = \frac{s}{N_V + N_A} \qquad (4-5)$$

with

N_V: number of words labeled &V
N_A: number of words labeled &A.

The variation in H due to each c_i is described in TRLR by Eq. (4−6), fractal dimension [8] at t = i, even though it has not yet been found a self-similarity function for H fluctuations.

$$D = \frac{\log_x N}{\log_x (1/r)} \qquad (4-6)$$

with

N: number of partitions
r: change rate
$x = 2$.

In the context of TRLR, N can be thought of as the total entropy variation (ET), at every c_i in $h(e, t)$. Then:

$N_i = \Delta ET_i = ET_i - ET_{i-1}$, the change in ET between two questions or sentences. Regarding r, it is the total entropy at c_i. Then: $r_i = ET_i$, ET value in question or sentence i. Eq. (4−7) shows the result after adaptations:

$$D_i = \frac{\log_2 \Delta ET_i}{\log_2 (1/ET_i)} = \frac{\log_2(ET_i - ET_{i-1})}{\log_2 (1/ET_i)}. \qquad (4-7)$$

Fig. 4−12 is the plot of Eq. (4−7) for the current use case.

As can be seen, the plot is like a pulse with a negative and a positive peak. The smoothed curve can be explained as a critical status where the class of the object represented needs to be determined (minimum peak) and a maximum where it is found. The following dots are a decreasing alteration to the obtained entropy since the subsequent interactions just provide further specificity to the features of e. This is one of the four strategies found in the analysis of the entire test set, revealing the alternate preferences of humans to approach the problem (considering that the AI just mimics human behavior). See [2] for more details.

Consider a second dimension analysis as in Eq. (4−8). Here, $N = \Delta ET(V) = ET(V)_i - ET(V)_{i-1}$, the change in ET due to V between two questions, and $r = ET(N)_i$, ET value due to N in question at the time i.

$$D_i = \frac{\log_2 \Delta ET(V)_i}{\log_2 (1/ET(N)_i)} = \frac{\log_2 (ET(V)_i - ET(V)_{i-1})}{\log_2 (1/ET(N)_i)}. \qquad (4-8)$$

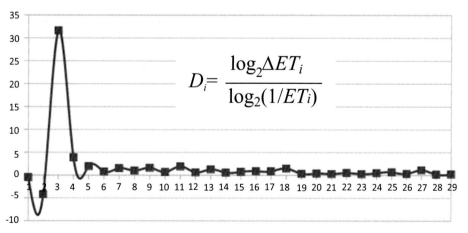

FIGURE 4–12 Fractal dimension evolution for test case 5

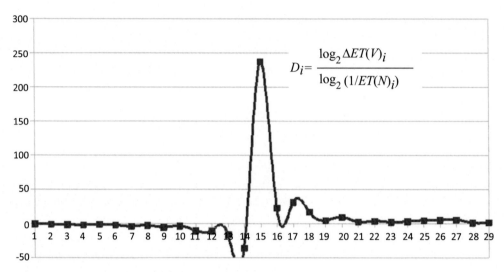

FIGURE 4–13 Fractal dimension evolution for $ET(V)_i$ variation due to $ET(N)_i$.

Fig. 4−13 shows the resulting plot for the use case.

This behavior is one of the most frequently found in the tests. There is a negative peak smaller than the positive. It is typical of the strategy already described in the previous figure, where the individual intends to get an idea of the type of target object before trying a specific name. Dimension as in Eq. (4−7) is good to identify when the player intends to discard main properties and to classify quickly. There are other alternatives to this two-step approach (for instance, to take more time to discard also minor features and/or to validate main features); all of them present different curves in Eq. (4−7) but similar curves for Eq. (4−6).

A peculiar symmetry is found between the curve obtained with Eq. (4−6) and the one with Eq. (4−8), with $N = ET(V) = ET(V)_i$, the value of ET due to V at the current question, and $r = ET(N)_i$, ET value due to N in question at the time i.

$$D_i = \frac{\log_2 ET(V)_i}{\log_2 \left(1/ET(N)_i\right)} \qquad (4-9)$$

Fig. 4−14 shows curves for Eqs. (4.7) and (4.8) overlapped with dark and light colors, respectively.

The positive peak compensates with a counterpart in the other curve. The same happens with the slopes. This is almost a kind of symmetric behavior. The figure represents the graph for Game ID 5. They lack perfect symmetry due to the influence of words labeled with A.

Rule 2 explains how the information is carried in sentences. When the analysis is centered on N and V, then H variations can be used to evaluate the efficiency of the process. Tests have shown that the evolution of H is neither linear nor perfect. It also shows a kind of complementary behavior between N and V that is not perfect and presents a certain rhythm and cycle. In this context, a cycle is events in a group that happens in a particular sequenced

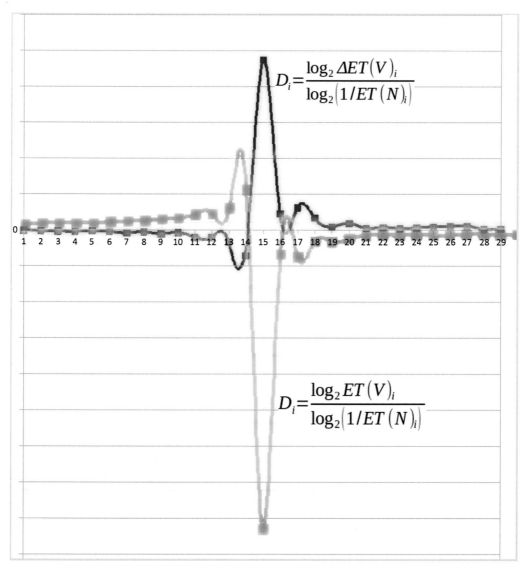

$$D_i = \frac{\log_2 \Delta ET(V)_i}{\log_2\left(1/ET(N)_i\right)}$$

$$D_i = \frac{\log_2 ET(V)_i}{\log_2\left(1/ET(N)_i\right)}$$

FIGURE 4–14 Dimension evolution for $\Delta ET(V)_i$ and $ET(V)_i$ due to $ET(N)_i$.

ordering and is often repeated. Rhythm is a regular movement or pattern of movements. Both have been found in the tests of this section.

4.4.3.3 Third rule: poles in c according to timelines

A communication in TRLR involves a polarized t (i.e., a $t \to +\infty$) that requires a counterpart ($t \to -\infty$). There is a t_f where the polarization ends, and it happens when $h(e, t)$ is complete. There is a special time in 20Q when the accumulated entropy reaches a level called H_s. It is important to determine if the transference is complete or not.

Note that any C performed by M requires a $t << \infty$ since its length covers the interchange between M and F (in the current use case during Dialog #5). During that lapse, E has an e made explicit in some way available in O (i.e., a text, a mimic, a picture, or any other channel). Note that the system keeps dual: timeless and time dependent, and in every case, it is a triplet (O, E, C).

This section evaluates the polarization evidence in Test 5 and the triplet constituents regarding t; as a summary, it can be said that any C is a certain evolution of the triplet in t due to the existence of e. The interchange C presents an evolution, an increasing entropy due to the growing participation of constituents pertaining to O until a critical value related to Φ, as will be shown here.

As mentioned, M polarizes E through a communication C that takes an e in t. The communication, when evaluated from the entropy evolution, presents a critical point in time called t_a in TRLR. For written interchanges the movements or alterations in t of $h(e, t)$, the polarization expresses with words as constituents, and they follow certain patterns that moderate the changes of $h(e, t)$. Note that the perspective of the receiver F is negentropy evolution more than entropy increasing, but for both M and F, E has a net balance of H at any time. There is a breakout in the evolution of $h(e, t)$ that impacts the entire quality of the process and can be used to evaluate whether the transference is complete or not between the sender and receiver.

In order to evaluate the breakout, consider the EI and ER entropy as in Eqs. (4−4) and (4−5), respectively. Fig. 4−15 shows the rate EI/ER for Test ID 5.

The figure shows a line in $EI/ER = 1.01$ which is a target value (there is a similar behavior in all the tests [2]). This value gets Hs as a value. In order to understand how it words

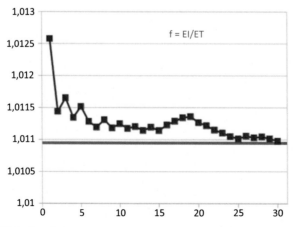

FIGURE 4.15 Relation EI/ER for Test 5.

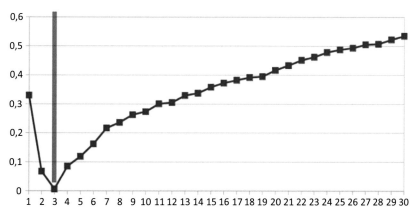

FIGURE 4–16 Curve of Eq. (4.10) for Test 5.

see the curve f in Fig. 4–16 [for Eq. (4–10) applied to Test 5] and f^{-1} in Fig. 4–17 [as Eq. (4–11)].

$$f = \left| \frac{\log_2(ET)}{\log_2(1/m)} \right| \qquad (4-10)$$

with

   ET as calculated in Eq. (4–3)
   $m = 30$, the number of sentences generated by M.

$$f^{-1} = \left| \frac{\log_2(ET)}{\log_2(1/m)} \right|^{-1} \qquad (4-11)$$

f is based on the fractal dimension, but this time N is ET, and r is the number of sentences generated by M at the time i. Note that f reaches an inflection value at time t_a, which is more evident in Fig. 4–17. The curves exhibit a change in the trend polarity. To remark on this behavior, the absolute values are considered.

Considering $E_{[1-k]}$ as in Eq. (4–11), every test that verifies Eq. (4–12) represents a game where AI wins (that is, the entire entropy is transferred, and e is understood by F)

$$E_{[1-k]} = \sum_{i=1}^{i=K} \sqrt{D_i^2} \qquad (4-11)$$

$$\left(E_{[1-k]} \right)^{\Phi} = \Phi1^{E_{[1-k]}} - 1 \qquad (4-12)$$

$$\Phi = \frac{(1 + \sqrt{5})}{2} = 1.6180339 \qquad (4-13)$$

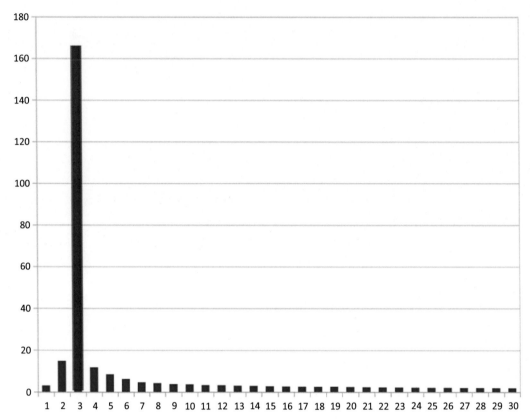

FIGURE 4–17 Curve of Eq. (4.11) for Test 5.

with

> D as in Eq. (4–10)
> Φ as in Eq. (4–13)
> $k = m = 30$, the number of sentences generated by M.

For the current use case, it verifies Eq. (4–12), $E_{[1 - k]} = 0.61$, $\Phi^{E[1 - k]} - 1 = 1.61$. It is interesting to note that in games where artificial neural networks (ANN) loses, the proportion is not perfect, and there are differences in the order of 10^{-2}.

4.4.3.4 Fourth rule: the physical expression of timelines
In TRLR, there are two types of movements:

> The generative (M): activates the movement using entropy portions as pulses $h(e, t)$, to transfer e contextualized (i.e., adapted in some way to the channel, culture, and several features available in O to reduce E)
> The receptive (F): reactive to an incoming pulse that uses the features encompassed by M in order to acquire e in a proper way.

NNR4 is a technical device designed to evaluate Rules 1−4 in TRLR. The neural network is described in section 4.1 (see [2] for further details).

This section focuses on specific values obtained with NNR4 applied to the use case, in order to analyze how Rule 4 expresses timelines.

Layer 1 for the use case obtains a set of coordinates (x, y, z) using Hilbert units. The statistical data are as follows:

Tuples: 13,939
hmin: 0
hmax: 65
Mean x: 6.9
Mean y: 7.8
Mean z: 17.0
Mean h: 37.0

where hmin is the minimum of the entropy variation values managed during the test, and hmax is the maximum. The coordinates x, y, and z present mean values that are low respecting other tests, but h is average.

The locality property of these units is useful to determine a timeless disposition of information. The mean values found indicate that the information is transferred in small portions; this is true since the number of sentences is relatively high (60, almost twice the normal in a play).

Layer 2 manages a classification of the data provided by Layer 1 as tuples $< id\_node, x, y, z, h >$. It intends to evaluate the main features of entropy management as a way to assess the information quality of every step in the process of communication. The classification, as mentioned in section 4.1, is performed with EM at every unit. EM considers the log-likelihood as a validation metric, which is the probability of current data given the estimated model parameters. The higher the probability, the better the fit is. The reason that they are negative (rather than between 0 and 1) is because of the logarithm used in its formulation. It is important to note that this type of clusterer does not produce density estimates and has to be wrapped in the MakeDensityBasedClusterer [31].

Weka EM clustering here uses all the variables but ID node. The validation considers a split of 66% for training data. For Test ID 5, it results in eight clusters with log-likelihood of −11.88274. The cluster distribution contains 3% and 28% of the data tuples. When h is considered as part of the clustering improves, and the distribution among the aggregations of the instances is bigger. Regression with REPTree confirms that nodes defined in Layer 1 are for managing information according to h. This can be observed with the plot of Cluster ID versus h; the distribution of the clouds of values present specific vertical patterns in Fig. 4−18 for this use case testing. As the distribution covers all the sentences of the test, then the configuration of h along axis y is also unique to the specific combination of sentences. Then, h represents extra information not given by the words, sentences, or sequences of words.

In Layer 3, the tuples include the clustering information provided by Layer 2: $< TestID, instance\_number, idNode, x, y, z, h, Cluster >$. They feed the 12 units in Layer 3, running with batch size 100, learning rate 0.3, momentum 0.2, and 500 epochs. The goal of this layer

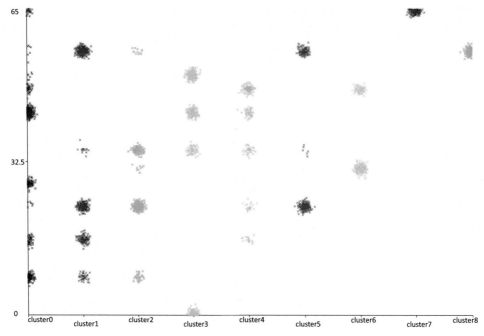

FIGURE 4–18 Distribution of h according to clusters in tests (x = cluster versus y = delta_h).

is to validate the quality of the process, so it infers the value that should take h at time t, given the current context. For testing, five values match exactly. NNR4 generates several logs that are to be used in the definition of validation metrics, in future work.

There are several features found with NNR4 for the use case that keep it valid for the entire corpus (see [1]):

1. There is a common behavior in delta_h distribution, and it serves to determine the relationship between context information and entropy gain. There is a locus promoted by the Hilbert mappers, which evolves with time (as $t \rightarrow +\infty$).
2. Empty spaces in the mappers of Layer 1 represent alternate ways of e, as other expressions of C are available in O and conforming to E.
3. Tests reveal that data, final disposition: when *idNode* is considered, there are fewer clusters, but they are in the neighborhood of the ones obtained without *idNode*. Then, *idNode* just collapsed close clusters.
4. *idNode* is relevant to the type of content, but the process of C involves several combinations of the attributes, and the nodes self-organize in a logical way according to semantics.
5. Every test presents a specific h pattern in Hilbert units, with no repetition in them across tests.

Classification with EM for Test 5 provides a cluster c as a compact evaluation of how good behaves h [2], which combined with h, y, and z, gives just 12 configurations (or clouds) for semantic administration even though the range for h is wider. This shows a good abstract way to automatically collapse the number of clusters following the semantic association criteria. Fig. 4−19 is a star graphics are used to represent in a concise way this information (and at the same time compare the associations obtained automatically from observations in Test 5).

This type of graphic is based on multivariate criteria where each variable is represented as a radio in a star. Here, the length is proportional to the value of the variable. In the figure, the 12 configurations present three variables (y, z, c) and a regressive value for h shown as a label.

Fig. 4−20 is the cluster distribution along the nodes defined by NNR4 in the Hilbert 3D space.

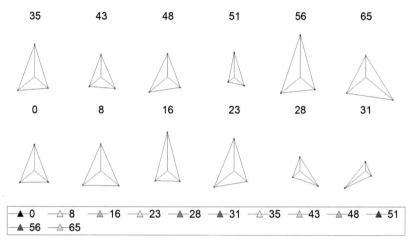

FIGURE 4–19 Star representation of the main semantic aggregations for Test 5.

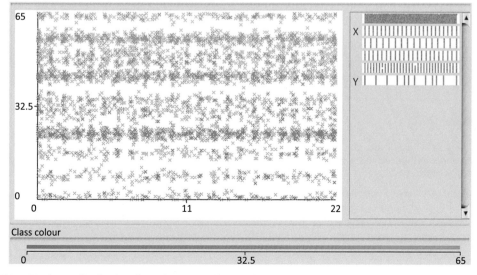

FIGURE 4–20 Cluster distribution along the NNR4 Hilbert nodes.

The distribution denotes that nodes organized their content according to not only the entropy variation degree but also the timing, morphology, semantics, or any other criteria. Here, the timeline is considered in the sequencing of the sentences (ID in the first column of Table 4−2). Note that during the construction of the testing, at every t of any dialog, the AI system (F) comes back to fetch and update the current local formulation of the remote e in M (the human player) and updates it, adding additional features according to the newly added portion of $h(e, t)$. The process keeps until a final version of e matches or not its remote version [which is validated using Eq. (4−12)].

4.5 Conclusions and future work

Theoretical physicists demonstrated that time is relative according to reference systems or the presence of mass, but this is far from being a valid explanation for the process of time perception in humans. This chapter explains the biological process of incorporating new knowledge is dual: declarative and episodic (space−time association and that the process of incorporating knowledge influences the perception of space−time).

From the presented information, it becomes feasible that each subject has their own perception of timeline, that temporal-spatial perception is altered by feelings and metabolism, and is able to evolve in time. There is a brief presentation of TRLR and its rules, and the NNR4 neural architecture as a device to explore and evaluate time, among other considerations regarding linguistic reasoning in the context of certain types of dialogs as future work remains to consider other languages besides Spanish for NNR4. It also remains to expand the corpus and evaluate the effect of biasing the experience limiting the type of target in the game. Other interesting pending work is to repeat the tests with a human on both sides (M and F) and to reapply with other types of communication channels such as vocal or visual interchanges. The characteristics of hit cycling in ET regions also need to be deeply studied to understand what it implies. Furthermore, there would be interesting to be able to find if the fractal dimension used here is associated with a current fractal function and eventually analyze its characteristics. Finally, there is still pending use of the logs generated by NNR4 to implement validation metrics.

References

[1] D. López De Luise, Hilbert curves for sentences interpretation in dialogs. Special Issue Outstanding Women contributions in theory and applications of artificial intelligence, Int. J. Intell. Decis. Technol. LAIS 24 (2023) 287−332.

[2] D. López De Luise, Language and reasoning by entropy fractals, Signals 2 (4) (2021) 754−770. Available from: https://doi.org/10.3390/signals2040044.

[3] L. Friesen, Using mental bias to construct a model of cognition, Acad. Lett. (2021). Available from: https://doi.org/10.20935/AL1681. Article 1681.

[4] M.F. Rodríguez Duch, Chaos, entropy and public health: Legal analysis from a multidimensional perspective (Caos, entropía y salud pública: Análisis desde una perspectiva jurídica multidimensional). Argentina Association of Administrative law Magazine. N 1. 2016.

[5] R.S. Siegler, J.L. Booth, Development of numerical estimation in young children, Child. Dev. 2 (75) (2004) 428−444. N 2.

[6] V. Evans, B.K. Bergen, J. Zinken, Chaos, fractals and dissipative structures, Syst. N. Paradig. Hum. Sci. Cogn. Linguistic Read. (2007).

[7] D. López De Luise, Linguistic intelligence as a root for computing reasoning, in: M. Virvou, G. A. Tsihrintzis, L.C. Jain (Eds.), Advances in Selected Artificial Intelligence Areas: World Outstanding Women in Artificial Intelligence Learning, first ed. Analytics in Intelligent Systems 24, 2022.

[8] V.W. Spinadel, *Fractal geometry and Euclidean thermodynamics* (Geometría fractal y geometría euclidiana), Mag. Educ. Pedagogy. Univ. Antioquia 1 (35) (2003) 85−91. XV, N.

[9] S. Widyarto, M. Syafrullah, M.W. Sharif, G.A. Budaya, Fractals study and its application, 6th International Conference on Electrical Engineering, Computer Science and Informatics (EECSI) (2019) 200−204. Available from: https://doi.org/10.23919/EECSI48112.2019.8977124.

[10] K. Nambiar, What is Laplace's demon? Does this demon know everything? Science ABC (2022).

[11] G. Peano, *On a curve, which fills an entire flat area* (Sur une courbe, qui remplit toute une aire plane), Math. Ann. 36 (1890) 157−160.

[12] I. Prigogine, The End of Certainties (La fin des certitudes). Editions O. Jacob, 1996.

[13] D. López De Luise, Entropy, Chaos and Language, IGI Global, 2021.

[14] V. Rüdiger, Tunnel through space and time. Einstein's Legacy—Black Holes, Time Travel and The Speed of Light (Tunnel durch Raum und Zeit. Einsteins Erbe—Schwarze Löcher, Zeitreisen und Überlichtgeschwindigkeit). Franckh-Kosmos, Stuttgart, ISBN 3−440-09360-3 (mit einem ausführlichen Kapitel über Tachyonen). 2006.

[15] G. Rains, Human Neurophysiology Principles (Princ. de. neuropsicología humana) (2004) 533 ISSN: 978-970-10−3972-4. Available from: https://biblioteca.uazuay.edu.ec/buscar/item/52728.

[16] W. Penfield, B. Milner, Memory deficits induced by bilateral lesions in the hippocampal zone, Arch. Neurol. Psych. 79 (1958) 475−497. Available from: https://www.ncbi.nlm.nih.gov/pmc/articles/PMC497229/.

[17] B. Milner, et al., Further analysis of the hippocampal amnesic syndrome: 14 year follow-up study of H. M, Neuropsychologia 6 (3) (1968) 215−234. Available from: https://www.sciencedirect.com/science/article/abs/pii/0028393268900213.

[18] D. Schacter, Forgotten Ideas, Neglected Pioneers. ISBN 9780203720134, https://www.taylorfrancis.com/books/mono/10.4324/9780203720134/forgotten-ideas-neglected-pioneers-daniel-schacter, 2001.

[19] R.A. Poldrack, M.G. Packard, Competition among multiple memory systems: converging evidence from animal and human brain studies, Neuropsychol 1497 (2003) 1−7. Available from: https://ww.sciencedirect.com/science/article/abs/pii/S0028393202001574. 2003.

[20] A. Martin, L.L. Chao, Semantic memory and the brain: Structure and processes, Curr. Neurobiol. 11 (2001) 194−201 2001. Available from: https://www.sciencedirect.com/science/article/abs/pii/S0959438800001963.

[21] R.A. Poldrack, D.A. Wagner, M.W. Prull, J.E. Desmond, G.H. Glover, et al., Functional specialization for semantic and phonological processing in the left inferior frontal cortex, Neuroimage 10 (1999) 15−35. Available from: https://www.sciencedirect.com/science/article/abs/pii/S105381199990441X. 1999.

[22] E. Tulving, How many memory systems are there? Am. Psychol. 40 (1985) 385−398. Available from: https://psycnet.apa.org/doiLanding?doi = 10.1037%2F0003-066X.40.4.385.

[23] Roberts, et al., Episodic-like memory in rats: is it based on when or how long ago? Science 320 (5872) (2008) 1152709. Available from: https://doi.org/10.1126/science, https://www.science.org/doi/abs/10.1126/science.1152709.

[24]   D. Dombeck, J. Heys, Evidence for a subcircuit in medial entorhinal cortex representing elapsed time during immobility, Nat. Neurosci. 21 (2018) 1574−1582. Available from: https://www.nature.com/articles/s41593-018-0252-8.

[25]   C.N. Smith, L. Squire, Medial temporal lobe activity during retrieval of semantic memory is related to the age of memory, J. Neurosci. 29 (2009) 930−938. Available from: https://www.jneurosci.org/content/29/4/930.short.

[26]   K. Healy, et al., Metabolic rate and body size are linked with perception of temporal information, Anim. Behav. 86 (4) (2013) 685−696. Available from: https://www.sciencedirect.com/science/article/pii/S0003347213003060#tbl1.

[27]   Hippocampus, Encyclopædia Britannica, Encyclopædia Britannica, Inc., 2022.

[28]   A. Kuljeet Singh, V. Dhikav, Hippocampus in Health and Disease: An Overview, Annals of Indian Academy of Neurology, Medknow Publications & Media Pvt Ltd., 2012.

[29]   G. Neal Perry, Brainy hormones the body's messengers. hormone health network. https://www.hormone.org, 2022.

[30]   Z. Shahid, E. Asuka, G. Singh, Hypothalamus, Available from: https://www.ncbi.nlm.nih.gov, Physiology, StatPearls Publishing, 2022.

[31]   R. Bouckaert, F. Eibe, M. Hall, R. Kirkby, P. Reutemann, A. Seewald, et al., WEKA Manual for Version 3−6-2, Waikato University, 2010.

[32]   20Q. http://www.20q.net/, 2021.

5

Hate speech detection using LSTM and explanation by LIME (local interpretable model-agnostic explanations)

Ravi Shekhar Tiwari

ÉCOLE CENTRALE SCHOOL OF ENGINEERING, COMPUTER SCIENCE AND ENGINEERING, MAHINDRA UNIVERSITY, HYDERABAD, TELANGANA, INDIA

5.1 Introduction

Detection of hate speech in social media is one of the main major crucial tasks for the government or for the respective social media organization. Many countries are in the process of regulating content in social media platforms. If the contents of these platforms are not regulated, then it can create chaos and disrupt the normal functioning of our society. In this chapter, we are going to learn how we can detect hate speech from any sentence. Hate speech detection on a Twitter dataset involves using natural language processing (NLP) techniques to identify tweets that contain harmful or offensive language. This can include racist, sexist, or homophobic language, among other forms of hate speech. Usually, the tweets are preprocessed to eliminate any extraneous data, such as hashtags and user mentions, and then machine learning algorithms are used to determine whether or not the tweets contain hate speech. The effectiveness of these algorithms is typically assessed using metrics such as precision, recall, and F1-score, and the results can be utilized to enhance the platform's ability to identify hate speech. The below flowchart shows the overall process of training the model and implementing XAI Explainable Artificial Intelligence (Fig. 5−1).

As we can see in the above figure, the dataset has been fetched from medium API, and the dataset is known as Twitter Hate speech dataset and saved/downloaded locally after that I have implemented Tensorflow Data Input pipeline, which consists of functions integrated into the pipeline such as punctuation removal, emoji removal, stopwords removal, and tokenization stemming to sanitize the dataset. After sanitizing or preprocessing the dataset, I have integrated three types of word-embedding techniques such as Bag of Words, Term Frequency (TF)−Inverse Document Frequency (IDF), and Glove. These embedding techniques are very essential for converting the word into a numerical vector representation. Finally, the Long

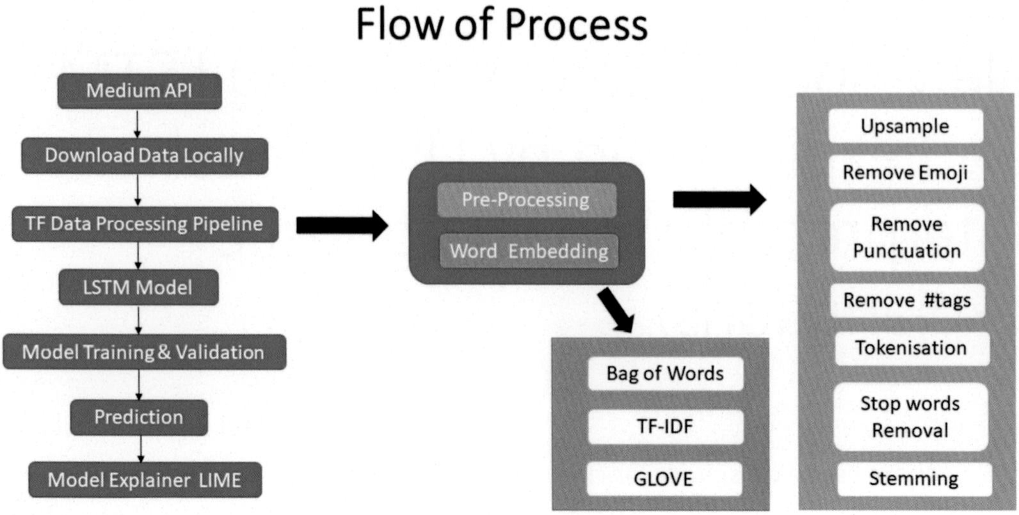

Flow of Process

FIGURE 5–1 Flow process.

Short Term Memory Deep Neural architecture is trained using the Data Input Pipelines. Once the model is trained, we are using the Local Interpretable Model—agnostic Explanations (LIME)—Model Agnostic Technique to explain why our model associates the input sentence to the specific class. In later sections, all these topics have been explained in depth.

5.2 Bag of words

Bag of words is a method used in NLP to represent text data in a numerical format [1]. It involves creating a vocabulary of all the unique words in a text corpus and then counting the number of times each word appears in each document [2]. The resulting representation is a vector of word counts, also known as a bag of word representation. This representation discards the grammar and word order in the text and only preserves the frequency of the words [2]. The text modeling technique known as "bag of words" is employed in NLP. To explain it formally, it is a method for feature extraction from text data. This approach makes it simple and flexible to extract features from documents.

A Bag of Words is a textual representation of word repetition in a document [3]. We only keep track of word occurances; we don't care about the grammatical rules or the word order. Because any information pertaining to the organization or structure of the words within the document is disregarded, it is referred as a "bag" of words [4]. The model is solely concerned with whether recognized terms are there or not, in the document. The bag-of-words (BoW) notion is extensively used in NLP and information retrieval [5]. Each word's frequency of use is used as a feature while training a classifier for techniques of classifying documents or sentences, where it is also used rather frequently. The Bag of Words paradigm is also used in some use cases for computer vision.

Table 5–1   BoW pseudocode.

Bag of Words

```
# Define a function to create a bag-of-words representation of a text document
def create_bow(text):

    # Tokenize the text into words
    words = text.split()

    # Create an empty bag-of-words representation
    bow = {}

    # Iterate over the words in the text
    for word in words:
        # If the word is not already in the bag, add it with a count of 1
        if word not in bow:
            bow[word] = 1
        # If the word is already in the bag, increment the count
        else:
            bow[word] += 1

    # Return the bag-of-words representation
    return bow
```

```
#Initiating the Function
document = "The cat in the hat."
bow_representation = create_bow(document)
print(bow_representation)
```

```
#This will output:
{'The': 1, 'cat': 1, 'in': 1, 'the': 1, 'hat.': 1}
```

The BoW model is most frequently used in the real world as a feature creation technique [6]. You can calculate a number of different measurements that can be used to describe the text once you have converted it into a Bag of Words. The below image shows an example of how we can convert the sentence into Bag of Words representation. The BoW model is a simple technique for representing text data as numerical feature vectors. Here is an example of pseudocode for creating a BoW representation of a text document (Table 5−1).

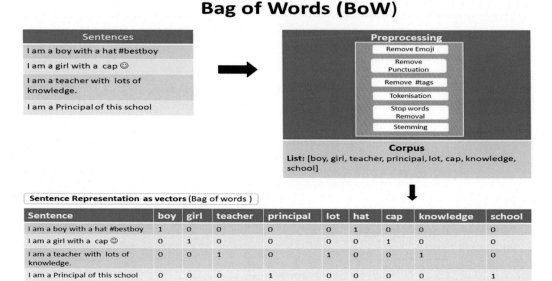

IMAGE 5–1 BOW in step by step.

This is a very simple example, there are many variations of the BoW model, such as using n-grams, or removing stopwords, and many other preprocessing steps [7]. The BoW representation is also commonly used as input for text classification tasks, such as hate speech detection on Twitter dataset. The below image describes how we can convert any sentence into a BoW model (Images 5−1 and 5−2).

5.2.1 Limitations of the Bag of Words

The dictionary and vocabulary should be well planned. It's size has an impact on the sparsity of the document representations, so it must be kept to a minimum [8]. The model eliminates context by ignoring the words intended meaning and focusing instead on their frequency of occurrence. This can be a big problem because the model doesn't account for how a phrase's word order might completely change what the statement means [9]. Another serious issue in this paradigm is its difficulties in modeling sparse representations. This is influenced by both informational and computational variables. It is difficult for the model to employ a small amount of information in a broad representational space. I've outlined the Bag of Word Embedding Techniques' limitations below:

It doesn't take into account the context of the words, which can change the meaning of a word. For example, "I am happy" and "I am not happy" have the same bag of words, but convey very different meanings.

It doesn't capture the relationship between words. For example, it can't distinguish between "I am happy" and "happy am I"

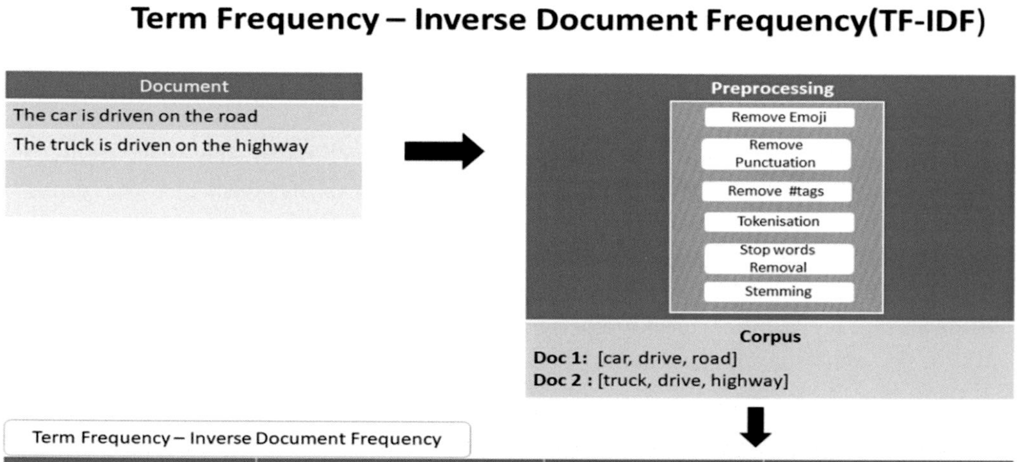

Term Frequency – Inverse Document Frequency(TF-IDF)

Document

The car is driven on the road

The truck is driven on the highway

Preprocessing

Remove Emoji

Remove Punctuation

Remove #tags

Tokenisation

Stop words Removal

Stemming

Corpus

Doc 1: [car, drive, road]
Doc 2 : [truck, drive, highway]

Term Frequency – Inverse Document Frequency

Word	TF		IDF	TF*IDF	
	Doc 1	Doc 2		Doc 1	Doc 2
car	1/3 = 0.33	0	log(2/1)= 0.3	0.099	0
drive	1/3 = 0.33	1/3 = 0.33	log(2/2)= 0	0	0
road	1/3 = 0.33	0	log(2/1)= 0.3	0.099	0
truck	0	1/3 = 0.33	log(2/1)= 0.3	0	0.099
highway	0	1/3 = 0.33	log(2/1)= 0.3	0	0.099

IMAGE 5–2 BoW example.

It doesn't handle morphological variations of words, for example, "happy," "happier," "happiest" would be considered as different words in bag of words representation
It creates a large sparse vector of word counts, which can be memory-intensive and computationally expensive to process.
It discards the information of the word order, which can be crucial for certain NLP tasks.
It is not suitable for small datasets, as it requires a lot of data to generate a good representation of the words.

5.2.2 Advantages of the Bag of Words

Because of its simplicity, Bag of Words is still commonly used. Before moving on to stronger word embeddings, NLP researchers typically build their initial model using Bag of Words to gage how well their work is performing. When we are working on a small number of documents that are very domain-specific, it is quite beneficial [10]. Working on political news data from Twitter, for instance, to gage sentiment. Below I have summarized the advantages of Bag of Word embedding Techniques:

1. Simplicity: It is a simple and intuitive method for representing text data in a numerical format, which makes it easy to understand and implement.

2. Efficiency: It is computationally efficient as it only requires counting the occurrences of words in a text corpus, which can be done quickly.
3. Scalability: It can handle large text corpora and is not affected by the size of the vocabulary.
4. Sparsity: The resulting vector representation is sparse, which means that most of the entries are zero. This is useful for text data as the majority of the words in a text corpus are not repeated frequently.
5. Suitable for high-dimensional data: The bag of word representation can handle high-dimensional data, which is common in text data.
6. Widely used: It is a widely used method in NLP and has been applied to many different NLP tasks such as text classification, sentiment analysis, and topic modeling.

The bag of words can be used as a feature for various machine learning models as well as deep learning (DL) models, which makes it a versatile representation of text data.

5.3 Term frequency–inverse document frequency

By using the statistical method TF-IDF (term frequency–inverse document frequency), one can determine how relevant a word is to each document in a group of documents [11]. To accomplish this, the frequency of a word within a document and its IDF across a collection of documents are multiplied. It has many uses, with automated text analysis being the most crucial, and is especially helpful for word scoring in machine learning algorithms for NLP [12].

TF-IDF was created for document search and information retrieval. It works by escalating in accordance with how frequently a term appears in a document, but is balanced by how many papers contain the word [12]. Because they aren't particularly crucial to that document, words such as this, what, and if rank low even if they may be used frequently.

However, it is most likely because it is highly relevant if the word "Bug" regularly appears in one document but not another. For instance, since most responses including the word "Bug" will be related to the topic "Reliability," the phrase "Bug" is likely to be connected to that topic if our purpose is to determine the topics to which particular NPS replies belong.

5.3.1 Why is TF-IDF?

Machine learning algorithms frequently deal with numbers; however, natural language is text, which is a big barrier to machine learning with natural language [13]. In order to turn the text into numbers, we must vectorize it first. It's an important step in the machine learning process of data analysis, and since the results of different vectorization algorithms can differ substantially, you need to choose one that will deliver the results you want.

The output of simpler methods like word counts can be significantly improved by feeding the TF-IDF score to algorithms such as Naive Bayes and Support Vector Machines [13], which can translate words into numbers that machine learning algorithms can understand. How does that work? In its most basic form, a word vector presents a text as a list of numbers, one for each word that can potentially exist in the corpus. By converting the text of a document into one of these vectors, the content of the text is in some way represented by the numbers of the vectors. We can quantify the importance of each word in a document by assigning it a numerical value with the aid of TF-IDF [14]. A machine learning system then looks for comparable vectors in documents that contain related, relevant terms [14].

5.3.2 How is it calculated?

To vectorize and score a word, its TF is multiplied by the IDF, as the name implies [5].

TF tracks how often a term or word appears in a document in comparison to all the other words inside [5].

$$TF = \frac{\text{Number of times the word appeared in the document}}{\text{Total number of the term in the document}} \tag{5-1}$$

The IDF, also known as IDF, represents the proportion of documents in the corpus that contain a phrase. For instance, technical jargon terms are more relevant than words that are only occasionally used in articles (e.g., a, the, and).

$$IDF = \log \frac{\text{Number of document in the corpus}}{\text{Number of document in the corpus contain the term}} \tag{5-2}$$

A term's TF-IDF is determined by multiplying the TF and IDF values [5].

$$TF - IDF = TF \times IDF \tag{5-3}$$

When a term appears frequently in one text and infrequently in another, it is said to be essential in plain English. In other words, rarity among papers as indicated by IDF and TF balances commonality within a document [15]. The final TF-IDF score reveals a phrase's importance for a particular corpus document.

The idea behind TF-IDF is that while a word that appears frequently in a document is significant, it is not as significant if it appears in numerous documents throughout the corpus. The words in a document that are most significant and different from the other documents can be found using TF-IDF by combining these two factors [16]. The TF-IDF is useful for many applications of NLP. For instance, Search Engines use TF-IDF to rate a document's relevance to a query.

Using the TF-IDF approach, text data can be visualized as numerical feature vectors [17]. It is used to determine how significant a term is in relation to the total corpus of documents. Here is an example of pseudocode for creating a TF-IDF representation of a text document (Table 5–2):

Additional uses for TF-IDF include topic modeling, text classification, and text summarization. Be aware that there are different ways to calculate the IDF score [18]. The base-10 logarithm is commonly used in the calculation. Step-by-step instructions for calculating the TF-IDF are shown in the image below (Image 5–3).

Table 5–2 TF-IDF pseudocode.

TF-IDF

```
# Define a function to create a TF-IDF representation of a text document
def create_tfidf(text, corpus):
    # Tokenize the text into words
    words = text.split()

    # Create an empty TF-IDF representation
    tfidf = {}

    # Iterate over the words in the text
    for word in words:
        # Calculate the term frequency (TF)
        tf = text.count(word) / len(words)
        # Calculate the inverse document frequency (IDF)
        idf = log(len(corpus) / sum(1 for doc in corpus if word in doc))
        # Calculate the TF-IDF score for the word
        tfidf[word] = tf * idf

    # Return the TF-IDF representation
    return tfidf
```

```
#Initiating the Function
text = "The cat in the hat."
corpus = ["The cat in the hat.", "The dog in the fog.", "A cat and a dog."]
tfidf_representation = create_tfidf(text, corpus)
print(tfidf_representation)
```

```
#This will output:
{'The': 0.0, 'cat': 0.3662040962227032, 'in': 0.0, 'the': 0.0, 'hat.': 0.3662040962227032}
```

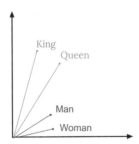

IMAGE 5–3 TF-IDF example.

As you can see, the TF-IDF representation assigns a weight to each word in the text based on its frequency in the document and its rarity across the corpus of documents. This can be useful for text classification tasks such as hate speech detection on Twitter dataset, as it allows words that are commonly used in hate speech to be distinguished from those that are not.

5.3.3 Advantages and disadvantages of TF-IDF

(Table 5–3)

5.4 Glove—word embedding

Language comprehension has long been a strength of the human race. The relationship between words is straightforward for people to understand, but it may be challenging for computers to accomplish. For instance, we humans are aware that phrases such as "king and queen," "man and woman," and "tiger and tigress" have certain relationships to one another, but how can a computer understand this?

Word embeddings, in their simplest form, are a kind of word representation that links a computer's understanding of language to that of a human. They have mastered n-dimensional text representations, in which words with comparable meanings are represented similarly [19]. This implies that two similar words are represented by very closely spaced vectors. These are critical for the vast majority of NLP issues (Image 5–4).

Table 5–3   Advantages and disadvantages of TF-IDF.

Advantages	Disadvantages
TF-IDF is easy to compute takes less resources for computation	TF-IDF is based on the bag-of-words model; therefore it does not capture position in text, semantics, cooccurrences in different documents, etc.
You have some basic metric to extract the most descriptive terms in a document	For this reason, TF-IDF is only useful as a lexical level feature
You can easily compute the similarity between two documents using it	Cannot capture semantics (e.g., as compared with topic models, word embeddings)

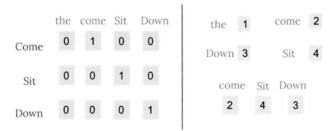

IMAGE 5–4 Vector representation of words.

When using word embeddings, each individual word is therefore represented by a real-valued vector in a specified vector space. Each word is mapped to a single vector, and the vector values are learned in a way approaching a neural network [1]. Word2Vec and Glove are the two most popular techniques for learning word embeddings using shallow neural networks. A technique for learning word vectors, sometimes referred to as word embeddings, called GloVe (Global Vectors for Word Representation) is trained using a global matrix of word cooccurrence statistics [1,5]. Contrary to other word vector techniques such as word2-vec, GloVe learns the vectors using a matrix factorization method rather than a neural network. The generated vectors are quite comprehensible and can be applied to a number of NLP tasks, including sentiment analysis, text classification, and language translation [16].

Since language cannot be processed by machine learning models, we must find a technique to turn this text into numerical data. This work can be accomplished using methods such as Bag of Words and TF-IDF, which have been described in the past. In addition, there are two other methods we can employ, such as one-hot encoding or assigning specific numbers to each word in a lexicon [20]. The latter method is more effective than one-hot encoding since we now have a dense vector instead of a sparse one. This strategy therefore functions even when our vocabulary is extensive.

In the example below, we'll assume that our vocabulary is minimal and only consists of four words. Using the two ways, we'll express the sentence (Image 5–5).

The integer encoding, however, is arbitrary because it ignores any link between words. A linear classifier, for instance, learns a single weight for each feature, making it difficult for the model to interpret the data. This feature—weight combination is meaningless since there is no connection between the similarity of any two words and the similarity of their encodings.

As a result, words with similar meanings can be grouped together in close proximity in vector space using word embeddings. For instance, when a term such as "frog" is being represented, the closest neighbors of a frog would be "frogs," "toads," and "Litoria." This suggests that while the two-word vectors are comparable, it is acceptable for a classifier to

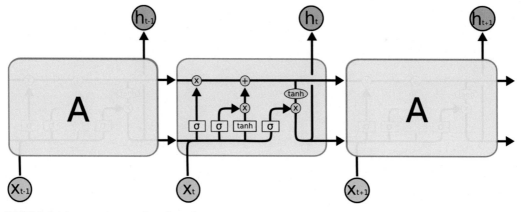

IMAGE 5–5 Integer representation of words.

only see the word frog during training and not see the word Litoria at all during testing. Word embeddings also discover relationships. Finding the equivalent word can be done by adding the vector differences between two words to another word vector. As an illustration, "man" + "woman" + "queen" "king."

5.4.1 What is glove?

Global Vectors for Word Representation (Glove) is a method for creating word embeddings. It is based on methods for word-context matrix factorization [21]. You create a sizable matrix of cooccurrence data and count the instances of each "word" (represented by the rows) in a specific "context" (represented by the columns) inside the corpus [21]. For each term, we look for context terms within a region defined by a window size before and a window size after the term. This is how we normally scan our corpus. We also give less weight to words stated far. There are obviously a lot of "contexts" because their size is virtually combinatorial. As a result, this matrix can be factored to produce a lower-dimensional matrix in which each row now contains a vector representation of each word. Usually, a "reconstruction loss" is reduced to achieve this. This loss searches for models with lower dimensions that can largely explain the variance in the high-dimensional data. Naturally, there are many "contexts" because their magnitude is essentially combinatorial. Thus, by factoring this matrix, a lower-dimensional matrix is created, with each row now containing a vector representation of each word. Typically, this is accomplished by reducing a "reconstruction loss." This loss looks for lower-dimensional models that can account for the majority of the variance in the high-dimensional data.

We use both GloVe and Word2Vec to actually embed our text, and both methods function equally well. Nevertheless, we train our model with Wikipedia text and a 5−10-pixel window for real-world applications. The corpus contains approximately 13 million words, thus constructing these embeddings takes a lot of effort and resources [10]. To prevent this, we can use the pretrained word vectors that have already been learned and are easy to employ. In this chapter, the text will be transformed into vectors using GLOVE pretrained word embedding.

5.5 Long short-term memory

Long Short-Term Memory (LSTM) is a type of recurrent neural network (RNN) architecture that is able to effectively retain information for longer periods of time [4]. RNNs are neural networks that handle time series or text written in natural language sequential data. However, traditional RNNs struggle to handle data with long-term dependencies, because they tend to forget information from earlier in the sequence as it processes new data [4]. A technique known as a memory cell, which has the ability to selectively store or discard information over time, is introduced by LSTMs to solve this issue. Gates, which are neural network layers that regulate the flow of information into and out of the memory cell, are another component of LSTM [18]. This allows LSTMs to selectively retain important information and discard irrelevant information as the network processes new data. Because of their ability to handle sequential data with long-term dependencies, LSTMs have been used in a wide variety of NLP tasks, such as language translation, text summarization, and sentiment analysis [4]. They are also used in speech recognition, stock market predictions, and anomaly detection. In hate speech detection, LSTMs are used to analyze sequential data such as tweets and and comments in order to classify them into hate speech or not hate speech.

5.5.1 Structure of LSTM

Four neural networks, often known as cells, and different memory building elements make up the chain structure of the LSTM. Information is stored by the cells, and the gates manipulate the memory. Three gates are present, which are shown in the below image (Image 5−6).

Forget Gate: The forget gate eliminates data that are no longer pertinent to the condition of the cell. Prior to bias being applied, the gate's two inputs—$x\,t$ (the input at the present time) and $h\,t-1$ (the output of the prior cell)—are multiplied using weight matrices [5]. The outcome is received as the activation function's binary output. If a cell state's output is 1, the information is preserved for use later; if it is 0, the information is lost [5].

Input gate: The input gate is in charge of updating the cell state with crucial information [8]. Beginning with the inputs $h\,t-1$ and $x\,t$, the information is regulated using the sigmoid function to filter the values that must be remembered in a manner akin to the forget gate [5]. The tanh function is then used to create a vector with all possible values between $h\,t-1$ and $x\,t$, with an output spanning from -1 to $+1$ [5]. The values of the vector and the controlled values are eventually multiplied to obtain the useful information.

Output gate: The output gate's responsibility is to collect relevant data from the current cell state and output it. A vector is first created in the cell using the tanh function [5]. Using the inputs $h\,t-1$ and $x\,t$, the information is then filtered by the values to be remembered, and the sigmoid function is used to regulate the information [5]. Finally, the values of the vector and the controlled values are multiplied and supplied, respectively, as input and output to the succeeding cell [5].

LIME

Input Sentence   Trained DL Model   Class 0   Class 1   Prediction   LIME   XAI   Human Makes Decision

XAI = Explainable Artificial Intelligence

IMAGE 5–6 LSTM cell.

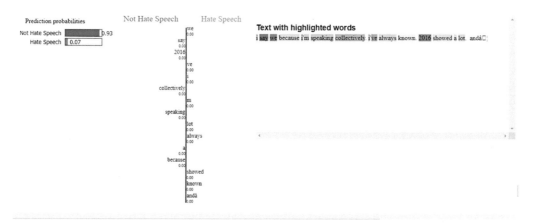

IMAGE 5–7 Explainable artificial intelligence (XAI).

5.6 LIME—local interpretable model–agnostic explanations

LIME is an algorithm for generating explanations for the predictions of any machine learning model. The goal of LIME is to provide an interpretable and accurate explanation for the predictions of a model, especially for those cases where the model is a black box, and its inner workings are not transparent (Image 5–7).

The basic idea behind LIME is to explain the predictions of a black-box model by training a simpler, interpretable model locally around the instance being explained. The interpretable model is trained on perturbed versions of the instance, which are chosen randomly from a neighborhood around the instance. The neighborhood is defined by applying a kernel to the input space, which creates a probability distribution over the input space [22]. Then, the algorithm samples instances from this distribution and trains the interpretable model on these instances. The interpretable model is trained to approximate the predictions of the black-box model in the neighborhood of the instance being explained.

LIME can be applied to any type of model, such as decision trees and neural networks. It's also model-agnostic, meaning that it can be applied to any type of model, regardless of its architecture or the type of data it's trained on. The main idea behind LIME is to fit a linear model to the local neighborhood of the instance being explained [22]. The linear model is then used to approximate the classifier's decision function in the vicinity of the instance. This allows for the interpretation of the classifier's predictions in terms of the features that are most important in the local region. To generate an explanation, LIME first samples a set of perturbed instances around the instance being explained. These perturbed instances are generated by randomly perturbing the feature values within a certain range. Next, the classifier is used to predict the class label for each perturbed instance. Then, LIME fits a linear model to the perturbed instances and their corresponding class labels [22]. The linear model is then used to approximate the classifier's decision function in the vicinity of the instance. Finally, the linear model's coefficients are used to identify which features are most important in the local region. These features are then used to generate an interpretable explanation of the classifier's predictions. It is useful to understand the context and assumptions of the problem, and the properties of the classifier to decide if LIME is a good choice for explaining the predictions and in which context it would be useful.

The process of generating explanations with LIME can be broken down into the following steps:

1. Define the black-box model and the instance to be explained.
2. Define the feature names and class names.
3. Create an explainer object by providing the training data, feature names, and class names.
4. Explain the prediction by calling the explain_instance method on the explainer object, passing the instance and the predict_proba function of the black-box model.
5. The explain_instance method returns an explanation object that can be used to display the explanation in different formats.

LIME has been used in a wide range of applications, such as detecting bias in machine learning models, improving the interpretability of models, and building trust with the users of the model [22,23]. By providing explanations, LIME allows one to understand how a model is making its predictions, which can be useful for detecting potential biases and building trust with the users of the model [22,23].

Many applications can benefit from the predictions made by deep learning models, but the developers are often unaware of the causes of certain correct or incorrect forecasts. These model-generated results are applied in several crucial situations when erroneous predictions can be useless. Therefore, it is always important to comprehend the logic behind the model's conclusion. We require a surrogate model to explain the results of AI-based models because machine learning and deep learning algorithms use a black-box approach. Local interpretable model-neutral explanation is one such substitute model (LIME) [22,23]. It is analogous to a human justification for making a choice. This interpretable model explains individual predictions. LIME is founded on two basic characteristics, namely:

Agnosticism to all the Models: According to this characteristic, any supervised learning model can be explained. LIME is capable of addressing any model that falls under the black-box approach category.

Local Fidelity: Based on the selected data samples from the data collection, LIME can provide explanations locally. The explanations will be restricted to the area surrounding the experimented-on data instance. The function of LIME in model interpretation is depicted in the following figure.

5.6.1 Working of LIME

Each data sample that is present in the dataset will be explained by LIME in terms of how it contributes features and any underlying meanings or explanations. This is accomplished by training these models to roughly comprehend the predictions. LIME is a powerful tool for explaining the predictions made by machine learning models in a human-understandable way [22,23]. In essence, LIME generates an interpretable explanation of a model's prediction by training an interpretable model that is locally faithful to the original model. Here's a more detailed explanation of how LIME works:

1. Select the instance you want to explain: This can be an image, a text document, or any other type of data that the machine learning model is making predictions on. The goal is to understand why the model made the prediction it did for this specific instance.
2. Perturb the instance: To generate a local explanation of the model's behavior, LIME creates a set of perturbed versions of the instance. This can involve adding random noise, removing or replacing parts of the image or text, or similar transformations.
3. Get predictions from the machine learning model: For each of the perturbed instances, the machine learning model provides a prediction, such as a label or a probability distribution over the possible labels.
4. Fit an interpretable model to the predictions: LIME uses these predictions to train an interpretable model, such as a linear regression, decision tree, or another simple model. The goal is to capture the relationship between the perturbations and the predictions, and use this relationship to generate a locally faithful explanation of the model's behavior.
5. Use the interpretable model to generate explanations: The interpretable model can then be used to generate explanations of the original model's predictions. For example, it can highlight the parts of the image that were most important in determining the prediction or the words in the text document that were most relevant to the prediction.
6. Evaluate the faithfulness of the explanation: LIME also provides a measure of the faithfulness of the explanation, which indicates how well the interpretable model approximates the behavior of the original model. This allows you to assess the quality of the explanation and determine whether it is trustworthy.

The key benefit of LIME is that it provides local explanations that are both human-understandable and model-agnostic, meaning that it can be applied to any type of machine learning model. This makes it a powerful tool for understanding the behavior of complex models in specific cases, as well as for identifying cases where the model may be making incorrect predictions.

5.6.2 Explaining LSTM model predictions

When individual predictions are interpreted, the overall model is considered to be a good one. LIME's main objective is to investigate how predictions change when the data change. As a result, LIME develops a dataset with chosen or altered samples and trains the model on it. Instead of concentrating on global approximation, this method lets us accomplish the local approximation.

LIME is aware of the significance of each feature that affects a sample's prediction. It includes the most important element that influences the sample's forecast [22,23]. Regression analysis examines the weighting of each sample relative to the total sample size.

The most crucial features are obtained using feature selection approaches. LIME APIs can provide explanations for datasets that are related to images, text, and tables (a sample result is shown in the figure below).

Image 5−8 shows the LIME on the prediction from the BoW-LSTM trained model. As we can see that the LIME has explained the prediction of the model word by word with the respected probability of input data association with the respected labels.

Image 5−9 shows the LIME on the prediction from the GLOVE-LSTM trained model. As we can see that the LIME has explained the prediction of the model word by word with the respected probability of input data association with the respected labels.

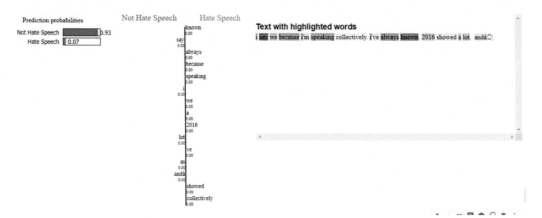

IMAGE 5–8 LIME (XAI) on BoW-LSTM model prediction.

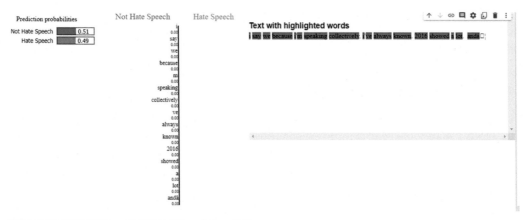

IMAGE 5–9 LIME (XAI) on GLOVE-LSTM model prediction.

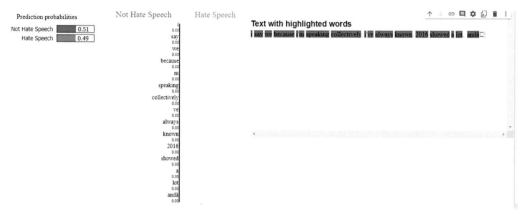

IMAGE 5–10 LIME (XAI) on TF-IDF LSTM model prediction.

Image 5−10 shows the LIME on the prediction from the TF-IDF-LSTM trained model. As we can see that the LIME has explained the prediction of the model word by word with the respected probability of input data association with the respected labels.

5.7 Code

The repository for the implementation and EDA can be found here.

References

[1] N. Badri, F. Kboubi, A.H. Chaibi, Combining FastText and Glove word embedding for offensive and hate speech text detection, Proc. Comput. Sci. 207 (2022) 769−778.

[2] D. Sookarah, L.S. Ramwodin, Combatting online harassment by using transformer language models for the detection of emotions, hate speech and offensive language on social media, In 2022 4th International Conference on Emerging Trends in Electrical, Electronic and Communications Engineering (ELECOM), IEEE, 2022, pp. 1−6.

[3] P. Badjatiya, S. Gupta, M. Gupta, V. Varma, Deep learning for hate speech detection in tweets. In Proceedings of the 26th international conference on World Wide Web companion, 2017, April, pp. 759−760.

[4] S. Poria, E. Cambria, D. Hazarika, P. Vij, A deeper look into sarcastic tweets using deep convolutional neural networks, (2016). arXiv preprint arXiv:1610.08815.

[5] R. Shinde, P. Udatewar, A. Nandargi, S. Mohan, R. Agrawal, P. Nirale, Evaluation of Fusion Techniques for Multi-modal Sentiment Analysis, in: 2022 International Conference on Advancements in Smart, Secure and Intelligent Computing (ASSIC), IEEE, 2022, pp. 1−9.

[6] J.S. Malik, G. Pang, A.V.D. Hengel, Deep learning for hate speech detection: a comparative study, (2022). arXiv preprint arXiv:2202.09517.

[7] R. Kaur, N. Sekhon, Application of Data Mining Tools and Techniques for Crime detection using Big Data, (2022). Available at SSRN 4143873.

[8]   Y. Sun, A.K. Wong, M.S. Kamel, Classification of imbalanced data: A review, International journal of pattern recognition and artificial intelligence 23 (4) (2009) 687−719.

[9]   T. Van Huynh, V.D. Nguyen, K. Van Nguyen, N.L.T. Nguyen, A.G.T. Nguyen, Hate speech detection on vietnamese social media text using the bi-gru-lstm-cnn model, (2019). arXiv preprint arXiv:1911.03644.

[10] F.A. Prabowo, M.O. Ibrohim, I. Budi, Hierarchical multi-label classification to identify hate speech and abusive language on Indonesian twitter, in: 2019 6th International Conference on Information Technology, Computer and Electrical Engineering (ICITACEE), IEEE, 2019, pp. 1−5.

[11] K.R. Mabokela, T. Celik, M. Raborife, Multilingual Sentiment Analysis for Under-Resourced Languages: A Systematic Review of the Landscape, IEEE Access, 2022.

[12] C. Viehmann, T. Beck, M. Maurer, O. Quiring, I. Gurevych, Investigating opinions on public policmies in digital media: setting up a supervised machine learning tool for stance classification, Commun. Methods Meas. 17 (2) (2023) 150−184.

[13] P. Chiril, E.W. Pamungkas, F. Benamara, V. Moriceau, V. Patti, Emotionally informed hate speech detection: a multi-target perspective, Cogn. Comput. (2022) 1−31.

[14] A. Sharma, A. Kabra, M. Jain, Ceasing hate with moh: hate speech detection in hindi−english code-switched language, Inf. Process. Manag. 59 (1) (2022) 102760.

[15] A. Bisht, H.S. Bhadauria, J. Virmani, A. Singh, Sentiment analysis of micro-blogging sites using supervised learning: a narrative review of recent studies, Int. J. Knowl. Learn. 15 (2) (2022) 89−119.

[16] S. Jain, K. Agarwal, Usefulness of graphemes in word-level language identification in code-mixed text, in: Advances in Distributed Computing and Machine Learning, Proceedings of ICADCML, 2021, Springer, Singapore, 2022, pp. 174−185.

[17] D. Robinson, Automated hate speech detection and the problem of offensive, language (2018).

[18] Z. Zhang, D. Robinson, J. Tepper, Detecting hate speech on twitter using a convolution-gru based deep neural network. In The Semantic Web: 15th International Conference, ESWC 2018, Heraklion, Crete, Greece, June 3−7, 2018, Proceedings, 15, Springer International Publishing, 2018, pp. 745−760.

[19] R. Kumar, A.K. Ojha, S. Malmasi, M. Zampieri, Benchmarking aggression identification in social media. In Proceedings of the first workshop on trolling, aggression and cyberbullying (TRAC-2018), 2018, August, pp. 1−11.

[20] A.S. Parihar, S. Thapa, S. Mishra, Hate speech detection using natural language processing: Applications and challenges. In 2021 5th International Conference on Trends in Electronics and Informatics (ICOEI), IEEE, 2021, June, pp. 1302−1308.

[21] A. Bisht, A. Singh, H.S. Bhadauria, J. Virmani, Kriti, Detection of hate speech and offensive language in twitter data using lstm model. Recent Trends in Image and Signal Processing in Computer Vision, (2020) 243−264.

[22] M.T. Ribeiro, S. Sameer, G. Carlos, Model-agnostic interpretability of machine learning, Proc. 22nd ACM SIGKDD Int. Conf. Knowl. Discov. Data Min. (2016).

[23] M.T. Ribeiro, S. Singh, C. Guestrin, "Why Should I Trust You?": Explaining the predictions of any classifier, Proc. 22nd ACM SIGKDD Int. Conf. Knowl. Discov. Data Min. (2016).

6

Enhanced performance of drug review classification from social networks by improved ADASYN training and Natural Language Processing techniques

P.M. Lavanya[1,2], E. Sasikala[3]

[1]DEPARTMENT OF COMPUTER SCIENCE & ENGINEERING, SRM INSTITUTE OF SCIENCE & TECHNOLOGY, KATTANKULATHUR, CHENNAI, TAMIL NADU, INDIA [2]DEPARTMENT OF INFORMATION TECHNOLOGY, EASWARI ENGINEERING COLLEGE, RAMAPURAM, CHENNAI, TAMIL NADU, INDIA [3]DEPARTMENT OF DATA SCIENCE & BUSINESS SYSTEMS, SRM INSTITUTE OF SCIENCE & TECHNOLOGY KATTANKULATHUR, CHENNAI, TAMIL NADU, INDIA

6.1 Introduction

Accessing healthcare has recently proven to be a big problem. People must be made aware of illnesses and symptoms in order to avoid becoming infected in the first place [1]. The propagation of falsehood, aided by social media and other digital platforms, has proven to be just as dangerous to global public health as the COVID-19 outbreak, actually. People can stay secure, informed, and connected because of technological developments and social media. According to the current research by the World Health Organization, 43.9% of two groups of respondents said they were inclined to share "scientific" material on social media [2]. Every year, about 250 million people in China and 100,000 in the U.S. are impacted by medication errors [3]. Around 40% of the time, physicians commit errors while prescribing since they assemble the remedy based on the information provided by their patients, which is quite limited [4,5]. With the rapid growth of the internet and the digitally commercial sector, item reviews are becoming an essential and vital part of the purchasing process for people all over the world. According to a U.S. Research Center study conducted in 2013 [5], around 60% of adults searched online for problems related to health issues, while around 35% of people searched for diagnostic health issues on social networks. In such cases, producing the better results in classifying the reviews from social network becomes mandatory.

Computational Intelligence Methods for Sentiment Analysis in Natural Language Processing Applications
DOI: https://doi.org/10.1016/B978-0-443-22009-8.00004-5

When a global health emergency like the present COVID-19 epidemic occurs, healthcare systems need solutions that can aid in the delivery of efficient care services and reduce their effect on society. Novel disease outbreaks place a heavy burden on public health and medical systems [6]. The present pandemic, meanwhile, happened at a time when public health organizations and healthcare systems had access to vast amounts of data. As a result, the difficulties brought on by the crisis present a chance to enhance public healthcare systems through the application of cutting-edge technology like data-driven AI [7]. Natural-language processing (NLP) is a subset of AI technologies that has a lot of potential, especially given the vast amount of textual data that are already accessible and are consistently developed via variety of channels, like digital health records, published medical journals, and social networks.

Nowadays, most scientists, especially those working in computational NLP, would like to create applications that utilize different classifiers. Text classification difficulties have been intensively explored and addressed in a number of diverse applications in the last few years [8−14]. The notion of converting unstructured textual data into structured data in the form of numbers so that statistical or mathematical methods may be used is the common thread that runs through all textual mining approaches [15]. The best results can be obtained by preprocessing the corpus, which is the initial step, by using some of the NLP techniques. In this paper, the drugs' dataset [16] is taken, where it contains the reviews and ratings of the drug name with the condition. Initially, the cleaning of raw text (i.e., reviews of the drug in the corpus) is performed by applying tokenization, removing the noise words from the reviews, and lemmatizing the textual data of the drug reviews. Once the data is cleaned, the features are extracted and converted into vectors by using word embedding techniques. The representation of reviews in a matrix, where each column represents a sentence and every row represents a specific term, is a typical technique. The frequency of the phrase in the corresponding document is then stored in the cells. Here are two issues: One of its key aspects in the depiction of text information in such a dataset matrix, as well as a possible weakness, is that it ignores the linguistic structuring inside a text, considering it a "bag of words." Furthermore, huge volumes of data can result in a highly textual data matrix or a high number of dimensions in scientific equations. Based on the vectors, the model is trained, and the performance is evaluated based on accuracy. There are various techniques to measure performance. Furthermore, the application might well be deployed at the edge, rather than in the cloud, because data saved in the cloud adds delay to the data processing. A mobile edge computing system may be implemented between IOT and cloud consumer devices to resolve this concern [17,18]. Recently, there has been a boom in the use of social media platforms that provide useful data for evaluating and comprehending user reactions, ideas, and emotions on a range of subjects, including medicine, government, academia, entertainment, science, and the arts. Users of social networks routinely update their statuses to share information about their current situations. They provide information about their day-to-day lives as well as any outbreak situations that may arise in a rapidly expanding area or if there is a viral illness [19].

Synthetic minority oversampling technique (SMOTE) is one of the first and the most well-known oversampling methods. it was developed based on the k-nearest neighbors approach for the minority class observations and includes synthesized minority class observations [20]. In order to balance out the disparity between the classes, more observations from the minority class are added to the data [21]. SMOTE's ability to generate synthetic data based solely on data from the minority class is one of its primary flaws. As a result, the class boundaries between both the positive class and the minority class after using SMOTE may not accurately reflect the distribution of the minority class as a whole [22]. The difficulty of learning certain minority class observations determines how many synthetic observations are generated by the improved adaptive synthetic sampling (ADASYN) algorithm; a higher number of synthetic observations is produced for minority class observations that are significantly more challenging to learn.

6.2 Related works

With the rapid progress of intelligence, a trend to use machine learning and deep learning methods has been increasing. Interestingly, there is still progress in the field of medication suggestion frameworks using text analytics since drug reviews are much more difficult to evaluate because they include medical phrasing such as condition names, symptoms, and synthesized names used in the medicine's manufacture [23]. The analysis [24] is built on the idea that the medicine that is prescribed should depend on the patient's ability. For example, if the patient's resistance is poor, trustworthy medications should be prescribed. In this study [25], a drug recommendation engine is developed that leverages patient's comments to identify sentiments via multiple vectorization methods, which can assist different classification algorithms in selecting select the best drug for a particular condition. Convolutional neural networks were used to train lexical phrase patterns and built a hashtag recommendation system that uses the skip gram model [26]. The results of this model outperform traditional models, such as support vector machine (SVM) and conventional RNN. This investigation is driven by the fact that it has been applied to standard methods such as SVM or content-based filtering approaches; the lexical characteristics are lost, and it has a significant impact on obtaining a reasonable expectation. Due to its suitability for understanding the intricate fundamental structure of sentences and the semantic proximity of different words, deep learning has been widely employed in NLP.

Overall, in this study [27], term frequency (tf) and stemmer feature extractor techniques are proposed, and the evaluation is done by using different classification techniques. Tf & inverse document frequency (tf-idf), a widely utilized feature extraction approach, is employed. For improved accuracy, the tf-idf method has been optimized [28−30] and has suggested a hybrid technique for extracting data characteristics. The methodology is developed by combining Linear discriminant analysis and word2vec. The relationship between concepts and texts is determined using this technique. It also incorporates the word's contextual connections. The findings suggest that the characteristics provided by this hybrid method can help improve classification performance. In [25], SMOTE is used for imbalanced dataset, and still there is a discrepancy between the positively and negatively classified metric from the predictive outcome, which shows that the training set must be correctly balanced via algorithms to get better results, but it doesn't fit for high-dimension data. [31] developed word2vec modeling, which uses a feed-forward-neural network approach to train word associations out of a textual corpus and can find synonyms and suggest new phrases on a partial phrase. It creates a distributed representation of words using either continuous bag-of-words or skip-gram modeling structures. [32] Our methods for classifying textual information rely on developing the features of a sizable collection of designs; these models indicate the semantic principles derived from the brief textual nuggets.

6.3 Proposed model

The drug corpus used in this research was downloaded from drugs.com at the UC Irvine ML repository. There are ten features used in the corpus, which contain unique ID (i.e., user), the drug name, reviews about the drug, condition, rating of the drug, the date on which the review is posted, and the useful count (i.e., number of times the drug has been used). The corpus contains 161,297 observations. There are 885 types of conditions in this corpus, such as left ventricular dysfunction, ADHD, birth control, opiate dependence, benign prostatic hyperplasia, etc., There are 3436 drug names based on conditions in this corpus, such as valsartan, guanfacine, lybral, ortho evra, etc. Initially, the preprocessing phase starts with data cleaning and preparation, like removal of unwanted words from the corpus. This is considered an important task for achieving a better performance (Fig. 6−1).

6.3.1 Tokenization

In NPL, tokenization is a typical activity. Both conventional NLP techniques like CountVectorizer and modern neural learning systems like transformers rely on this phase. Tokenization is a

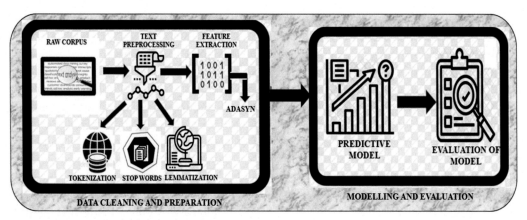

FIGURE 6–1 Architecture of the proposed model.

mechanism for breaking down a large chunk of text into smaller tokens. Based on the corpus taken here, the reviews of the drug dataset are tokenized. Once tokens are formed, they are utilized to create a vocabulary. The collection of identical tokens in the corpus is referred to as the vocabulary. In order to enhance the performance of text preprocessing, each and every token in the corpora can be considered individually, or the top N commonly encountered phrases might be considered.

Fig. 6–2 shows the description of number of features used in the drug dataset, which is indicated in red. The feature review describes the drug used by the patients or users. The rating is given by some of the users based on the condition. The maximum rating provided by the users is 10, and the minimum rating is 1. The total number of instances taken to train the model is shown in Fig. 6–3. In order to remove the duplicity, a unique ID is considered in the dataset. The data is structured in such a way that a patient with unique ID purchases a medicine/drug that is appropriate for his condition and then reviews and rates the drug on the date of purchase. If more people read that review and find it beneficial, they will click useful count button, which will increase the variable by one.

	uniqueID	drugName	condition	review	rating	date	usefulCount
0	206461	Valsartan	Left Ventricular Dysfunction	"It has no side effect, I take it in combinati...	9	20-May-12	27
1	95260	Guanfacine	ADHD	"My son is halfway through his fourth week of ...	8	27-Apr-10	192
2	92703	Lybrel	Birth Control	"I used to take another oral contraceptive, wh...	5	14-Dec-09	17
3	138000	Ortho Evra	Birth Control	"This is my first time using any form of birth...	8	3-Nov-15	10
4	35696	Buprenorphine / naloxone	Opiate Dependence	"Suboxone has completely turned my life around...	9	27-Nov-16	37
5	155963	Cialis	Benign Prostatic Hyperplasia	"2nd day on 5mg started to work with rock hard...	2	28-Nov-15	43
6	165907	Levonorgestrel	Emergency Contraception	"He pulled out, but he cummed a bit in me. I t...	1	7-Mar-17	5
7	102654	Aripiprazole	Bipolar Disorde	"Abilify changed my life. There is hope. I was...	10	14-Mar-15	32
8	74811	Keppra	Epilepsy	" I Ve had nothing but problems with the Kepp...	1	9-Aug-16	11
9	48928	Ethinyl estradiol / levonorgestrel	Birth Control	"I had been on the pill for many years. When m...	8	8-Dec-16	1

FIGURE 6–2 Features in the drug corpus.

	uniqueID	drugName	condition	review	rating	date	usefulCount
161292	191035	Campral	Alcohol Dependence	"I wrote my first report in Mid-October of 201...	10	31-May-15	125
161293	127085	Metoclopramide	Nausea/Vomiting	"I was given this in IV before surgey. I immed...	1	1-Nov-11	34
161294	187382	Orencia	Rheumatoid Arthritis	"Limited improvement after 4 months, developed...	2	15-Mar-14	35
161295	47128	Thyroid desiccated	Underactive Thyroid	"I've been on thyroid medication 49 years...	10	19-Sep-15	79
161296	215220	Lubiprostone	Constipation, Chronic	"I've had chronic constipation all my adu...	9	13-Dec-14	116

FIGURE 6–3 Total number of instances used in the drug corpus.

Fig. 6–4 shows the high availability of drugs based on the condition. For each of the top 8 conditions, there are around 100 medicines available. Let's take a glance at the review. The HTML characters like \t \n, as well as portions that communicate sentiments in brackets like (quite uncommon for someone) and (a nice thing) and terms in capital letters like MUCH, are the first parts that stand out.

From Fig. 6–5, this study shows the traditional data preparation procedures such as verifying missing values, duplicating rows, eliminating redundant values, and removing text from rows. Following that, in the condition column, all 1200 null entries rows are eliminated. Fig. 6–6, shows the user rating based on the drugs. The rating given by the user is 10 as maximum and 1 as minimum. The drugs are rated based on the remedial actions of users. Fig. 6–7 shows the result of tokenization of reviews column, where the reviews are divided into tokens.

6.3.2 Stop words removal

A stop-word is a widely used term (i.e., "us," "of," "thus," and "is") that even a search engine has been designed to disregard when processing and retrieving results as the result of a search query. This might take upspace and lead to increased processing time. Even though it saves space and time, stop words cannot be used for sensitive type of dataset. An example is depicted as follows: Before the removal of Stop words: ["This," "is," "the," "first," "time," "that," "I", "have," "not," "been," "suffering," "from," "severe," "fever"].

After removal of stop words: ["first," "time," "suffering," "severe," "fever"].

The overall meaning of the resultant statement is negative for the emotion purpose of analysis, which is not a scenario in reality. In this study, the performance is evaluated by both using stop words and not using stop words.

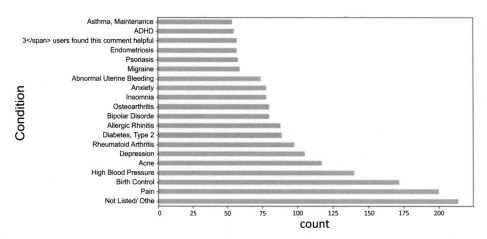

FIGURE 6–4 High availability of drugs based on condition.

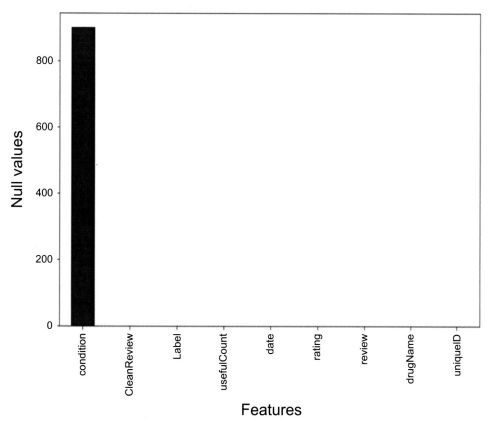

FIGURE 6–5 Null values in the dataset.

6.3.3 Normalization

The other form of text noise that occurs is when a single word exhibits numerous interpretations. Normalization is an important phase since it transforms high-dimensional characteristics into low-dimensional data, which is a perfect task for any ML model. Stemming and lemmatization are two often-used approaches for normalizing. In this study, stemming approach is not suitable as it affects the morphological relationship between words in the review column. So, lemmatization is used for specifying the part-of-speech (POS) tag for the particular phrase, and it performs on a given phrase if and only if it has POS tagging. The desired output is called lemma. The words are related morphologically to each other in a sentence. In this study, Wordnet lemmatizer is used to normalize the words in the drugs' dataset, which is being imported from the NLTK package. As a result, lemmatization helps to determine the word's context. Hence, it is more efficient with stemming.

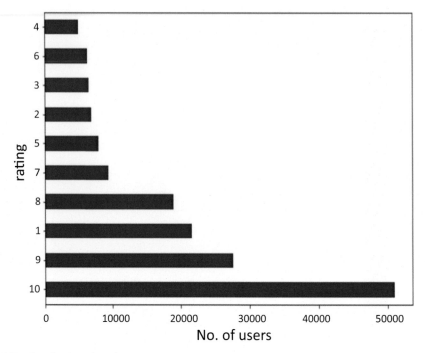

FIGURE 6–6 User's rating based on drugs.

	uniqueID	drugName	condition	review	rating	date	usefulCount	CleanReview
0	206461	Valsartan	Left Ventricular Dysfunction	"It has no side effect, I take it in combinati...	9	20-May-12	27	[it, has, no, side, effect, i, take, it, in, c...
1	95260	Guanfacine	ADHD	"My son is halfway through his fourth week of ...	8	27-Apr-10	192	[my, son, is, halfway, through, his, fourth, w...
2	92703	Lybrel	Birth Control	"I used to take another oral contraceptive, wh...	5	14-Dec-09	17	[i, used, to, take, another, oral, contracepti...
3	138000	Ortho Evra	Birth Control	"This is my first time using any form of birth...	8	3-Nov-15	10	[this, is, my, first, time, using, any, form, ...
4	35696	Buprenorphine / naloxone	Opiate Dependence	"Suboxone has completely turned my life around...	9	27-Nov-16	37	[suboxone, has, completely, turned, my, life, ...

FIGURE 6–7 Result after performing tokenization.

6.3.4 Feature extraction

Once the data is cleaned, the next step is to convert the cleaned dataset to numerical vectors so that machines can comprehend. To proceed with this step, vectorization is performed. Each review is transformed into a number vector that represents the label within the context. In this study, three techniques, such as CountVectorizer, tf-idf, and Word2Vec, are applied to the dataset, and it is compared with the ML model to calculate its performance. Here, the classification is done based on the rating, and a new target label is created that contains classes such as highly recommended, recommended, and not recommended as mentioned in Fig. 6–8. The users ratings on the drugs were classified, thus highly recommended drugs are rated by 97,410, recommended drugs are rated by 35063, and not recommended drugs are rated by 28824 users.

6.3.4.1 CountVectorizer

CountVectorizer is used to encode the review texts into numeric data. The purpose of adopting these algorithms is to capture the impact of the existence of specific phrases, and these methods do so in a variety of ways. If it is applied to real text data, the outcome will be very large vectors; however, a highly accurate estimate of the phrases in the textual data will be obtained. For example, from drug names

Valsartan = [1,0,0,0,0,...0] → Each word counts to 1 in its vector space if it is present.
Lybral = [0,1,0,0,0...0]
Ortho Evra = [0,0,1,0,0...0]

From Fig. 6–9, it shows that the useful count distribution has a difference between the lowest and highest of 1291, which is rather large. Furthermore, the deviation is enormous, at 36. The cause seems to be that the more medicines people can read reviews of, independent of whether they are positive or negative reviews, the higher the useful count is. As a result,

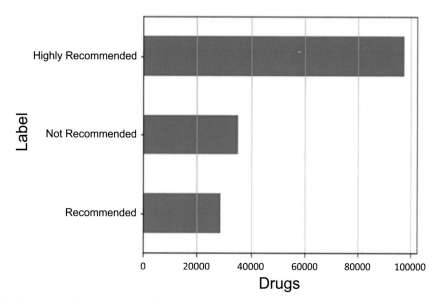

FIGURE 6–8 Extraction of the target label (drugs used by total number of users in each category).

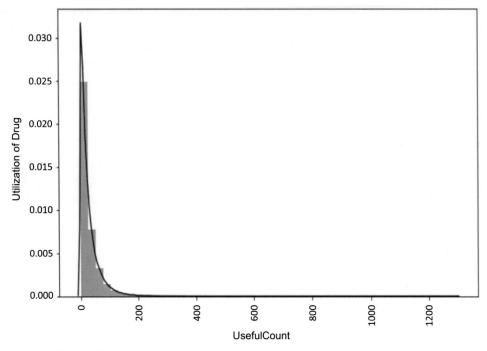

FIGURE 6–9 Utilization of drugs.

whenever a model is built, it is normalized based on conditions, which is taking into account people's accessibility.

6.3.4.2 Term frequency and inverse document frequency

This is meant to demonstrate the importance of a term in a group or corpus of texts. It is a statistical method for determining the numerical importance of words in texts [30]. The tf-idf value rises in relation to the amount of time in which a word occurs in the review and is balanced mostly by the number of words in the review column that include the term; this helps to justify the fact that certain words appear more frequently than others in total. It is calculated as, for every term in the review column,

$W_{i,j} = tf_{i,j} \times \log(N/df_i)$
$tf_{i,j}$ = No. of occurrence of i in j
df_i = No. of words in i
N = Total no. of words

6.3.4.3 Word2vec

Word2vec is a collection of similar models used for generating word vectors. It takes huge corpora of words and results in an output a vector matrix with several hundred dimensions, where each of the particular words is assigned to an associated vector in the space. The complete corpora are examined, as well as the vector generation procedure, which is carried out by calculating which phrases contain the phrases most frequently [33]. The word2vec produces a vocabulary, with each word having a vector associated with it as an output.

6.3.4.4 Improved adaptive synthetic sampling (ADASYN)

Oversampling occurrences of the minority class or undersampling occurrences of the majority class is the easiest approach to balancing an uneven dataset. The model will be biased if the dataset is indeed unbalanced. Consider this: if a model is fed to 0, for each and every possible combo, the model will return 0 for each and every given input. To make the drug dataset balanced and improve accuracy, ADASYN technique is used. In a nutshell, the ADASYN method enhances data distribution learning in two ways: (1) decreasing the bias induced by imbalanced data and (2) dynamically extending the classifier limit more toward the difficult cases.

One common question is: how to find out whether the dataset is balanced or imbalanced?

- To consider a data collection as balanced, the ratio of dependent categorical values should be 10:1.
- The confusion matrix has to be checked once the prediction is completed. From Fig. 6–10, it shows that if any of the variables are equal to zero, then the dataset is said to be unbalanced and the model is said to be biased

The reason for decreasing the dataset is to give the model less data to work upon. For illustration, there are 10,000 reviews in a dataset with just 100 data points of 1 and 0. Therefore, after applying undersampling technique, the reviews are reduced to 1.1,000 samples, which consists of 1000 are 0 and 100 of which are 1. As a result, approximately 9000 samples, which led to more error, were discarded and fed to the model. Although various models employ different strategies for undersampling, the overall outcome is the same: the dataset contains fewer rows. To enhance the range of instances in the dataset, this system

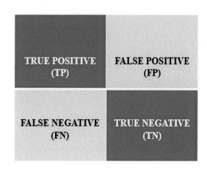

FIGURE 6–10 Confusion matrix.

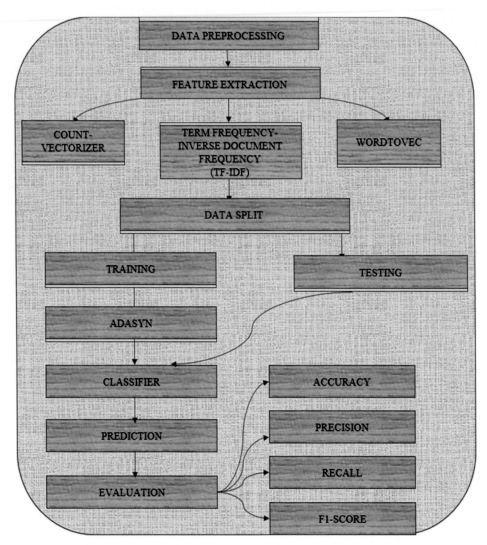

FIGURE 6–11 Flow process of the proposed model.

employs synthetic data generation. By producing synthetic observations based on existing minority instances, it enhances the minority class and makes the dataset more balanced. Fig. 6–11 shows the process of the proposed model, where it contains ADASYN which is trained on the classifier of Naïve-Bayes and SVM for better performance accuracy.

Algorithm

After creating the synthetic data, select k and α to represent the no. of closest neighbors and the required degree of class balanced, respectively. Then

1. Let m_l signify the majority-class number of instances, and let m_s represent the minority-class's number of instances. Now, Calculate $A = (m_l\text{-}m_s) * \alpha$
2. Let y_i, i = 1,2…. m_s denotes the instances belong to the minority instances and let G denotes the set of all y_i, such that $G \ni y_i$
3. To find the k-nearest neighbors y_i, determine the Euclidean-distance between y_i, and every other components of G.
4. Let's denote R_{ik}, the group of the k-closest neighbors of y_i.
5. Define γ_i as the no. of instances in the k-closest neighbor's section of y_i, which belongs to the majority-class. Compute the ratio r_i which is defined as $r_i = \gamma_i/k$, i = 1, 2… m_s
6. Now normalize r_i to $\hat{r}_i = r_i / \sum_{i=1}^{ms} ri$, i.e $\hat{r}_i$ is probability which is equal to 1
7. Compute $g_i = r_i{}^*A$, the no. of synthetic instances which is generated for y_i.
8. By randomly sampling g_i, synthetic instances denotes $y_{ij} = (j = 1, 2,…g_i)$ with replacement from R_{ik}
9. Let π denotes the no. in a range [0,1]. For given y_{ij}, synthetic instances are generated to
$$y_k = y_i + \pi (y_i\text{-}y_{ij}) \text{ where } \pi \text{ is drawn uniformly for each } y_k.$$
10. Stop algorithm

6.4 Results and discussion

All reviews were categorized as to whether a drug could be recommended for usage based on the patient's rating scale. Highly recommended drugs are ranged from above 8, recommended drugs are ranged between 4 and 7, while not recommended drugs are ranged between 1 and 3. At first, the number of training data for highly recommended, recommended, and not recommended was 97410, 35063, and 28824 respectively. After applying ADASYN, the dataset is balanced. Fig. 6−12 shows that none of the diagonal labels in the confusion matrix produced 0, as the dataset is balanced after applying ADASYN. It also determines the predicted and true values of a multiclass label based on the condition in the drug dataset. A confusion matrix is the sum of the number of times a classifier makes a valid or wrong interpretation, or, to put it another way, the number of time a classifier correctly finds the facts (true class) and the number of times it gets annoyed in distinguishing one category from another. Here, two classifiers, SVM and Naïve Bayes, are trained after preprocessing steps in order to evaluate the performance measure of the classification of reviews based on accuracy, precision, recall, and F1 score. Fig. 6−13 shows that SVM performs well by using tf-idf with stop words and produces 92.2% accuracy. The F1 score of SVM with tf-idf (using stop words) is 83.23%, which is

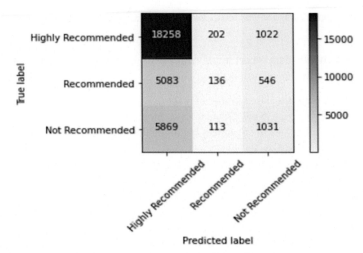

FIGURE 6–12 Confusion matrix of multiclass label based on condition after using ADASYN.

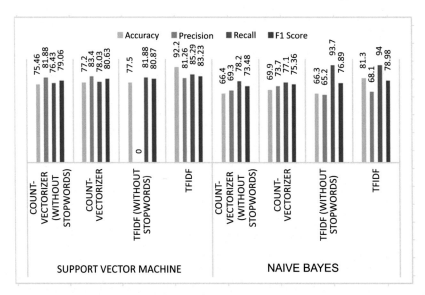

FIGURE 6–13 Performance evaluation of SVM and Naive Bayes based on accuracy, precision, recall, and F1-score.

higher when compared to the other preprocessing techniques. The recall of SVM is better when compared with Naïve Bayes and the result produced is 85.29%. When it comes to precision, SVM performs better but the count vectorizer (without using stop words) performs well by producing the result of 81.88%. Even tf-idf (with stop words) performs better and there is only a slight difference in the performance range between the two. Overall, SVM produced better performance results by using with tf-idf preprocessing technique.

6.5 Conclusion

Review sites are becoming more common in our everyday lives. Preprocessing a dataset can help enhance its quality generally and for classifying text in particular. But, in order for the algorithms to work more efficiently, they must focus on preprocessing operations such as cleaning the data and extracting features. Addressing the issue of unbalanced data distribution by incorporating a novel technique, ADASYN, is examined. These characteristics were fed into a classification model (i.e., SVM and Naïve Bayes). Finally, the performance is evaluated based on the metrics of accuracy, precision, recall, and F1-score. As a future work, the preprocessing techniques can be optimized further, either semantically or fusionally to train the classification model for producing better performance.

References

[1] S. Locke, A. Bashall, S. Al-Adely, J. Moore, A. Wilson, G.B. Kitchen, Natural language processing in medicine: a review, Trends Anaesth. Crit. Care 38 (2021) 4−9.

[2] https://www.who.int/news-room/feature-stories/detail/social-media-covid-19-a-global-study-of-digital-crisis-interaction-among-gen-z-and-millennials.

[3] S. Garg, Drug Recommendation System based on Sentiment Analysis of Drug Reviews using Machine Learning, 2021 11th International Conference on Cloud Computing, Data Science & Engineering (Confluence), Noida, India, 2021, pp. 175−181. Available from: https://doi.org/10.1201/9781315364094-12310.1109/Confluence51648.2021.9377188.

[4] C.M. Wittich, C.M. Burkle, W.L. Lanier, Medication errors: an overview for clinicians, Mayo Clin. Proc. 89 (8) (2014) 1116. -25.

[5] M.R. Chen, H.F. Wang, The reason and prevention of hospital medication errors, Pract. J. Clin. Med. (2013) 4.

[6] S. Vijayarani, M.J. Ilamathi, M. Nithya, Preprocessingtechniques for text mining-an overview, Int. J. Comput. Sci.Commun. Netw. 5 (1) (2015) 7−16.

[7] A. Bouaziz, C. Dartigues-Pallez, C. da Costa Pereira, F. Precioso, P. Lloret, Short text classification using semantic random forest, International Conference on Data Warehousing and Knowledge Discovery (2014) 288−299. Available from: https://doi.org/10.1007/978-3-319-10160-6_26.

[8] C. Giovanelli, X. Liu, S. Sierla, V. Vyatkin, R. Ichise, Towards an aggregator that exploits big data to bid on frequency containment reserve market, in: IECON 2017-43rd Annual Conference of the IEEE Industrial Electronics Society, IEEE, October 2017, pp. 7514−7519.

[9] K. Kowsari, D.E. Brown, M. Heidarysafa, K.J. Meimandi, M.S. Gerber, L.E. Barnes, Hdltex: hierarchical deep learning for text classification, in: 2017 16th IEEE International Conference on Machine Learning and Applications (ICMLA), IEEE, 2017, pp. 364−371.

[10] A. McCallum, K. Nigam, A comparison of event models for naive bayes text classification, AAAI-98 Workshop on Learning Text Categorization 752 (1) (1998) 41−48.

[11] K. Kowsari, M. Heidarysafa, D.E. Brown, K. Jafari Meimandi, L.E. Barnes, RMDL: random multimodel deep learning for classification. in: Proceedings of the 2018 International Conference on Information System and Data Mining, Lakeland, FL, USA, 9−11 April 2018; Available from: https://doi.org/10.1145/3206098.3206111.

[12] M. Heidarysafa, K. Kowsari, D.E. Brown, K.J. Meimandi, L.E. Barnes, An improvement of data classification using random multimodel deep learning (RMDL), arXiv Preprint. arXiv 1808 (2018) 08121.

[13] S. Lai, L. Xu, K. Liu, J. Zhao, Recurrent convolutional neural networks for text classification, Twenty-Ninth AAAI Conference on Artificial Intelligence. (2015).

[14] C.C. Aggarwal, C. Zhai, A survey of text classification algorithms, Mining Text Data, Springer, Berlin/Heidelberg, Germany, 2012, pp. 163−222.

[15] G. Miner, J. Elder IV, A. Fast, T. Hill, R. Nisbet, D. Dursun, Practical Text Mining and Statistical Analysis for Non-structured Text Data Applications, Academic Press, Waltham, MA, 2012.

[16] Drug Review corpus link <https://archive.ics.uci.edu/mL/datasets/Drug%2BReview%2BDataset%2B%2528Drugs.com%2529#>.

[17] M. Chary, S. Parikh, A.F. Manini, E.W. Boyer, M. Radeos, A review of natural language processing in medical education, West. J. Emerg. Med. 20 (1) (2019). Available from: https://doi.org/10.5811/westjem.2018.11.39725.

[18] S. Amin, et al., Recurrent neural networks with TF-IDF embedding technique for detection and classification in tweets of dengue disease, IEEE Access. 8 (2020) 131522−131533. Available from: https://doi.org/10.1109/ACCESS.2020.3009058.

[19] P. Lavanya, E. Sasikala, Deep learning techniques on text classification using natural language processing (NLP), in: Social Healthcare Network: A Comprehensive Survey, 2021 3rd International Conference on Signal Processing and Communication (ICPSC), 2021, pp. 603−609, Available from: https://doi.org/10.1109/ICSPC51351.2021.9451752.

[20] T. Joachims, Text categorization with support vector machines: learning with many relevant features, in: Machine Learning: ECML-98: 10th European Conference on Machine Learning Chemnitz, Germany, April 21−23, 1998 Proceedings, Berlin, Heidelberg, Springer Berlin Heidelberg, 2005, pp. 137−142.

[21] R. Rajput, A. Solanki, Real time sentiment analysis of tweets using machine learning and semantic analysis, The International Conference on Communication and Computing Systems (ICCCS-2016) (2016) 687−692. Available from: https://doi.org/10.1201/9781315364094-123.

[22] K. Archer, R. Kimes, Empirical characterization of random forest variable importance measures, Comput. Stat. Data Anal. 52 (2008) 2249−2260.

[23] T.N. Tekade, M. Emmanuel Probabilistic aspect mining approach for interpretation and evaluation of drug reviews, in: 2016 International Conference on Signal Processing, Communication, Power and Embedded System (SCOPES), Paralakhemundi, 2016, pp. 1471−1476. https://doi.org/10.1109/SCOPES.2016.7955684.

[24] K. Shimada, H. Takada, S. Mitsuyama, et al., Drug-recommendation system for patients with infectious diseases, AMIA Annu. Symp. Proc. 2005 (2005) 1112.

[25] S. Garg, Drug recommendation system based on sentiment analysis of drug reviews using machine learning, arXiv (2021).

[26] J. Li, H. Xu, X. He, J. Deng, X. Sun, Tweet modeling with LSTM recurrent neural networks for hashtag recommendation, in: 2016 International Joint Conference on Neural Networks (IJCNN), Vancouver, BC. 2016, pp. 1570−1577. https://doi.org/10.1109/IJCNN.2016.7727385.

[27] S. Vidhya, D.A.A.G. Singh, E.J. Leavline, Feature extraction for document classification, Int. J Innov. Res. Sci.Eng.Technol. 4, Special Issue 6, May 2015.

[28] Patil, Leena H., and Mohammed Atique. "A novel approach for feature selection method TF-IDF in document clustering." In *2013 3rd IEEE international advance computing conference (IACC)*, pp. 858−862. IEEE, 2013.

[29] L.-P. Jing, H.-K. Huang, H.-B. Shi, Improved feature selection approach Tfidf in text mining, in: Proceedings of the First International Conference on Machine Learning and Cybernetics, Beijing, 4−5 November 2002.

[30] A. Aizawa, An information-theoretic perspective of tf−idf measures, Inf. Process. Manag. 39 (1) (2003) 45−65. Available from: https://doi.org/10.1016/S0306-4573(02)00021-3.

[31] T. Mikolov, I. Sutskever, K. Chen, G. Corrado, J. Dean, Distributed representations of words and phrases and their compositionality. arXiv preprint arXiv:13104546, 2013.

[32] P.M. Lavanya, E. Sasikala, Auto capture on drug text detection in social media through NLP from the heterogeneous data, Meas.: Sens (2022 Nov 1) 100550.

[33] Tomas Mikolov, et al., Efficient estimation of word representations in vector space. arXiv:1301.3781 (2013).

Emotion detection from text data using machine learning for human behavior analysis

Muskan Garg[1], Chandni Saxena[2]

[1]MAYO CLINIC, ROCHESTER, MN, UNITED STATES [2]THE CHINESE UNIVERSITY OF HONG KONG, MA LIU SHUI, HONG KONG

7.1 Introduction

With the recent surge in awareness about social and mental wellbeing, affective computing has emerged as an active area of research, as evident from its exponential growth. The major focus of the social natural language processing (NLP) research community underlies an integrated and in-depth analysis of quantitative and computing methods for social and mental wellbeing. Amid COVID-19, a recent recommendation of the World Health Organization replaces the term "social distancing" with "physical distancing" thereby focusing on the importance of social connections and human emotions, which impact human behavior. Such initiatives suggest the importance of emotion detection and affective computing, which may impact millions of minds with personalized recommendation systems and personalized healthcare therapy. Imagine the world being treated by a conversational agent in a personalized way. Emotions can be captured from different sources of information, such as YouTube videos, verbal or nonverbal communications, sensors, and Internet of Things devices. Automatic emotion detection is a part of affective computing deployed on different modalities of data such as text, image, audio, and video [1]. To reduce complexity and simplify the task of emotion detection, we focus on text data, which acts as an indicator of mental state discovered through writing style, the use of specific words and knowledge that they impart.

7.1.1 Human behavior analysis

Human behavior is the potentially expressed capacity of individuals or groups of people to respond to external and internal stimuli throughout their lives. People express their emotions in face-to-face communication through their speech with different gestures, such as facial expressions, or they can share them by writing their thoughts. There are several psychological theories that provide insight into human behavior and emotion detection. Some of the most notable include:

7.1.1.1 Theories of emotion

The theories of emotion attempt to explain the physiological and cognitive processes that underlie emotions. For example, the James-Lange theory states that emotions are the result of physiological changes in the body [2], while the Cannon-Bard theory posits that emotions are the result of both physiological and cognitive processes [3].

7.1.1.1.1 Social cognitive theory

Social cognitive theory (SCT) emphasizes the role of cognitive processes in understanding and predicting human behavior. It posits that people learn and understand behavior by observing others and interpreting their actions.

Self-perception theory: This theory suggests that people infer their own emotions and attitudes by observing their own behavior and the context in which it occurs.

7.1.1.2 Theories of personality

These theories attempt to explain how different personality traits are related to behavior and emotions. For example, the Big Five personality traits (openness, conscientiousness, extraversion, agreeableness, and neuroticism) (Cobb-Clark et al., 2012) have been found to be related to different emotions and behavior patterns.

7.1.1.2.1 Social identity theory

This theory posits that people identify with certain social groups, and that these social identities influence their behavior and emotions.

7.1.1.2.2 Self-determination theory

This theory emphasizes the role of autonomy, relatedness, and competence in motivation and well-being and suggests that people are more likely to experience positive emotions when they feel a sense of autonomy and relatedness with others.

Such theories influence human behavior and emotions that can be used to inform the development of emotion detection systems. However, it's important to note that psychological theories are not always mutually exclusive, and different theories can provide complementary perspectives. Additionally, the field of emotion detection is a relatively new field, and more research is needed to fully understand the psychological processes underlying human behavior and emotions.

7.1.2 Models of emotion

An emotion detection system is a software application that uses various technologies such as NLP, machine learning, and deep learning algorithms to recognize and analyze human emotions from text, speech, or facial expressions. The primary goal of an emotion detection system is to identify and classify the emotional states of individuals, such as happiness, sadness, anger, fear, and disgust, among others. Since emotion models form the foundation of emotional detection systems, and it is crucial to concentrate on characterizing and explaining their creation. Although there is no well-defined system for emotion detection, the most popular models employed in research on emotion detection are twofold: (1) *emotions as categories* and (2) *dimensional models of emotions.*

1. According to the *emotion category theory*, emotions are distinguished based on neural, behavioral, physiological, and expressive features regardless of culture (Colombetti 2009). Ekman's basic emotion model [4] concludes with the six basic emotions are ANGER, SADNESS, FEAR, HAPPINESS, DISGUST and SURPRISE [5] defines a hybrid model consisting of eight primary complex emotions (JOY, DISGUST, SADNESS, ANGER, SURPRISE, FEAR, TRUST and ANTICIPATION). According to Plutchik, emotions are classified into four categories: primary, secondary, tertiary, and opposite emotions. These basic emotions can be organized into four sets: JOY versus SADNESS, ANGER versus FEAR, TRUST versus DISGUST and SURPRISE versus ANTICIPATION.

2. According to the *Emotional dimension technique*, emotions can be represented in dimension form. A model by Russell is one of the most illustrative models of these strategies [6]. According to Rusell's Circumplex Model of Affect [7], emotions are spread in a circular, two-dimensional region: the *valence dimension* and the *arousal dimension*. The valence dimension describes the extent of a certain emotion to be PLEASANT or UNPLEASANT. The arousal dimension refers to the level of activation or energy associated with an emotional state. Arousal can be described as the intensity of emotional experience, ranging from low to high, and is often measured using physiological indicators such as heart rate, blood pressure, or skin conductance. The PAD (pleasure, arousal, and dominance) [8] model developed by Mehrabian is based on a three-dimensional depiction.

Due to their simplicity and familiarity, *emotional categories* form the foundation for the majority of computational techniques. However, emotional categories are constrained, they might not adequately encompass all emotions. A key *advantage* of emotional dimensional models is that they are capable of capturing nuanced emotion ideas that just slightly differ and are not associated to a specific emotional state. The selection of emotional dimension models depend on the range of emotions that we need to identify.

7.1.3 Affective computing for emotion detection

Affective computing is a subdomain of artificial intelligence (AI) that enfolded the development of systems that can recognize, understand, and respond to human emotions. In the context of emotion detection, affective computing approaches aim to identify emotions in natural language text, speech, or other forms of human communication. There are several different modalities used in affective computing for emotion detection, such as:

1. Text mining: Text mining is used for inferring mental states and sentiment analysis tasks such as identifying positive, negative, or neutral emotions in text.

2. Speech recognition: Audio mining analyzes the tone, pitch, and other characteristics of speech to identify emotions.
3. Facial expression recognition: Images and video frames are extracted to analyze the facial expressions for identifying emotions of a person in image or frame, respectively.
4. Biometric sensor data: The physiological data, such as rate of heartbeat and skin conductance, provide significant insights about emotional well-being conducted through intelligent sensors to infer emotions.

Furthermore, the learning-based mechanisms are trained on the labeled data to learn patterns that are associated with different emotions.

The accuracy of emotion detection using affective computing can be affected by several factors, such as external commonsense knowledge and domain-specific knowledge infusion, the quality of the data used for training, cultural variations, and individual differences. Additionally, the ethical and societal implications of emotion detection systems need to be considered, such as privacy and bias.

7.1.4 Natural language processing for emotion detection

NLP is particularly important for emotion detection, as it allows the system to understand and identify emotions in text, speech, or other forms of human communication. Some of the key tasks in which NLP is used for emotion detection are:

1. Sentiment analysis identifies the emotional tone of a piece of text as positive instances, negative instances, or the neutral ones. Sentiment analysis can be used to detect emotions such as happiness, anger, sadness, and more.
2. Opinion mining: Subjective information extraction from text, such as opinions, evaluations, appraisals, and emotional states, in order to understand the emotions and attitudes of the author.
3. Emotion recognition in speech: NLP techniques such as speech recognition and prosody analysis are used to identify emotions in speech by analyzing the tone, pitch, and other characteristics of the speaker's voice.
4. Text generation: The generated text expresses a specific emotion and can be used for creating emotionally expressive chatbots and virtual assistants.
5. Dialog and conversation understanding: NLP techniques can be used to understand the emotional state of the conversation and its context, which is useful for identifying the emotions of the interlocutors.

7.1.4.1 Applications

The potential of these tasks lies in their major applications. Emotion detection using text data is a prominent area of research due to its applications in the areas of marketing, political science, human-computer interaction, and psychology. It is useful in several AI-based applications domains, such as question answering systems, sentiment analysis, text summarization, recommendation systems, information extraction, and healthcare applications. There are several real-time applications of NLP for emotion detection, such as:

1. *Customer service*: Companies can use NLP for emotion detection to analyze customer feedback and identify patterns in customer emotions, which can be used to improve customer service.
2. *Marketing*: Companies can use NLP for emotion detection to analyze customer feedback on products and services, which can be used to improve marketing strategies.
3. *Social media monitoring*: Companies can use NLP for emotion detection to monitor social media for mentions of their brand and identify patterns in customer emotions, which can be used to improve marketing strategies.
4. *Sentiment analysis*: Companies can use NLP for sentiment analysis to analyze customer feedback on products and services, which can be used to improve marketing strategies.
5. *Mental health*: Clinicians, researchers, and healthcare providers use NLP-based emotion detection systems to identify emotions in text data generated by their patients, like social media posts, journal entries, or speech transcripts, which can be used to help identify mental health issues [9].
6. *Human resource*: Companies use NLP-based emotion detection to identify and manage employee emotions and morale, which can be used to improve employee satisfaction and retention.
7. *Virtual assistants and chatbots*: NLP-based emotion detection can be used to improve the effectiveness of virtual assistants and chatbots by allowing them to respond appropriately to user emotions.
8. *Voice-enabled devices*: NLP-based emotion detection can be used to improve the effectiveness of voice-enabled devices by allowing them to respond appropriately to user emotions.

The accuracy of NLP-based emotion detection can be affected by several factors, such as the quality of the data used for training, cultural variations, and individual differences. Furthermore, the ethical and societal implications of emotion detection systems need to be considered, such as privacy and bias.

7.1.4.2 Challenges

After extensive literature, the following major challenges are observed by the research community for applying NLP to emotion detection mechanisms:

1. *Language variability*: Different people express emotions in different ways, which makes it difficult to identify emotions in text.
2. *Ambiguity*: Words and phrases can have multiple meanings, making it challenging to identify the intended emotion.
3. *Lack of labeled data*: There is a scarcity of labeled data that can be used to train emotion detection models.
4. *Context*: Emotions may change due to the context while conveying the expression, making it difficult to accurately identify emotions in text.

5. *Cultural differences*: Different cultures express emotions in different ways, which can make it challenging to identify emotions in text written in different languages or from different cultures.
6. *Multimodality*: Emotions can be expressed both in verbal and nonverbal way, such as facial expression or voice tone.
7. *Fine-grained emotion detection*: Differentiating between similar emotions like happiness, excitement, etc.

7.2 Available tools and resources

The research community constructs and releases many language resources, datasets, and dictionaries on subjectivity and emotion, most of which are publicly available [10]. This section describes the tools and datasets used to build AI models for emotion detection in a given text.

7.2.1 Tools for emotion detection

The following tools embrace NLP in emotion detection:

1. **Sentiment analysis tools** are the machine learning algorithms that classify the text data into one of the predefined classes of being positive, negative, or neutral based on the emotions expressed. The most common tools are VADER [11], TextBlob,[1] and NLTK Sentiment Intensity Analyzer.[2]
2. **Emotion lexicons** are prebuilt lists of words or phrases associated with different emotions, used to analyze text data, such as National Research Council Canada (NRC) Emotion Lexicon, SenticNet, and EmoLex, ANEW [12], LIWC.[3] The most commonly used lexicons are:
   - WordNet-Affect [13] is one of the main lexicon resources employed to detect emotion in the text. For a relatively small number of words, it indicates whether a particular word is associated with one or more of the six basic emotions but has no information about the intensity of the emotion; for example, words *angered* and *infuriated* have the same emotion label in WordNet-Affect.
   - The NRC-Emotion Lexicon [14] NRC, also called EmoLex, assigns 14182 emotion lexicons into one or more of the eight basic classes (anger, fear, anticipation, trust, surprise, sadness, joy, and disgust) of Plutchik. These emotion classes are manually annotated by Mechanical Turk users.
   - The SenticNet 3.0.3 [15] is used for concept-level sentiment analysis and opinion mining. SenticNet assigns 13,741 concepts, which also include multiword concepts.
   - The Intensifier Lexicon [16] provides a set of 112 modifiers (adverbs) that can be used to determine fine-grained attitude labels and the strength of the attitude.
   - The Prior-polarity Lexicon [17] is a prior-polarity subjectivity lexicon resource. It assigns lexicons the classes of strong subjectivity and weak subjectivity clues.

[1] https://textblob.readthedocs.io/en/dev/.
[2] https://www.nltk.org/api/nltk.sentiment.html.
[3] https://www.liwc.app/.

3. **Deep learning-based models** are the neural network models, such as LSTMs and CNNs, which extract features from text data and classify them into different emotions.
4. **Emotion detection API's:** There are many multinational companies providing application programming interface (API) for emotion detection, such as Google Cloud Natural Language API,[4] Microsoft Azure Text Analytics API,[5] and Amazon Comprehend.[6]

These available resources are used in combination or separately, depending on the specific use case and the amount of data available. However, there are no prior works that are benchmarked and thus need a lot of data to be trained, validated, and fine-tuned to achieve better results.

7.2.2 Datasets

The publicly available datasets are:

- EmoReact[7]:The EmoReact dataset is a collection of audiovisual recordings of participants watching emotionally charged videos [18]. The dataset was constructed to develop and evaluate AI models for automatic emotion recognition from audiovisual data. The dataset contains a total of 5360 recordings, with each recording consisting of a participant watching a video and their emotional reactions captured on video and audio.
- Sentiment140[8]: The Sentiment140 dataset is a collection of tweets that have been annotated for sentiment analysis. The dataset was created to support research on automatic sentiment analysis and contains a total of 1.6 million tweets.
- EmoContext[9]: The EmoContext dataset is a collection of short text messages that have been annotated for emotion and context. The dataset was created to support research on emotion recognition in text and contains a total of 7835 messages. The messages in the dataset were collected from various sources, including Twitter, Reddit, and SMS messages. Each message was labeled with one of four emotion categories: joy, sadness, anger, or no emotion. In addition to emotion labels, each message was also labeled with one of six contextual dimensions: social support, socializing, achievement, enjoyment, bonding, or loss.
- EmoInt[10]: The EmoInt dataset is a collection of short texts in English that have been annotated for emotion intensity. The dataset was created to support research on automatic emotion intensity recognition and contains a total of 5000 texts. The texts in the dataset were collected from various sources, including social media, blogs, and news articles. Each text was annotated with an intensity score for each of the following emotions: anger, fear, joy, and sadness. The intensity scores range from 0 (no intensity) to 1 (maximum intensity).

---

[4] https://cloud.google.com/natural-language.
[5] https://azure.microsoft.com/en-us/products/cognitive-services/text-analytics.
[6] https://aws.amazon.com/comprehend/.
[7] https://github.com/bnojavan/EmoReact.
[8] http://help.sentiment140.com/for-students.
[9] https://github.com/sedflix/EmoContext.
[10] https://github.com/SEERNET/EmoInt.

- SentiHood[11]: The SentiHood dataset is a collection of short texts in English that have been annotated for sentiment and aspect polarity. The dataset was created to support research on aspect-based sentiment analysis and contains a total of 5704 texts. The texts in the dataset are related to different aspects of urban neighborhoods and were collected from various online sources, such as Yelp and Google reviews. Each text was annotated with a sentiment label for the overall sentiment and an aspect polarity label for the sentiment toward each aspect mentioned in the text.
- EmoBank[12]: The EmoBank dataset is a collection of short texts in English that have been annotated for emotion intensity and valence. The dataset was created to support research on automatic emotion detection and contains a total of 10,563 texts. The texts in the dataset were collected from various online sources, including news articles, blog posts, and social media. Each text was annotated with an intensity score for each of the following emotions: anger, disgust, fear, joy, sadness, and surprise, and a valence score ranging from 1 (negative) to 5 (positive).
- CARER − An emotions dataset[13]: This dataset is obtained from English Twitter messages to discover indicators of six basic emotions: sadness, anger, joy, fear, love, and surprise [19].
- GoEmotions[14]: The GoEmotions dataset was created to support research on fine-grained emotion recognition and contains a total of 58,466 comments. The Reddit comments in the dataset were collected using Reddit's API and were filtered to include only those that contained English text and expressed some form of emotion. Each comment was then annotated with labels indicating the presence or absence of 27 different emotion categories, including amusement, anger, contentment, disappointment, and pride.
- Emotions Detection Dataset[15]: The dataset supports exploration of multiclass classification problems to classify each given text among 40,000 texts in 13 different emotions, making it challenging to build an efficient multiclass classifier.
- Emotions Dataset- LiveJournal[16]: This dataset contains the text samples, which are classified as per the mood of the authors into one of three classes: either positive (1), negative (−1), or neutral (0).

7.2.3 Feature extraction tools

Feature extraction is the process of extracting relevant information from the text data that can be used to identify the emotions expressed. The extracted features can be used as input

---

[11] https://github.com/Nix07/Utilizing-BERT-for-Aspect-Based-Sentiment-Analysis.
[12] https://github.com/JULIELab/EmoBank.
[13] https://huggingface.co/datasets/emotion.
[14] https://ai.googleblog.com/2021/10/goemotions-dataset-for-fine-grained.html.
[15] https://www.kaggle.com/datasets/pashupatigupta/emotion-detection-from-text.
[16] https://data.syr.edu/get/EmotionPatterns/.

to a machine learning algorithm for classification. The following methods are used to extract features from text data for emotion detection:

- Bag-of-Words: Here, each word is treated as a separate feature. The frequency or presence of each word in the text is used as a feature. This method is simple, but does not take into account the context or order of the words.
- N-grams: This method considers a sequence of N words as a feature. This allows for the capture of context and meaning within the text.
- Word Embeddings: Word embeddings are a way of representing words as numerical vectors. These vectors capture the meaning and context of a word in a high-dimensional space. Common examples of word embeddings include GloVe, word2vec, and BERT.
- Lexical Features: These features include the use of certain words or phrases that are associated with certain emotions. Examples include the use of words such as "happy," "sad," "angry," etc., in the WordNet-Affect lexicon [20]
- Syntactic features: These features include information about the structure of the text, such as the use of certain grammatical structures or patterns.
- Sentiment lexicons: These are prebuilt lists of words or phrases associated with different emotions that can be used to analyze text data. Examples include NRC Emotion Lexicon, SenticNet, and EmoLex.

7.3 Methods and materials

Although the prior literature is composed of many different approaches for emotion detection, they are majorly categorized into the following approaches:

7.3.1 Rule-based approaches

A rule-based approach for emotion detection involves using a set of predefined rules or heuristics to identify emotions in text. This approach typically involves manually creating a list of keywords or phrases that are associated with specific emotions, and then using these keywords to identify emotions in a given piece of text.

7.3.1.1 Lexicon-based approach

One common way to implement a rule-based approach is to use a lexicon, which is a list of words and their associated emotions. For example, words like "happy," "joyful," and "content" may be associated with the emotion of happiness, while words like "sad," "depressed," and "miserable" may be associated with the emotion of sadness. The lexicon can be constructed manually by experts in the field or by using unsupervised learning techniques. Once the lexicon is created, the process of emotion detection can be performed by scanning the text for keywords or phrases that match those in the lexicon. If a match is found, the corresponding emotion is assigned to that text.

7.3.1.2 Keyword-based approach

It is the simplest approach to emotion analysis, which directly characterizes emotions [6]. The approach is based on finding the related set(s) of keywords in a given text. These keywords are emotional categories for a target problem of emotion detection, which can be labeled as fear, anger, happiness, disgust, sadness, surprise, etc. Keyword-based approach can be described as a sequence of steps as shown in Fig. 7−1.

7.3.1.3 Regular expressions

Another way of rule-based approach is to use regular expressions, which are patterns that can be used to match certain text [11]. For example, a regular expression might be used to match all occurrences of the word "happy" in a piece of text, regardless of whether it is in the form of a verb, noun, or adjective. This approach can be relatively straightforward to implement and can provide accurate results for certain types of text. However, it can be limited by the quality and coverage of the lexicon, which are highly dependent on the quality of the data and the expertise of the people who created it. Additionally, it can be challenging to identify more complex or nuanced emotions using a rule-based approach, as it may not be able to capture the context and meaning of the text as well as other approaches, such as machine learning-based methods.

7.3.2 Statistical learning

Statistical learning is a method for using statistical models to make predictions or detect patterns in data. In the context of emotion detection, statistical learning approaches involve training a model on a dataset of text or speech data that has been labeled with emotional categories (e.g., "happy," "sad," "angry"). The model learns the statistical patterns in the data that are associated with different emotions, and can then be used to classify new, unlabeled text or speech data into the appropriate emotional categories. Common techniques used in statistical learning for emotion detection include decision trees, support vector machines, and neural networks.

7.3.2.1 Machine learning-based approaches

Emotion detection using machine learning-based approaches can be broadly divided into four types: supervised learning, unsupervised learning, and semisupervised learning.

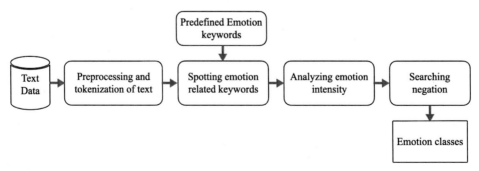

FIGURE 7–1 General steps of keyword-based approach.

A supervised learning algorithm analyzes the training data and derives a function that it uses to map new examples [21]. Unsupervised learning approaches attempt to find hidden structures in unlabeled data to build models of emotion detection [22]. Semisupervised learning approaches intend to use training data without the intervention of human annotators [23]. One of the most commonly used classification algorithms is SVM, a supervised machine learning algorithm [24]. The logistic regression model can also be used to extract meaningful features for emotions classification [10].

7.3.2.2 Deep learning methods

Major deep learning approaches are:

- Recurrent Neural Networks (RNNs): RNNs are a type of neural network that processes sequential text data. They can be used for emotion detection by processing the text data and using the output of the network to classify the text data into different emotions.
- Long Short-Term Memory (LSTM) Networks: LSTMs are a type of RNN that accommodate the sequential data with long-term dependencies. They can be used for emotion detection by processing the text data and using the output of the network to classify the text data into different emotions.
- Convolutional Neural Networks (CNNs): CNNs are a type of neural network that are particularly well-suited for processing image and text data. They can be used for emotion detection by processing the text data and using the output of the network to classify the text data into different emotions.
- Transformer-based models: These are a type of neural networks that are developed to process sequential data, such as text data. They have been shown to be very effective in a variety of NLP tasks, including emotion detection. The most popular models in this category include the BERT and GPT-2.

Deep learning approaches further advance in: (1) Attention-based models: These models use attention mechanisms that allow the model to focus on specific parts of the text data when making predictions. This can help the model to better understand the context and meaning of the text data, which is important for emotion detection. (2) Multimodal models: These models combine information from multiple modalities, such as text, images, or speech, to improve emotion detection.

These deep learning methods are able to learn complex patterns and features from text data that are indicative of different emotions and can achieve high accuracy rates in emotion detection tasks. However, they require a huge amount of annotated training data and fine-tune them, which can be difficult to interpret and explain.

7.3.2.3 Contextual adaptation

Contextual adaptation in NLP for emotion detection refers to the process of adapting the models to the specific context in which they will be used. This is done to improve the performance of the models by making them more robust to variations in the input data. Contextual adaptation in NLP for emotion detection is performed in the following ways:

- Fine-tuning pretrained models: This involves using pretrained models, such as BERT or GPT-2, and fine-tuning them on a specific dataset of emotion-labeled text. This allows the model to learn the specific patterns and features of the text data relevant to the emotion detection task.
- Domain adaptation: This involves adapting models to a specific domain, such as customer service or mental health, by training them on a dataset of text data from that domain.
- Data augmentation: Multiplying the size of the dataset by constructing new text data using techniques such as back-translation, paraphrasing, or adding noise to the data.
- Multitask learning: This involves training models on multiple related tasks, such as emotion detection and sentiment analysis, at the same time. This allows the model to learn more general representations of the text data and improve performance on the specific task of emotion detection.
- Multimodal learning: This involves incorporating other modalities, such as speech or facial expressions, into the model to improve performance.

Contextual adaptation can help improve the performance of models by allowing them to learn the specific patterns and features of the text data relevant to the emotion detection task. It also enables models to be more robust to variations in the input data, such as changes in language, dialect, or domain, and improves the generalization of models.

7.3.2.4 Personalized bots

Personalized bots for NLP in emotion detection are chatbots that are specifically tailored to the emotional needs of an individual user. These bots can be used in various applications, such as emotional and mental health, customer service, and market research. Personalized bots can be created using machine learning algorithms and NLP techniques. The bots are trained on a dataset of text data that is labeled with emotions and can understand and respond to text input from users. The bots can then analyze the text input, identify the emotions expressed, and respond in a way that is tailored to the specific emotional needs of the user. For example, in emotional and mental health, a personalized bot can be used to monitor the emotional well-being of an individual and provide targeted support. The bot can be trained to understand and respond to text input related to mental health and provide resources or referrals to professionals as needed.

In customer service, personalized bots can be used to analyze customer feedback and identify areas for improvement. The bot can be trained to understand and respond to text input related to customer service and provide helpful responses or troubleshoot issues. In market research, personalized bots can be used to analyze social media data and gauge public sentiment about a brand or product. The bot can be trained to understand and respond to text input related to market research and provide insights about public sentiment. Personalized bots for NLP in emotion detection can be a powerful tool for providing targeted support and understanding the emotional needs of users. With the help of machine learning and NLP, these bots can understand and respond to text input with a high level of accuracy and provide tailored support and help.

7.3.3 Explainable AI for emotion detection

Explainable AI (XAI) for NLP in emotion detection refers to the use of AI models that can provide clear and interpretable explanations of their predictions or decisions. This is particularly important in emotion detection, as the ability to understand the reasoning behind a model's predictions can be critical for ensuring that the model's decisions are fair, trustworthy, and aligned with ethical principles. The AI models are made more explainable in the context of NLP for emotion detection:

- Feature importance: This involves providing an understanding of which features of the text data are most important for the model's predictions. For example, a model might indicate that a specific word or phrase was particularly important in determining a particular emotion.
- Attention mechanisms: Attention mechanisms are a way of identifying which parts of the input text the model is paying the most attention to when making its predictions. This can provide insight into which parts of the text are most important for the model's predictions.
- Counterfactual analysis: This involves analyzing how small changes to the input text would affect the model's predictions, which can provide insight into how the model is making its decisions.
- LIME (Local Interpretable Model-Agnostic Explanations): LIME is a technique that allows one to understand the predictions of any classifier, by learning an interpretable model locally around the prediction.
- SHAP (SHapley Additive exPlanations): SHAP values are a unified measure of feature importance that can be used to explain the output of any machine learning model.

They rely on cooperative game theory to attribute the importance of features. By providing clear and interpretable explanations of their predictions, XAI models can help build trust and confidence in the use of AI for emotion detection. It can also help identify potential biases or errors in the model's predictions and improve the overall performance of the model.

7.4 Outlook

The futuristic idea for NLP in emotion detection would be the development of a technology that can accurately and effectively detect and respond to a wide range of emotions and mental states in real-time. This technology would be able to understand the nuances of human emotions and mental states, and respond in a way that is tailored to the specific needs of the individual. One potential application of this technology would be in the field of emotional and mental health. A futuristic idea would be to develop a personalized chatbot that can provide real-time emotional support to individuals experiencing mental health issues.

The chatbot would be able to understand the user's emotional state and respond with appropriate resources, referrals, or advice.

Another application would be in customer service, where a futuristic idea would be to develop personalized chatbots that can understand the emotional state of customers and respond in a way that is tailored to the specific needs of the individual. The chatbot would be able to understand the customer's emotional state and provide helpful responses or troubleshoot issues. Additionally, in market research, personalized chatbots could be used to analyze social media data and gauge public sentiment about a brand or product. The chatbot would be able to understand the emotional state of the users and provide insights about public sentiment.

7.4.1 Ethical considerations

The use of NLP for emotion detection raises a number of ethical considerations, including:

1. Privacy: The use of NLP for emotion detection often involves the collection and analysis of personal text data, such as social media posts or text messages. This raises concerns about the protection of personal privacy and the potential for misuse of the data.
2. Bias: NLP models for emotion detection are trained on large datasets of text data, which can contain biases based on factors such as gender, race, and socioeconomic status. This can result in models that are not fair or equitable and may produce biased predictions.
3. Explainability: NLP models for emotion detection can be complex and difficult to understand, making it difficult to understand the reasoning behind their predictions. This can make it difficult to identify and address potential biases or errors in the model's predictions.
4. Transparency: The use of NLP for emotion detection can be opaque, making it difficult for users to understand how the technology works and what data is being collected. This can make it difficult for users to make informed decisions about the use of the technology.
5. Fairness: The use of NLP for emotion detection can be used for some decision-making processes, such as hiring, lending, or insurance, which can have a significant impact on people's lives. It's important to make sure that the models are fair and unbiased, and that the predictions are not used in a way that discriminates against certain groups of people.
6. Accountability: The use of NLP for emotion detection raises questions about who is responsible if something goes wrong, such as if a model produces biased or inaccurate predictions.

To address these ethical considerations, it is important to consider the use of techniques such as XAI, counterfactual analysis, and fairness metrics, as well as the use of human oversight and ethical guidelines. Furthermore, it is important to have transparency in the data collection and use, as well as clear and fair policies for data sharing and privacy. Additionally, it is important to consider the potential impact of the technology on different groups of people and to take steps to ensure that the technology is used in a way that is fair and equitable.

7.4.2 Limitations of NLP in emotion detection

There are several limitations of NLP in emotion detection, including:

1. Complexity of human emotions: Human emotions are complex and nuanced, and it can be difficult to accurately detect and classify them using NLP techniques. The models can be biased by the dataset they were trained on, and may not be able to understand the nuances of emotions in different cultures, languages, or idioms.
2. Ambiguity and context: Text data is often ambiguous and context-dependent, which can make it difficult for NLP models to accurately detect emotions. Models may struggle to understand the intent or meaning behind certain words or phrases, or may misinterpret the tone of a message.
3. Lack of labeled data: NLP models for emotion detection require large amounts of labeled text data for training. The lack of labeled data can limit the performance of the models and make it difficult to fine-tune them for specific use cases.
4. Limited interpretability: Many NLP models for emotion detection are complex and difficult to interpret, making it difficult to understand the reasoning behind their predictions. This can make it difficult to identify and address potential biases or errors in the model's predictions.
5. Privacy: The use of NLP for emotion detection often involves the collection and analysis of personal text data, such as social media posts or text messages. This raises concerns about the protection of personal privacy and the potential for misuse of the data.
6. Fairness and accountability: The use of NLP for emotion detection raises questions about who is responsible if something goes wrong, such as if a model produces biased or inaccurate predictions.

Additionally, it's important to make sure that the models are fair and unbiased, and that the predictions are not used in a way that discriminates against certain groups of people.

7.5 Conclusion

The futuristic idea for NLP in emotion detection would be a technology that can accurately detect and respond to a wide range of emotions and mental states in real-time and that is tailored to the specific needs of the individual. This technology would have a wide range of applications, from emotional and mental health to customer service and market research.

References

[1] M. Garg, S. Wazarkar, M. Singh, O. Bojar, Multimodality for NLP-centered applications: resources, advances and frontiersJune Proc. Thirteen. Lang. Resour. Eval. Conf. (2022) 6837−6847.

[2] W.B. Cannon, The James-Lange theory of emotions: a critical examination and an alternative theory, Am. J. Psychol. 39 (1/4) (1927) 106−124.

[3] O.E. Dror, The Cannon−Bard thalamic theory of emotions: a brief genealogy and reappraisal, Emot. Rev. 6 (1) (2014) 13−20.

[4] E. Paul, Basic Emotions in Handbook of Cognition and Emotions, Chapter 3, T Dalgleish, M Power (Eds.), 1999.

[5] R. Plutchik, The nature of emotions: human emotions have deep evolutionary roots, a fact that may explain their complexity and provide tools for clinical practice, Am. Sci. 89 (4) (2001) 344−350.

[6] L. Canales, P. Martínez-Barco, Emotion detection from text: a surveyOctober Proc. Workshop Nat. Lang. Process. 5th Inf. Syst. Res. Working Days (JISIC) (2014) 37−43.

[7] J. Posner, J.A. Russell, B.S. Peterson, The circumplex model of affect: an integrative approach to affective neuroscience, cognitive development, and psychopathology, Dev. Psychopathol. 17 (3) (2005) 715−734.

[8] A. Mehrabian, Pleasure-arousal-dominance: a general framework for describing and measuring individual differences in temperament, Curr. Psychol. 14 (4) (1996) 261−292.

[9] M. Garg, Mental health analysis in social media posts: a survey, Arch. Comput. Methods Eng. (2023) 1−24.

[10] D. Ghazi, D. Inkpen, S. Szpakowicz, Prior and contextual emotion of words in sentential context, Comp. Speech Lang. 28 (1) (2014) 76−92.

[11] C. Hutto, E. Gilbert, Vader: a parsimonious rule-based model for sentiment analysis of social media textMay Proc. Int. AAAI Conf. Web Soc. Media 8 (1) (2014) 216−225.

[12] S. Shaikh, K. Cho, T. Strzalkowski, L. Feldman, J. Lien, T. Liu, et al., ANEW + : automatic expansion and validation of affective norms of words lexicons in multiple languagesMay Proc. Tenth Int. Conf. Lang. Resour. Evaluati(LREC'16) (2016) 1127−1132.

[13] C. Strapparava, A. Valitutti, Wordnet affect: an affective extension of wordnetMay Lrec 4 (1083−1086) (2004) 40.

[14] S.M. Mohammad, P.D. Turney, NRC emotion lexicon, Natl Res. Council, Can. 2 (2013) 234.

[15] E. Cambria, D. Olsher, D. Rajagopal, SenticNet 3: a common and common-sense knowledge base for cognition-driven sentiment analysisJune Twenty-eighth AAAI Conf. Artif. intelligence. (2014).

[16] A. Neviarouskaya, H. Prendinger, M. Ishizuka, @ AM: Textual attitude analysis modelJune Proc. NAACL HLT 2010 Workshop Computational Approaches Anal. Gener. Emot. text. (2010) 80−88.

[17] T. Wilson, J. Wiebe, P. Hoffmann, Recognizing contextual polarity: An exploration of features for phrase-level sentiment analysis, Comput. Linguist. 35 (3) (2009) 399−433.

[18] B. Nojavanasghari, T. Baltrušaitis, C.E. Hughes, L.P. Morency, Emoreact: a multimodal approach and dataset for recognizing emotional responses in childrenOctober Proc. 18th ACM Int. Conf. Multimodal Interact. (2016) 137−144.

[19] E. Saravia, H.C.T. Liu, Y.H. Huang, J. Wu, Y.S. Chen, Carer: contextualized affect representations for emotion recognition, Proc. 2018 Conf. Empir. Methods Nat. Lang. Process. (2018) 3687−3697.

[20] H. Khanpour, C. Caragea, Fine-grained emotion detection in health-related online posts, Proc. 2018 Conf. Empir. Methods Nat. Lang. Process. (2018) 1160−1166.

[21] M. Hasan, Automatic emotion detection in text messages using supervised learning, Doctoral dissertation, University of Massachusetts Boston, 2021.

[22] A. Agrawal, A. An, Unsupervised emotion detection from text using semantic and syntactic relations, 2012 IEEE/WIC/ACM Int. Conf. Web Intell. Intell. Agent. Technol., Vol. 1, IEEE, 2012, pp. 346−353. December.

[23] Z. Zhang, F. Ringeval, B. Dong, E. Coutinho, E. Marchi, B. Schüller, Enhanced semi-supervised learning for multimodal emotion recognition, 2016 IEEE Int. Conf. Acoustics, Speech Signal. Process. (ICASSP), IEEE, 2016, pp. 5185−5189. March.

[24] C.O. Alm, D. Roth, R. Sproat, Emotions from text: machine learning for text-based emotion predictionOctober Proc. Hum. Lang. Technol. Conf. Conf. Empir. Methods Nat. Lang. Process. (2005) 579−586.

8

Optimization of effectual sentiment analysis in film reviews using machine learning techniques

S. Balamurugan[1], E. Gurumoorthi[2], R. Maruthamuthu[3], N. Naveenkumar[3]

[1]SCHOOL OF COMPUTERS, MADANAPALLE INSTITUTE OF TECHNOLOGY AND SCIENCE, MADANAPALLE, ANDHRA PRADESH, INDIA [2]DEPARTMENT OF IT, CMR COLLEGE OF ENGINEERING AND TECHNOLOGY, HYDERABAD, TELANGANA, INDIA [3]DEPARTMENT OF COMPUTER APPLICATIONS, MADANAPALLE INSTITUTE OF TECHNOLOGY AND SCIENCE, MADANAPALLE, ANDHRA PRADESH, INDIA

8.1 Introduction

The advent of social media in the last 10 years, including web logs and community networks, has increased attention to sentiment analysis. With the growth of assessments, grades, commendations, and other online expressions, online belief has essentially become a virtual currency for companies wanting to advertise their goods, find new business prospects, and maintain their reputations [1]. Many are now looking to the field of sentiment analysis to systematize the procedure of sifting out the noise, interpreting the dialogs, recognizing the key material, and taking necessary measures. An issue with most sentiment analysis algorithms is that they describe sentiment regarding a good or service in straightforward words [2]. However, it can be very challenging to distill a body of written content into a straightforward pro or con attitude due to cultural considerations, sentence negation, sarcasm, terseness, language ambiguity, and many settings [3].

Categorizing the polarity of a specified text in the article, sentence, or part level is a crucial problem in sentiment analysis. It focuses on whether a document, a sentence, or a characteristic or attribute expresses an opinion that is positive, negative, or neutral. Sometimes, it looks at emotions other than polarity, such "angry," "sad," and "happy." Subjectivity/objectivity identification is a task in sentiment analysis that focuses on categorizing a specified text (often a sentence) into one of two classifications (objective or subjective) [4]. Because the subjectivity of words and phrases may depend on their context and because an objective document may contain subjective sentences (such as a news article that quotes people's opinions), this challenge might occasionally be more difficult than polarity classification [5,6].

Computational Intelligence Methods for Sentiment Analysis in Natural Language Processing Applications.
DOI: https://doi.org/10.1016/B978-0-443-22009-8.00003-3

Existing sentiment analysis techniques can be divided into four primary types. They are concept-level strategies, statistical methods, lexical affinity, and keyword detection [7]. Based on the existence of clear-cut affect terms such as joyful, sad, fearful, and bored, a technique called keyword spotting organizes text according to the affect categories. Lexical affinity enhances keyword-based approaches by taking into account more subtle influence terms [8]. In addition, it gives arbitrary words a potential "affinity" for certain emotions. Semantic analysis, support vector machines (SVMs), sack of words, and semantic alignment are examples of machine learning (ML) components that are influenced by statistical methodologies [9,10].

With the introduction of Web 2.0, a number of sites such as Facebook, Twitter, LinkedIn, and Instagram enable users to share their opinions on a wide range of subjects, from entertainment to education [11]. These platforms have a massive quantity of data available in the method of tweets, web logs, status informs, postings, etc. Sentiment analysis looks at the texts, reviews, and postings that are available online on various platforms to assess the separation of emotions, including gladness, distress, anguish, abhorrence, rage, and fondness, as well as feelings [12,13]. Opinion mining determines the text's attitude toward a specific content source. The use of slang terms, misspellings, abbreviations, repeated characters, regional languages, and new, emerging emoticons hampers sentiment analysis [14].

The popularity of sentiment analysis is due to its effectiveness. Sentiment analysis may be applied to thousands of documents [15]. It has several uses because it is a productive process that offers good accuracy: Buying Goods or Services: Making the right decision while buying goods or services is no longer a difficult task [16]. People can quickly assess reviews and opinions of any good or service and compare competing companies by using sentiment analysis. Enhancing and upgrading the quality of a product or service is possible by using opinion mining, which allows producers to gather customer feedback on their goods or services, whether positive or negative [17,18].

Recommendation systems can determine which items should be recommended and which ones should not by assessing and classifying people's opinions [19] in accordance with their preferences and areas of interest. Making a decision with individual opinions, feelings, and sentiments of other people is a crucial consideration. Users read comments and reviews of a product before purchasing it, whether it is a book, outfit, or electronic gadget. These reviews have a significant influence on users' decisions, especially in marketing research [20]. Sentiment analysis techniques' output can be used in this type of research in which many methods can be used to study consumer perceptions of new government policies, goods, or services.

8.2 Literature Survey

Markle-Huß et al. [21], developed and contrasted a number of methods for using semantic information to enhance sentiment analysis, including bag of words models and n-grams. The semantic relationships between sentences or document elements were not taken into account by prior methods. Hogenboom et al. [22] did not compare the different methodological approaches or offer a strategy for merging disclosure units in the best way possible. Using rhetoric structure theory (RST), which provides an ordered representation at the article level, they sought to enhance sentiment analysis. They suggested integrating the RST tree's grid emotion. Feature engineering was used to encode the binary data into the random forest, considerably reducing the complexity of the original RST tree. They concluded that ML improved well-adjusted accuracy, yielding a head-to-foot F1 score of 72.9%.

Yazdavar et al. in their research [23] offered a fresh interpretation of the sentiment analysis problem incorporating numerical data in drug evaluations. They looked at sentences with quantitative terms to determine if they were opinionated or not, and they also used fuzzy set theory to determine the polarity expressed. Several doctors from different medical centers were interviewed to create a fuzzy knowledge base. Although numerous studies have been conducted in this area [24], these do not take into account the numerical (quantitative) data found in the reviews while acknowledging the polarity of sentiment. In addition, because of the significant domain dependency of the training data, it cannot be applied to other domains. They concluded that their suggested method of information engineering based on fuzzy sets was meaningfully more straightforward, effective, and accurate to the tune of over 72% F1.

Murthy in his study [25] defined the functions that tweets serve in political campaigns. He emphasized that despite several research and study efforts to determine the Twitter's political activity, no effort was made to determine whether or not these tweets were predictive. He concluded in his paper that tweets are less predictive and more reactive. He discovered that electoral success was in no way tied to Twitter success and that numerous social media sites were used to boost a candidate's popularity by creating a buzz about them.

Kamal in his paper [26] built an opinion-mining framework that makes it easier to analyze objectivity or subjectivity, extract features, and summarize reviews, among other things. He classified the subjectiveness and objectivity of reviews using supervised ML. He employed a number of methods, including naive Bayes, decision trees, multilayer perceptions, and bagging, avoiding noise and useless extraction as in Kamal's paper [27].

Shaziya et al. [28] used the WEKA tool to categorize film reviews for sentiment analysis. They improved earlier work on sentiment categorization, which classifies opinions as either good or negative based on their emotional content. They took into account both positive and negative attitudes that might be expressed in a single review as well as reviews that contain comments from multiple people in this study. They carried out their experiment on WEKA and found that naive Bayes performs significantly better than SVM for both text and film reviews. The accuracy of naive Bayes is 85.1%.

The dataset was constructed using tweets from film reviews and related tweets about those films by Amolik et al. in their study [29]. These tweets are subjected to sentiment analysis at the sentence level. There are three stages to it. Pre-processing is the first step. Then, utilizing pertinent features, a feature vector is produced. Finally, tweets were divided into positive, negative, and neutral classes using a variety of classifiers, including naive Bayes, SVMs, ensemble classifiers, K-means, and artificial neural networks. The findings indicate that we obtain an SVM accuracy of 75%. He refuted the assertion made in the research by

Wu et al. [30], which noted that the presence of a @username in a tweet affects possibility and an accomplishment has been described after exceedingly roughly 45 epochs for all realized models.

8.3 Proposed System

Tab-separated files containing words and phrases from the Film Review dataset make up the dataset offered for this competition. For benchmarking purposes, the dataset has been split into training and test sets, although the original order of the sentences has been changed. The Stanford parser has broken down each sentence in the dataset into many phrases. There is a phrase ID for each one. There is a sentence ID for each one. Recurring phrases (such as short, popular words) are only recorded once in the data.

The phrases and their corresponding sentiment labels can be found in train.csv. There are only phrases in test.csv. Each sentence in the test file needs to have a sentiment label applied to it.

The dataset's sentiment labels are as follows:

0 - negative
1 - little bit negative
2 - neutral
3 - little bit positive
4 - positive.

There are a number of phrases in the training dataset, and their sentiment scores are distributed as follows:

It is evident from Fig. 8−1 that the majority of the sentences have an emotion value of 2, which is considered neutral. Most ML algorithms anticipate that the incoming data will be vectors with numerical properties. Therefore, it is necessary to turn each word into a feature vector at first. In this project, feature vectors for each sentence are created using the tf-idf transformation. The terms "tf" and "tf-idf" stand for term frequency and inverse document frequency, respectively. This word-weighting technique is widely used in information retrieval and is very effective in document classification.

Using tf-idf rather than using raw frequencies of occurrence of a token in a given document, characteristics that present in a small portion of the training corpus and are experimentally more informative than tokens that occur very frequently in a particular corpus are scaled down. Count vectorizer, tf-idf transformer, and tf-idf vectorizer are only a few of the tf-idf transformers available in the scikit Python package. To convert text data to tf-idf data, there are two methods.

1. Create feature vectors with frequency values using the count vectorizer first. Then, using the tf-idf transformer, convert them to tf-idf values.
2. Tf-idf vectorizer combines the capabilities of tf-idf transformer with count vectorizer. Text data are directly converted to features with tf-idf values.

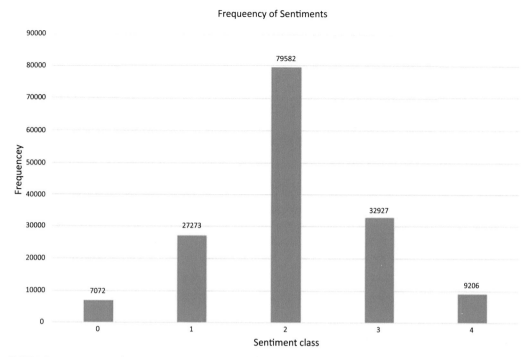

FIGURE 8–1 Frequency of sentiments.

When converting the text data to tf-idf format, all tokens are made lowercase to prevent duplicates. Stop words, or words that do not affect decision-making, are typically eliminated from text data processing in ML and data mining to reduce the complexity of the data. Since each phrase only contains a few words and some phrases just contain stop words, stop word reduction was not performed in this research.

8.3.1 Hybrid algorithm Design

The C5.0 Bayesian network (C5.0BN) is an extension of the C5.0 algorithm that is also a C4.5 extension. This is a classification algorithm suitable for very large datasets. It is higher than C4.5 in terms of execution time, performance contrast, and accuracy recalled. The C5.0BN model works by splitting the data on training and maximizing effectiveness. The C5.0BN actually contains more attributes and omits them from the film quality rating dataset. In this paper, we use training quality data to build a C5.0 decision tree when predicting outcomes for research evaluations.

Decision trees can then be used to identify subsequent test sets. As an improved version of the acclaimed and widely used C4.5 classifier, the enhanced C5.0BN has many key elements over its predecessor. The rules generated are more accurate, and the time used to generate them is lower (in some datasets, even around 360 times).

8.3.2 Solution Representation

Use top-down method, C5.0BN decision tree expands. The resulting tree is minimized for evaluation. It can also accept numeric characteristics, released values, and noisy data. This creates a threshold to keep the attributes continuous and splits the array into attribute values greater than, less than, or equal to the threshold. Bayesian networks previously formed by decision trees try to eliminate useless branches by replacing them with leaf nodes.

Algorithm to generate C5.0BN
Input

  a. Data Partition, DaPa, a set of training tuples and their associated class labels
  b. quality_list, the rest of applicant qualities
  c. $quality_{choosing_{procedure}}$, a method to decide the dividing principle partition the data tuples into entity classes. This measure consists of a dividing_principle and either a divide—point or dividing subset.

    Output
    C5.0 BN
    Method

  1. Produce a node N0
  2. if tuples in DaPa are all of the similar class, C0, then
  3. return R as a leaf node categorized with the class C0
  4. if quality_list is empty, then
  5. return R as a leaf node labeled with the mainstream class in DaPa
  6. apply $quality_{choosing_{procedure}}(DaPa, quality_{list})$ to discover the most excellent dividing_principle
  7. label node R with dividing_measure
  8. if dividing_principle is discrete—valued and more number of way divides approved then
  9. quality_list quality_list—dividing_principle
  10. For each result j of dividing_principle
       Let DPj be the set of data tuples in DP gratifying result j
       if DPi is empty, then connect a leaf considered with mainstream class in DP to node N0,
       else connect the node revisited by producing C5.0 decision tree (DPj, $quality_{list}$) to node N0
  11. Return R.

8.3.3 Improved Flowchart for C5.0BN

The flow map for the algorithm suggested is symbolized in Fig. 8—2B.

The C5.0BN calls for the noticeability of attribute values as for absent attributes. Missing attribute values are not used in calculating gain and entropy. The C5.0BN algorithm generally builds decision trees and creates branches to fully control and categorize the training data. With execution time, accuracy contrast, and accuracy—recall, this method works well.

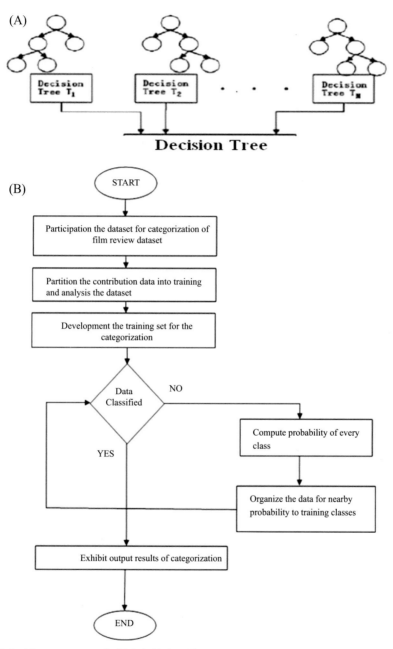

FIGURE 8–2 (A) Decision tree approach, (B) hybrid algorithm process.

However, mostly, this algorithm is heading toward over fits other data into the training case. There are actually several methods that are being used widely to prevent this overfitting in the learning of decision tree.

8.3.4 Importance of Splitting Criteria in Decision Tree Algorithms

Splitting necessities are mandatory for all decision tree algorithms to interrupt a node into a tree construction. The different division functions are univariate in many instances. Univariate implies the division of a domestic node according to the importance of an attribute of an individual. The method used examines on which to classify the most outstanding attribute. There are a variety of criteria for splitting, based on the node contamination. The key goal in separating parameters is to decrease node toxicity. There are many slicing techniques that can be used to find the right way to split the data. Such separating strategies are distinct in the class distribution situations of the documents before and after separation.

1. Entropy analysis: It is used to establish a node's deprivation. It is particular as:

$$\text{Entropy(t)} = -\sum p(i/t)\log 2p(i/t) \qquad (8-1)$$

2. Gini index: The computation of the dissimilarity between the probability distributions of the values of the objective attribute is dissimilar from that of impurity and is defined as:

$$\text{Gini index} = 1 - \sum [p(i/t)]2 \qquad (8-2)$$

3. Classification error: It is computed as:

$$\text{Classification error(t)} = 1 - \max[p(i/t)] \qquad (8-3)$$

   where $p\left(\frac{i}{t}\right)$ is a specified node and t denotes the fraction of records belonging to class i.
4. Information gain: Information gain is a variable based on impurity that utilizes entropy calculations as the impurity quantifies. It is the differentiation between parent node entropy and child node entropy.

$$\text{Information gain} = \text{Entropy(parent node)} - \text{entropy(child node)} \qquad (8-4)$$

5. Benefit ratio: The benefit ratio "normalizes" the advantage of information as follows

$$\text{Advantage ratio} = \text{Information gain/entropy} \qquad (8-5)$$

   Entropy and the Gini index are two impurity metrics that are likely to handle attributes with a very large number of different values. The quality of a break is then assessed using the gain ratio, which is then determined. Each splitting criterion has a keep analysis and rule that is specific to its purpose and type features.

6. Twoing criteria: Problems with the Gini index can arise once the goal characteristic domain is quite extensive. Twoing criteria, a differential condition, may be used in this situation. This requirement is what we define as:

$$\text{Twoing criteria(t)} = PLPR\left(\Sigma\left(\left|p\left(\frac{i}{tL}\right) - p\left(\frac{i}{tR}\right)\right|\right)\right). \qquad (8-6)$$

8.4 Computational Experiments and Result Analysis

In this segment, we inspect the steps of the modification and the investigation to get the end result in Table 8–1. The 50 K film review files in the IMDB dataset are entirely written in English, with 25 K favorable and 25 K negative evaluations. A file size of 1 KB to 15 KB has been used. The text files did not include any rating information. The dataset was divided into two parts: a training set and a testing set.

8.4.1 Implementation of C5.0BN using scikit-learn

First, we import the necessary libraries of the python for exhibition of the Decision Tree Classifier.

```
import pandas as pd

from sklearn.metrics import accuracy_score

from sklearn.model_selection import train_test_split

from sklearn.tree import DecisionTreeClassifier
```

Table 8–1   Simulation process.

Simulation parameter	Meaning
Software	Google Co laboratory
Output	Decision Tree Classifier
Libraries	Pandas, Numpy, Matplotlib and Sklearn
Dataset characteristics	Multivariate
Attribute characteristics	Real
Associated tasks	Classification
Number of instances	1599
Number of attributes	12
Missing values?	N/A
Area	Business

Read the data of the review quality from the csv file using read_csv function of pandas data frame

```
data = pd.read_csv('./train.csv')
```

Checking is that there exist null values in the dataset or not

data[data.isnull().any(axis=1)].head()

Filter the values which contain more than four qualities.

clean_data = data.copy()

clean_data['quality_label'] = (clean_data['quality'] >4) *1

clean_data['quality_label'].head()

y = clean_data[['quality_label']].copy()

y.head()

	quality_label
0	1
1	1
2	1
3	1
4	1

8.4.2 Perform Test and Train Split

Using train_test_split, we have split the data into training datasets and testing datasets.

```
▶  X_train,X_test,y_train,y_test = train_test_split(x,y,test_size=0.33,random_state=120)
```

```
[ ]  X_train.shape
```

```
(1071, 11)
```

```
[ ]  X_test.shape
```

```
(528, 11)
```

```
[ ]  y_train.shape
```

```
(1071, 1)
```

```
[ ]  y_test.shape
```

```
(528, 1)
```

8.4.3 Fit on Train Set

We have made a classifier for making the Decision Tree and for training the data using this classifier.

```
[ ]  quality_classifier = DecisionTreeClassifier(max_leaf_nodes=10,random_state=0)
     quality_classifier.fit(X_train,y_train)

     DecisionTreeClassifier(ccp_alpha=0.0, class_weight=None, criterion='gini',
                            max_depth=None, max_features=None, max_leaf_nodes=10,
                            min_impurity_decrease=0.0, min_impurity_split=None,
                            min_samples_leaf=1, min_samples_split=2,
                            min_weight_fraction_leaf=0.0, presort='deprecated',
                            random_state=0, splitter='best')
```

```
[ ]  type(quality_classifier)

     sklearn.tree._classes.DecisionTreeClassifier
```

8.4.4 Predict on Test Set

Using quality_classifier, we have predicted the value for the X_test and stored it to y_predicted.

```
[ ]  y_predicted = quality_classifier.predict(X_test)
```

```
[ ]  y_predicted[:10]

     array([1, 1, 1, 1, 1, 1, 1, 1, 1, 1])
```

```
[ ]  y_test['quality_label'][:10]

     44        1
     1019      1
     838       1
     49        1
     1509      1
     1046      1
     461       1
     898       1
     1577      1
     494       1
     Name: quality_label, dtype: int64
```

8.4.5 Measure Accuracy of the Classifier

Checking our accuracy of the model using accuracy_score function from sklearn metrics which in this case is with around 96% accuracy.

```
[ ]  accuracy_score(y_test, y_predicted)*100

     96.21212121212122
```

from sklearn. externals. six import StringIO

from IPython. display import Image

from sklearn. tree import export_graphviz

import pydotplus

dot_data = StringIO()

export_graphviz (quality_classifier, out_file = dot_data,

filled = True, rounded = True,

special_characters = True)

graph = pydotplus. graph_from_dot_data(dot_data. getvalue())

Image(graph. create_png())

The returning determination of decision-based model form training instances over ID3, C5.0, CART, and enhanced C5.0 BBN is specified in Fig. 8–3. It appears from the aforementioned investigations and creating the model, highlights the highest number of tree instances are in experiment 1 with ID3 and has the highest percentages 17%. However, the highest number of trees with C4.5 is in experiment 2. The total amount of instances with the decision tree percentage is demonstrated in Fig. 8–4.

On the other hand, the smallest number of instances can be found in experiment 3 with the smallest percentage. However, experiment 4 has the lowest number of instances, and it depends only on his CART output. Results of applying decision-based models to test dataset instances through simple ID3, advanced C5.0BN, and CART algorithms.

Performance is evaluated based on the following parameters:

8.4.5.1 Accuracy

As shown by the findings, running the Bayesian network classifier with the C5.0 algorithm dramatically enhanced decision tree performance. The accuracy performance comparison between the proposed C5.0BN algorithm and ID3, C4.5, and C5.0 is shown in Fig. 8–5. It is

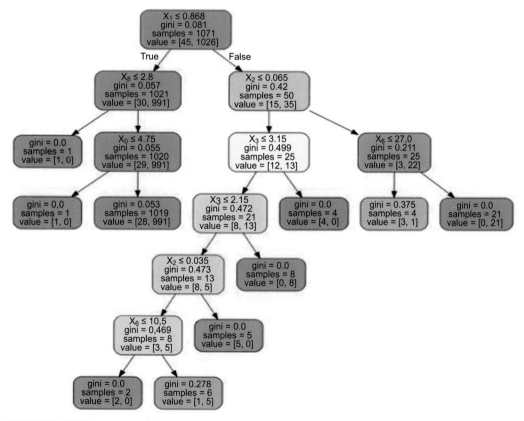

FIGURE 8–3 C5.0BN output model.

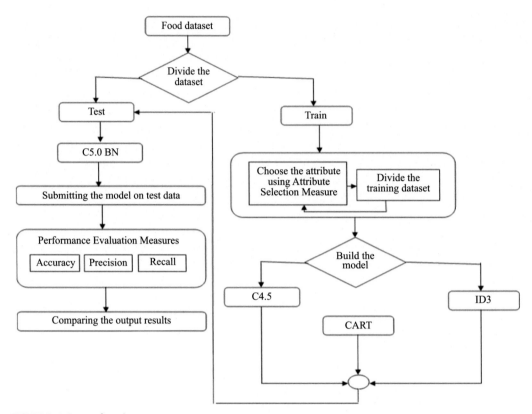

FIGURE 8–4 Steps of work.

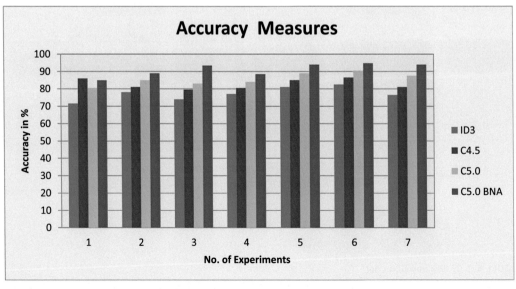

FIGURE 8–5 Accuracy measure.

obvious that the proposed C5.0BN algorithm's accuracy has increased. From the foregoing, it follows that the *C5.0BN* outperforms earlier classification algorithms like the *ID3*, *C4.5*, and *CART* algorithms in terms of classification accuracy.

8.4.5.2 Memory used

A detailed breakdown of the memory usage of *ID3*, *C4.5*, and *CART*, as well as the proposed C5.0BN algorithms and their evaluation, is provided which displays the relative memory requirements of the proposed algorithms C5.0BN, *ID3*, *C4.5*, and *CART*. The obtained findings show that the suggested C5.0BN method uses less memory than the ID3, C4.5, and CART algorithms. Preliminarily from the above, the *C5.0BN* has relative memory usage over previous classification algorithms, such as the *ID3*, *C4.5*, and *CART* algorithms. An evaluation of the memory usage of the decision tree classifiers is shown in Fig. 8−6.

8.4.5.3 Training time

The training time needed to estimate the data is longer than that of the *ID3*, *C4.5*, and *CART* algorithms, according to the results. Therefore, the *ID3*, *C4.5*, and *CART* algorithms must function well to specify the training time. The training times are also provided using Fig. 8−7, which includes the intended C5.0BN of the implemented method along with the training durations of *ID3*, *C4.5*, and *CART*.

8.4.5.4 Search time

Fig. 8−8 compares the proposed algorithm's training times to those of the ID3, C4.5, and CART algorithms. The proposed C5.0BN algorithm trains the model more quickly than the

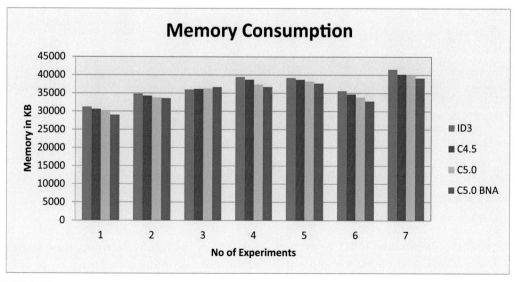

FIGURE 8−6 Memory consumption.

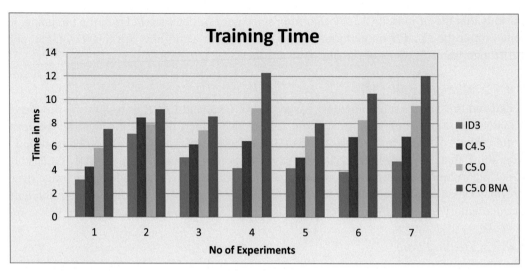

FIGURE 8–7 Training time.

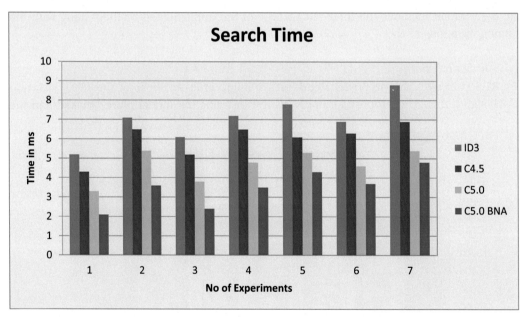

FIGURE 8–8 Search time.

ID3, C5.0 evaluations, and CART algorithms, as shown by the results. In comparison to *ID3*, *C4.5*, and *CART* algorithms, the proposed classification algorithm's performance is quite good, according to the approximate output findings. Using the graphic, the decision tree algorithm's relative search time is also computed.

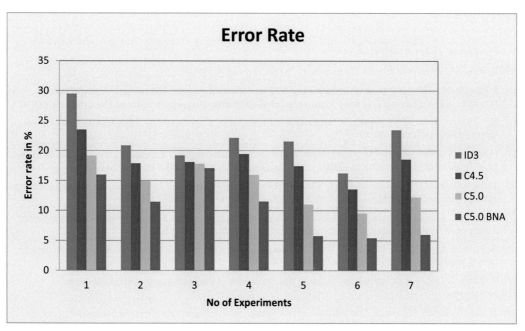

FIGURE 8–9 Error rate.

8.4.5.5 Error rate

Fig. 8–9 compares the error rate of the revised C5.0 algorithm with that of the traditional C5.0 algorithm. It has been determined that the enhanced C5.0 algorithm makes fewer mistakes. Fig. 8–9 provides the typical C5.0 decision tree algorithm's percentage mistake rate.

8.5 Conclusion

In this study, a sentiment analysis classifier for the 50 K film reviews from the IMDB dataset was developed utilizing three ML networks, *ID3*, *C4.5*, and *CART*, as well as the hybrid C5.0BN algorithm. Words were embedded using the decision tree approach. The outcomes demonstrated that the C5.0BN algorithm beat all other ML methods used. The results demonstrated that the suggested ML techniques (C5.0 and Bayesian networks) have outperformed *ID3*, *C4.5*, and *CART*. In addition, the attained precisions have been associated with correctness reported by formerly available works that have used several ML techniques.

Finding the review polarity can be helpful in a variety of areas. Without the need for the user to read through individual reviews, intellectual schemes can be established that can give users wide-ranging appraisals of films, products, facilities, etc. The user can then make decisions based on the outcomes that the intellectual schemes provide without having to read individual reviews.

References

[1] S. Poria, A. Gelbukh, Aspect extraction for opinion mining with a deep convolutional neural network, Knowl. Syst. 108 (2016) 42–49.

[2] K. Kim, M.E. Aminanto, H.C. Tanuwidjaja, Deep Learning, Springer, Singapore, 2018, pp. 27–34.

[3] J. Einolander, Deeper customer insight from NPS-questionnaires with text mining - comparison of machine, representation and deep learning models in finnish language sentiment classification, 2019.

[4] P. Chitkara, A. Modi, P. Avvaru, S. Janghorbani, M. Kapadia, Topic spotting using hierarchical networks with self attention, Apr. 2019.

[5] F. Ortega Gallego, Aspect-based sentiment analysis: a scalable system, a condition miner, and an evaluation dataset, Int. J. Data Mining Knowledge Management Process (IJDKP) 9(2/3), May 2019.

[6] M.M. Najafabadi, F. Villanustre, T.M. Khoshgoftaar, N. Seliya, R. Wald, E. Muharemagic, Deep learning applications and challenges in big data analytics, J. Big Data 2 (1) (2015) 1.

[7] B. Pang, L. Lee, S. Vaithyanathan, Thumbs up?, In Proceedings of the Acl-02 Conference on Empirical Methods in Natural Language Processing - Emnlp '02, 2002, Vol. 10, pp. 79–86.

[8] R. Socher, A. Perelygin, J.Y. Wu, J. Chuang, et al., Recursive deep models for semantic compositionality over a sentiment treebank, PLoS One (2013).

[9] B. Pang, L. Lee, S. Vaithyanathan, Thumbs up? Sentiment classification using machine learning techniques.

[10] H. Cui, V. Mittal, M. Datar, Comparative experiments on sentiment classification for online product reviews, In Aaai'06 Proceedings of the 21st National Conference on Artificial Intelligence, 2006.

[11] Z. Guan, L. Chen, W. Zhao, Y. Zheng, S. Tan, D. Cai, Weakly-supervised deep learning for customer review sentiment classification, Ijcai Int. Jt. Conf. Artif. Intell. (2016).

[12] B. Ay Karakuş, M. Talo, İ.R. Hallaç, G. Aydin, Evaluating deep learning models for sentiment classification, Concurr. Comput. Pract. Exp. 30 (21) (2018) E4783.

[13] M.V. Mäntylä, D. Graziotin, M. Kuutila, The evolution of sentiment analysis—a review of research topics, venues, and top cited papers, Computer Sci. Rev. (2018).

[14] Y. Goldberg, O. Levy, Word2vec Explained: Deriving Mikolov Et Al.'S Negative-Sampling Word-Embedding Method, Feb. 2014.

[15] D. Ciresan, U. Meier, J. Schmidhuber, Multi-column deep neural networks for image classification, 2012 IEEE Conf. Computer Vis. And. Pattern Recognit. (2012) 3642–3649.

[16] Y. Kim, Convolutional neural networks for sentence classification, Aug. 2014.

[17] R. Jozefowicz, O. Vinyals, M. Schuster, N. Shazeer, Y. Wu, Exploring the limits of language modeling.

[18] N. Kalchbrenner, E. Grefenstette, P. Blunsom, A convolutional neural network for modelling sentences, Apr. 2014.

[19] X. Li, X. Wu, Constructing long short-term memory based deep recurrent neural networks for large vocabulary speech recognition, Oct. 2014.

[20] H. Strobelt, S. Gehrmann, H. Pfister, A.M. Rush, Lstmvis: a tool for visual analysis of hidden state dynamics in recurrent neural networks, Ieee Trans. Vis. Comput. Graph. (2018).

[21] J. Markle-Huß, S. Feuerriegel, H. Prendinger, 2017. Improving sentiment analysis with document-level semantic relationships from rhetoric discourse structures, In Proceedings of the 50th Hawaii International Conference on System Sciences.

[22] A. Hogenboom, F. Frasincar, F. de Jong, U. Kaymak, Using rhetorical structure in sentiment analysis, Commun. ACM 58 (7) (2015) 69–77.

[23] A.H. Yazdavar, M. Ebrahimi, N. Salim, Fuzzy based implicit sentiment analysis on quantitative sentences, Faculty of Computing, UniversitiTechnologi Malaysia, Johor, Malaysia, J. Soft Comput. Decis. Support. Syst. 3 (4) (2016) 7−18.

[24] R.S. Bhatia, A. Graystone, R.A. Davies, S. McClinton, J. Morin, R.F. Davies, 2010, Extracting information for generating a diabetes report card from free text in physicians notes. Paper presented at the Proceedings of the NAACL HLT 2010 Second Louhi Workshop on Text and Data Mining of Health Documents.

[25] D. Murthy, Twitter and elections: are tweets, predictive, reactive, or a form of buzz?, Inf. Commun. Soc., 18:7, 816−831, Available from: https://doi.org/10.1080/1369118X.2015.1006659.

[26] A. Kamal, 2015. Review mining for feature based opinion summarization and visualization.

[27] A. Kamal, Subjectivity classification using machine learning techniques for mining feature- opinion pairs from web opinion sources, Int. J. Computer Sci. Issues 10 (5) (2013) 191−200.

[28] H. Shaziya, G. Kavitha, R. Zaheer, Text categorization of film reviews for sentiment analysis, Int. J. Innovative Res. Sci. Eng. Technol. 4 (11) (2015).

[29] A. Amolik, N. Jivane, M. Bhandari, M. Venkatesan, Twitter sentiment analysis of film reviews using machine learning techniques, School of Computer Science and Engineering, VIT University, Vellore.

[30] Y. Wu, F. Ren, Learning sentimental influence in twitter, Future Computer Science and Application (ICFCSA), 2011, International Conference, IEEE, vol. 119122, 2011.

9

Deep learning for double-negative detection in text data for customer feedback analysis on a product

Deepika Ghai[1], Ramandeep Sandhu[2], Ranjit Kaur[3], Mohammad Faiz[2], Gurleen Kaur Walia[1], Suman Lata Tripathi[1]

[1]SCHOOL OF ELECTRONICS & ELECTRICAL ENGINEERING, LOVELY PROFESSIONAL UNIVERSITY, PHAGWARA, PUNJAB, INDIA [2]SCHOOL OF COMPUTER SCIENCE & ENGINEERING, LOVELY PROFESSIONAL UNIVERSITY, PHAGWARA, PUNJAB, INDIA [3]SCHOOL OF COMPUTER APPLICATIONS, LOVELY PROFESSIONAL UNIVERSITY, PHAGWARA, PUNJAB, INDIA

9.1 Introduction

Sentiment analysis is also named as Natural Language Processing technique, which determines the positivity, negativity, or neutrality of data. It is often referred to as opinion mining. In order to observer that how the specific brands and products are perceived by its customer in terms of their reviews, businesses routinely do sentiment analysis on datasets. Customer satisfaction, decision-making, processes, and other areas can all be improved by sentiment analysis. Analysis based on sentiments is primarily concerned with a text's polarity (i.e., whether it is positive, negative, or neutral), but it similarly goes further than polarity to recognize specific moods and emotions (i.e., being joyful, angry, or unhappy, etc.), importance (i.e., whether it is important or not), and even intents (i.e., intrigued and not intrigued). Evaluating things purchased online has become a routine task for individuals as e-commerce has grown. As a result, both consumers and e-commerce activities must examine client remarks [1−4].

Electronic Word-of-Mouth (eWOM) is growing quickly, posing a new challenge to online retailers and marketers as paid reviewers flood websites with reviews of goods and services that may mislead and turn off potential customers [5,6]. This study investigated how paid reviewers' posts—specifically their bad reviews—affected buyers' perceptions of risk, attitudes toward the products, and intention to buy. You can construct and customize your groupings to tie your sentiment breakdown requirements to be based on how you demand to read user remarks and inquiries. Fig. 9−1 shows the various categories of sentiment analysis.

a. Emotion Analysis: It categorizes different emotion types such as joy, dissatisfaction, frustration, and pain as shown in Fig. 9−2. Various emotion recognition systems

Computational Intelligence Methods for Sentiment Analysis in Natural Language Processing Applications
DOI: https://doi.org/10.1016/B978-0-443-22009-8.00012-4

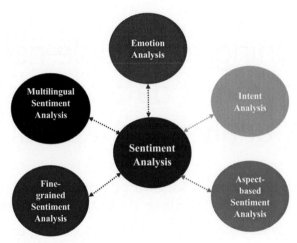

FIGURE 9–1 Categories of sentiment analysis.

FIGURE 9–2 Emotions.

FIGURE 9–3 Fine-grained sentiments.

make use of either sophisticated machine learning algorithms or lexicons (collections of words and the feelings they signify) [7].

b. Multilingual Sentiment Analysis: The practice of extracting emotional insights from data that may be in numerous languages is known as multilingual sentiment analysis. This is typically true when analyzing customer feedback data from diverse audiences or various geographic places with a consistent customer base.

c. Fine-Grained Sentiment Analysis: If the company places a premium on polarity exactness, one can think about mounting polarity groupings to do various intensities of positive and negative like: positive, very positive, negative, very negative, and neutral [8,9]. It is possible to comprehend reviews with 5-star ratings by using a technique called graded or fine-grained sentiment analysis as shown in Fig. 9–3.

d. Intent Analysis: The focus of intent analysis is on the user's goals. We can better direct the user if we know what he wants to do. For instance, knowing that a customer has a purchase purpose when he browses a shopping site enables us to present him with the appropriate goods [10].

e. Aspect-based Sentiment Analysis: While analyzing the emotions of the texts, the emphasis is often on determining whether the comment or view is positive or negative [11−17]. We do not, however, focus on the positive or negative parts of the text. To put it more plainly, the consumer complains about the purchase and expresses discontent with the products by saying, "I did not like the product at all; its battery life is not good." Aspect-based sentiment analysis additionally places emphasis on the remark "its battery life is not good," which would be classified as negative by conventional sentiment analysis. In this work, we concentrated on double-negative detection in text data for customer feedback analysis regarding a purchased product.

9.2 Related work

Numerous techniques have been done for the negative detection of customer feedback analysis on a product. The Allard et al. [18] study shows how unfairly perceived unfavorable reviews might evoke feelings of pity for businesses that have been mistreated. Converging data from six studies and four further tests shows that consumers' empathy for the company inspires positive behaviors such as paying more for products and saying they want to do business with them more often. Both positive and negative evaluations have a significant impact on consumers' purchasing decisions. This study identifies elements that may heighten or lessen empathy for a company. By emphasizing the impact of perceived (un)fairness, the knowledge of how consumers respond to word-of-mouth in the marketplace is expanded through this work. The findings' theoretical and practical ramifications are discussed by the writers to improve customer review management. Positive reviews increase the favorability of the company's evaluations, whereas negative reviews decrease it. In this study, we found that unfair kind of negative reviews are not inevitably bad always for the corporate and that the impact of negative reviews on customers' future reactions to the focus business varies depending on how fair the review is perceived to be. In a preliminary study, authors examined a sample of randomly chosen one- and two-star hotel ratings scraped from TripAdvisor, a prominent hotel review website, for the top 10 hotels in Chicago, Hong Kong, London, Los Angeles, Paris, and Singapore to show the prevalence of unfair Word of Mouth (WOM). Two independent coders who were not aware of the assumptions examined the total 1000 number of reviews from these 60 hotels for perceived fairness and the justifications for the rankings. The findings showed that overa quarter of negative evaluations had injustice in them (26.3%, assessed as unfair or somewhat unfair). Therefore, it seems that unjustified bad customer evaluations are rather common. It has been discovered that unfavorable reviews might increase empathy, inspiring following acts of kindness and positive thoughts toward the company as well as qualities that increase the review's credibility (e.g., time signals, misreferred indicators, deviatory reviews, emotionality).

In this research, Study 1a and Study 1b compare consumer reactions to a company non-profit in Study 1a and a for-profit in Study 1b after reading an unfairly critical review to those following both a fair criticism and a favorable one using consequential metrics.

Study 2 sheds light on the circumstances in which unjustified bad ratings may lead to firm results that are better than (or comparable to) those in response to positive comments.

By demonstrating how participants' empathy levels affect how customers respond favorably to unfairly negative evaluations, Study 3 contributes to the body of research establishing empathy as the underlying mechanism.

Study 4 examined if a managerial interpolation may augment empathetic emotional state and favorable responses to the firm.

In Study 5, with the aid of a separate managerially pertinent intervention, the moderating impact of increased empathy for the company is examined. We focus on how companies might use a narrative to encourage increased perspective-taking to increase client empathy.

Overall, it is demonstrated how perceived unfairness can cause consumers to feel sympathy for the firm's hardships, which then encourages them to assist the business. The current investigation broadens the understanding of how emotional mechanisms might affect and direct consumers' responses to unfavorable reviews by examining this empathy-driven account. The authors also showed how to apply a cognitive-emotional (e.g., perceived unfairness! empathy) sequence to WOM in order to have customers support for businesses.

Online negative Word of Mouth (nWOM) is defined by Azemi et al. [19], an empirical study from 2020, as an interaction between the complainant (i.e., the one who starts the online nWOM) and the recipient (i.e., the consumer who interacts with the online nWOM), looking at their quirks to see how they interpret the experience. Through phenomenological hermeneutics, interviews, and focus groups, data from millennials in Albania and Kosovo were collected, which led to narratives of complex and distinctive online nWOM realities. Variances in frustration-aggression identified in online nWOM led to the development of tolerable online nWOM customers, rigorous online nWOM customers, and confrontational online nWOM consumers. Regardless of the nWOM environment, the findings resulted in satisfying recovery procedures that were linked to customer interpretations. The study's data were collected using focus group and semistructured interviews. Prior to the focus group interviews, there were two pilot focus groups (one per country). In the semistructured interviews, the complainant was spoken with first, followed by the beneficiary. A total of 48 interviewees made upthe sample size, with 12 in-depth interviews (6 each nation) and 6 focus groups with 6 participants each (3 focus groups per country). Six consumers who had propagated nWOM (i.e., complainants) and six consumers who had participated in online nWOM (i.e., recipients) were interviewed in-depth. Two emails were sent to participants: the first one was an invitation to an interview, and the second one was a reminder 48 hours before the interview. Access to the real online nWOM thread for each case was made available to participants.

The thread was sent to the researchers by email 24 hours before the in-depth/focus group interviews; this helped to strengthen their knowledge before the data collection instances, which, in the opinion of social constructivists, is a requirement for a comprehensive conceptualization of phenomena. The interviews consisted of 15 open-ended questions, the last five of which were phenomenologically organized after the first 10 were "loosely" structured.

Future studies may broaden the conceptualization of nWOM construction to include additional generations and offer useful advice for all consumers kinds. For this study, information was also acquired from complainants and beneficiaries on several social media platforms. A comparison study to decode conclusions about particular social media sites will provide a better understanding to enable an effective recovery approach. The complainant−recipient model of online nWOM should also is empirically tested in future studies to ensure that the conclusions apply to a variety of contexts and settings.

The most recent research of Dang et al. [20] using deep learning to state various issues linked to sentiment analysis, such as sentiment polarity, is reviewed in this publication. Data preprocessing methods included word embedding and Term Frequency−Inverse Document Frequency (TF-IDF). The experimental results for various models and input attributes have also been compared in this work. The most recent research on deep learning models, such as Deep Neural Networks (DNN), Convolutional Neural Networks (CNN), and Recurrent Neural Networks (RNN), is examined in this work. These models have been used to address various issues with sentiment analysis, such as sentiment polarity and aspect-based sentiment. Researchers of this study have concentrated on important elements of research, including datasets, methodologies offered in each study, and the domains in which they might be employed.

In tests on sentiment polarity analysis, eight datasets were employed. Three of these eight contain tweets; the largest has 1.6 million with labels for happy or negative mood, while the other two datasets have 14,640 and 17,750 with positive, negative, or neutral labels, respectively. The last five datasets comprise 125,000 user reviews of films, books, and songs that have been classified as either positive or negative attitudes. In this study, two techniques, namely word embedding and TF-IDF, are compared, which are used for supplying input to the classification algorithms. Word2vec was used, which includes models such as skip-gram and Continuous Bag-of-Words for word embedding. The scikit-learn library's vectorizer class was utilized for TF-IDF. Accuracy, recall, precision, Area Under Curve, and F-score remained the metrics used to calculate the models' performance throughout all experiments.

When performing sentiment analysis, the findings demonstrate that the deep learning methods in conjunction with word embedding are preferable to TF-IDF. CNN beats other models, according to the experiments, striking a fair compromise between accuracy and CPU runtime. RNN reliability is discovered to be slightly higher than CNN dependability for the majority of datasets, but its computational time is substantially greater.

The study also found that the properties of the datasets have a significant impact on the algorithms' efficacy. It highlights the benefit of testing deep learning techniques on larger datasets in order to take a greater range of characteristics into account.

Future studies will focus on exploring hybrid approaches, which integrate many models and techniques to increase the accuracy of sentiment categorization reached by the individual models or techniques while also reducing the computational cost.

Mukherjee et al. [21] provide a novel end-to-end sentiment analysis approach in addition to negation identification and negation scope marking to handle negations. For explicit negation identification, a special negation marking technique is presented, and tests with sentiment analysis of Amazon reviews are conducted obtained from Kaggle, specifically reviews of cell phones, using a variety of machine learning algorithms, including Naive Bayes, Support Vector Machines, Artificial Neural Networks (ANN), and RNN. To handle negations in sentences, the mentioned methodology involves several processes, including data collection and preparation, text preprocessing, negation identification and marking, TF-IDF feature extraction, training, and model evaluation. The results showed that when standard text classification classifiers and negation identification were combined, the sentiment classifier performed better.

Singh et al. [22] examined the phrase's cue and scope, two negation components that affect how the polarity of the sentence changes. An LSTM-based deep neural network model is proposed to handle negations, where the model automatically extracts the required features from a training set with labeled input. The Conan Doyle narrative corpus is used for model testing and training. The proposed model first recognizes the negation cues in each phrase, and then, using bidirectional LSTM, determines the relationship between the cue and other words, in order to ascertain the breadth of the cue in sentences. The results demonstrate that nonlinear language models based on LSTM outperform more established models based on SVM, HMM, or CRF. A suggested baseline deep neural network model for handling negations makes use of a probabilistic CRF model for scope detection along with a linear SVM classifier for cue identification. The proposed deep-learning linguistic model for handling negations divides the task into two subtasks: binary classification and sequence labeling. The model's approach to the cue (negation) identification task divides each token in a sentence into the cue or noncue class. The comparative analysis of the existing state-of-the-art methods on sentiment analysis is shown in Table 9−1.

9.3 Proposed methodology

Different deep learning models, including CNN, SVM, RNN, and LSTM, are given the properly formatted data as input. 20% of the data are used to evaluate the model, and 80% are used to train the model. The output classes are "positive review," "negative review," "double negative" and "neutral review." For the purpose of analyzing customer reviews of a product, the suggested method is based on a deep learning technique for double-negative detection in text data. Fig. 9−4 depicts the flowchart of the sentiment analysis method that has been suggested. The secret to identifying the emotion in customer reviews is sentiment analysis. It works for a better phase of sentiment analysis. Competitors in the world are highly dependent on their customer feedback. Some of the researchers have used their own created datasets, but others prefer to work on public benchmark datasets of reputed companies. There are various datasets dealing with sentiment analysis such as Flipkart dataset, Kaggle, and Amazon. In these datasets, the first column is product_name, which consists of the name of

Table 9–1 Comparative analysis of the existing state-of-the-art methods on sentiment analysis.

Author (Year)	Techniques, features, datasets, parameters, remarks
Allard et al. [18]	**Techniques:** **Study 1:** Baseline Effect: **Study 1a:** 4ocean {Generalized Linear Model (GLM) analysis} **Study 1b:** Bottle Choice {Variance Analysis} **Study 2:** Mediation by empathy for the firm (Sushi Scenario) {GLM analysis} **Study 3:** Moderation by empathy manipulation (Panini Scenario) {Dummy-Coded Multicategorical Predictors} **Study 4:** Empathy-based moderated mediation of firm response type and review type (Garden Tools Scenario) {Dummy-Coded Multicategorical Predictors} **Study 5:** Empathy-based moderated mediation of firm response type and employee spotlight (Garden Tools Scenario) {Dummy-Coded Multicategorical Predictors} **Features:-** **Study 1a:** This study found that biased bad ratings elicited just as many supportive comments as favorable reviews. Importantly, it is demonstrated that the observed effect does not appear to be driven by the perceived rudeness of the review, as evidenced by the fact that the findings persist even after adjusting for harshness statistically. **Study 1b:** When the behavioral choice measure was taken into account, Study 1b demonstrates that unfair unfavorable reviews led to higher firm support. **Study 2:** Study 2 looked for proof of empathy as a fundamental mechanism. The outcomes show that empathy mediates the effects that have been noticed impacts, according to the findings that empathy mediates the effects that **Study 3:** By using a moderation technique to alter participants' ability to feel sympathy for either the reviewer or the firm's staff, the study lends support to the idea that empathy is the mechanism underlying our findings. One important hypothesis holds that unjustified unfavorable reviews inevitably cause people to feel sympathetic for the company. **Study 4:** It has been discovered that, in response to evaluations that aren't naturally empathic, by reacting to the review with more empathy, a company can evoke consumer empathy in addition to more favorable purchase intentions. **Study 5:** It has been discovered that replies with empathy to reviews that don't usually generate empathy (i.e., fair negative and positive assessments) can be effectively increased by an employee spotlight. Higher firm support resulted from this elevated empathy. Together, the findings support the idea that businesses might boost empathic customer responses to reviews by assisting customers in identifying with staff. **Dataset:** TripAdvisor **Parameters:** **Study 1a:** Fair Negative, Unfair Negative, and Positive based on Fairness, Donation, and Rudeness. **Study 1b:** Fair Negative, Unfair Negative, Positive based on Purchase intensions, Empathy, and Bottle Choice. **Study 2:** Fair Negative, Moderately Unfair Negative, Highly Unfair Negative, Positive based on Empathy, Willingness to Pay (WTP), and Rudeness. **Study 3:** Fair Negative (Employee Perspective, Reviewer Perspective, and Control), Unfair Negative (Employee Perspective, Reviewer Perspective, and Control), and Positive (Employee Perspective, Reviewer Perspective, and Control) based on Empathy, Evaluation, Manipulation, and Rudeness.

(Continued)

Table 9–1   (Continued)

Author (Year)	Techniques, features, datasets, parameters, remarks
	Study 4: Fair Negative (Neutral, Empathetic), Unfair Negative (Neutral, Empathetic), and Positive (Neutral, Empathetic) based on Empathy, Purchase Intensions, and Rudeness. **Study 5:** Fair Negative (Absent, Present), Unfair Negative (Absent, Present), and Positive (Absent, Present) based on Empathy and Voucher Value. **Remarks:** **Study 1:** The key finding is that unjustified negative evaluations can result in customer responses that are just as favorable as those that accompany unjustified positive ratings. **Study 2:** The most important conclusion is that, while unfair negative reviews can result in consumer reactions that are just as favorable as those after positive reviews, extremely unfair negative reviews can result in reactions that are even more favorable than those after positive reviews. This conclusion is motivated by sympathy for the business. **Study 3:** The key finding is that when participants' capacity for empathy is suppressed, the reactions of consumers to unfairly bad reviews are less favorable. **Study 4:** The key finding is that exposure to a review that naturally inspires increased empathy is more effective than responding to a review in a manner that elicits empathy in the customer who would not otherwise experience a rise in empathy (i.e., fair negative and positive evaluations) (i.e., unfair negative reviews) **Study 5:** Like Study 4, employee highlights may move customers who wouldn't typically experience an increase in empathy and a positive consumer response for particular review types. • Future studies would benefit from looking into how consumers react to thoughts of unfairness brought on by excessively positive reviews. • Additional research is needed to better understand how consumers interpret and react to a large number of unfair negative reviews because the current study is limited to scenarios in which consumers' reactions are assessed after reading a single unfair negative review. • Overall, this study shows how empathy for businesses can have a significant impact on consumer intentions and behaviors that may support a company that has experienced unfair treatment, a relatively novel and understudied aspect of consumer-firm interaction. A more thorough analysis of customers' emotional interactions with brands, especially one that uses an empathy method, can be beneficial to both businesses and researchers.
Azemi et al. [19]	**Techniques: -** • Semistructured Interviews: Stimulus-response format • Focus Group Interviews • A thematic approach was used for data analysis. **Features:-** • Total of 15 open-ended interview questions, the last five of which are phenomenologically structured after the first 10 are loosely structured. • Two emails were sent to participants: the first one was an invitation to an interview, and the second one was a reminder 48 h before the interview. • The researchers received the thread via email 24 h before the in-depth and focus group interviews. • Duration of Interview: 60 min. • Before the interviews, participants received consent forms outlining their responsibilities and rights in the process of data gathering.

(Continued)

Table 9–1   (Continued)

Author (Year)	Techniques, features, datasets, parameters, remarks
	Datasets:
	• Social media platforms like Facebook, Twitter, etc.
	• In-depth Interviews
	• Data gathered from millennials in Albania and Kosovo
	• Sample Size: 48 Interviewees
	Parameters:
	• There are three types of online nWOM: lenient, moderate, and severe.
	• Three types of customers: tolerable, rigorous, and confrontational.
	• Demographic characteristics of participants: Age, Gender, Occupation.
	Remarks:
	• The study only included millennials; thus, it offers no information about how people of different ages understand nWOM.
	• Future research may broaden our understanding of how nWOM is constructed to encompass additional generations and provide insightful guidance for all types of consumers.
	• Online nWOM's complainant-recipient model should also be empirically tested in future studies to ensure that the conclusions apply to a variety of contexts and settings.
Dang et al. [20]	**Techniques:**
	Deep Neural Networks (DNN), Recurrent Neural Networks (RNN), Convolutional Neural Networks (CNN), Word Embedding, Term Frequency-Inverse Document Frequency (TF-IDF), K-Fold Cross Validation.
	Features:
	• The studies for sentiment analysis included three deep learning models (i.e., DNN, CNN, and RNN).
	• It was found that the CNN model offers the best compromise between processing speed and result accuracy.
	• The RNN model had the highest level of accuracy when combined with word embedding, but its processing time was ten times longer than that of the CNN model.
	• Text data (such as tweets and reviews) is converted into a numeric vector and then fed into a deep learning model using related techniques (TF-IDF and word embedding).
	• In comparison to other datasets containing reviews, the outcomes from the IMDB movie review datasets and the datasets containing tweets are superior.
	• Models derived from the Tweets Airline dataset, which concentrate on a specific issue, outperform those derived from datasets on general themes.
	Datasets:
	• Sentiment140 was collected from Stanford University.
	• Cornell Movie Reviews
	• Tweets SemEval
	• Tweets Airline
	• IMDB Movie Reviews from Stanford University.
	• Book Reviews and Music Reviews collected from the Multidomain Sentiment of the Department of Computer Science of Johns Hopkins University.
	Parameters:
	Classification of Tweets: favorable, unfavorable, or neutral

(Continued)

Table 9–1   (Continued)

Author (Year)	Techniques, features, datasets, parameters, remarks
	Remarks: • The findings demonstrate that while conducting a sentiment analysis, instead of using TF-IDF, it is advised to combine word embedding with deep learning methods. • CNN beats other models, according to the experiments, striking a fair compromise between accuracy and CPU runtime. • It has been discovered that while RNN reliability is slightly higher than CNN reliability for the majority of datasets, its computational time is noticeably longer. • Future research will focus on investigating hybrid approaches, which combine numerous models and methods to improve sentiment categorization accuracy. • Future studies on deep learning models may concentrate on approaches to better balance processing speed and result accuracy.
Mukherjee et al. [21]	**Techniques:** Multinomial Naive Bayes (MNB), Support Vector Machines (SVM), Artificial Neural Networks (ANN), Recurrent Neural Networks (RNN), TF-IDF feature extraction, SentiWordNet. **Features:** Considered Negations in product reviews: Morphological and syntactic considerations. Double negations are handled by using the "_NEG" suffix. **Datasets:** Amazon reviews were obtained from Kaggle. Gold standard dataset for NegAIT. **Parameters:** **Brand Reviews:** no. of reviews, average word count, average token count, average sentence count, average words in the sentence. **Comparison of classifiers' performance**: Positive Class and Negative Class (Precision, Recall, F1 Score), Accuracy, Area underReceiver Operating Characteristic (ROC) curve. **Remarks:** • According to the results, the sentiment classifier performed better when conventional text classification classifiers were combined with negation identification. • Future methods can take emotion recognition in the text into account when calculating the market mood toward the product.
Singh et al. [22]	**Techniques:** Long Short-Term Memory (LSTM), Bidirectional Long Short-Term Memory (BiLSTM), linear SVM, probabilistic Conditional Random Fields (CRF), Dijkstra Algorithm, RNN, Hidden Markov Model (HMM). **Features:** Implementation is done in Tensorflow **Datasets:** Movies, Books, Cras, Computers, Cookware, Hotels, Music, Phones, Conan Doyle's story. **Parameters:** Learning rate, dropout, and activation function selection. **Hyper Parameters:** Kernel_Initializer, Recurrent, Initializer, Bias_Initializer, dropout, stateful, embedding dimension, batch size, epoch. **Remarks:** • For managing negations, a deep neural network model based on LSTM is suggested. • For training and testing, Conan Doyle story is used. • The results demonstrate that nonlinear language models based on LSTM outperform more than established models based on SVM, HMM, or CRF. • BiLSTM obtained the best outcome.

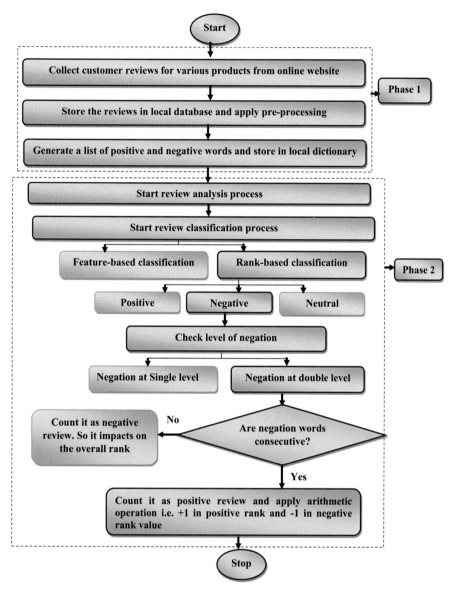

FIGURE 9–4 Flowchart of the proposed methodology on sentiment analysis.

the product with few details about it. The second column is a text-based review that consists of customer opinions about the product. It may be a one-word sentence or can be a collection of words. Here, preprocessing is mandatory to apply to these datasets. The third column is the last column of the dataset, which is named rating, wherein each review is assigned a rating.

There are two phases to the suggested technique: Phase 1 and Phase 2.

Phase 1:

i. To start the process of sentiment analysis for a deep understanding of various reviews. A total of 2304 reviews have been collected for the year 2022. We have considered the Flipkart dataset for the year 2022 which is available at the link: https://www.analyticsvidhya.com/blog/2022/09/sentiment-analysis-on-flipkart-dataset/. These reviews contain various columns like Serial number, Product_name, Review (in text form), and Rank (integer value) [23].

ii. In the local hard disk, store these reviews in a.csv file (comma-separated values) format for flexible extraction.

iii. In the next step, create two dictionaries named d_pos and d_neg. The d_pos contains only positive words and d_neg contains only a list of negative words.

iv. Complete phase 1 and shift to phase 2 of the proposed system.

Phase 2:

i. To start the review analysis process, sort all reviews based on ascending order of their rank. As it is clear from input reviews, each review has been assigned one unique rank value that can range from 1 to 5.

ii. After the sorting operation, reviews are classified based on their rank value. Based on the sorted output, assign 3 different categories to the reviews, such as positive, neutral, and negative as shown in Table 9–2. For further processing, we need reviews of only rank 1 (strongly disagree) and rank 2 (disagree) of online reviews.

iii. Moving to the next step, the study is towards better resolution of negative reviews only. So, at a further level, reviews with only ranks 1 and 2 have been selected for further classification.

iv. Here, it is required to consider the level of negation. There are further two more cases.

Table 9–2 Text reviews categorization as per the Likert scale (rank value).

Column no. 1	Column no. 2	Column no. 3				
Product_name	Text-based review	Rating as per Likert scale (rank value)				
		Strongly agree	Agree	Neutral	Disagree	Strongly disagree
		5	4	3	2	1
		Positive reviews		Neutral reviews		Negative reviews

Table 9–3   Examples of single-negation and double-negation reviews.

Earlier rank	Negative review_text	Is single negation?	Is double negation?
1	Bad performance	Yes	No
1	Awkward look	Yes	No
1	Not bad speed	No	Yes
1	No lose if buy it	No	Yes
1	Don't buy, don't waste your money	Yes	No
2	Battery drains very fast	Yes	No

    a. This case includes negative reviews with a single negation. Refer to Table 9–3 for a better understanding of the concept of single-negation and double-negation reviews.

    b. This case includes negative negation reviews with double negation as shown in column 2 of Table 9–3. Here, green cell values are those negations that are ranked towards negative feedback provided by a customer. But these types of reviews are positive because double negations come if in consecution then make opposite sense of the review.

    c. After the successful applicability of negation level classification, now check the position of negation words. If index [first negation word] and index [second negation word] are consecutive, then change the rank value of such reviews and it implies that such reviews are not negative, but rather positive.

The process of data cleaning and data segregation applied on input text review attributes is given as under:

a. Data Cleaning: Using stemming, stop words, and regular expressions, the review column's data is cleaned. During stemming, similar words are considered underthe same roof. For example, play, plays, playing, and played are reduced to play. Hence, the root word is play.

b. Data Segregation: From the Flipkart dataset of a total of 2304 reviews, it has been found that 1800 reviews are unique. From these 1800 reviews, the rank values ranging between 5 and 1 (where 5 is the highest rank also called too high or positive rank and 1 is the lowest rank or negative rank) have been described in the pie chart in Fig. 9–5.

The percentage reviews on different feedbacks such as positive, neutral and negative is shown in Table 9–4. It can be easily found that the range of positive reviews is very high compared to neutral and negative reviews. Here, rank 5 and rank 4 are positive reviews, rank 3 are neutral reviews, and rank 2 and rank 1 are negative reviews. Only 2% of reviews are identified in the original dataset as negative reviews which have been submitted online.

Fig. 9–6 shows WordCloud Visualization of device feature words and feedback rank words.

It is well clear that the reputation of one product depends on all rank values. The reputation is directly linked to the product's high demand. As shown in Fig. 9–6, a word Cloud

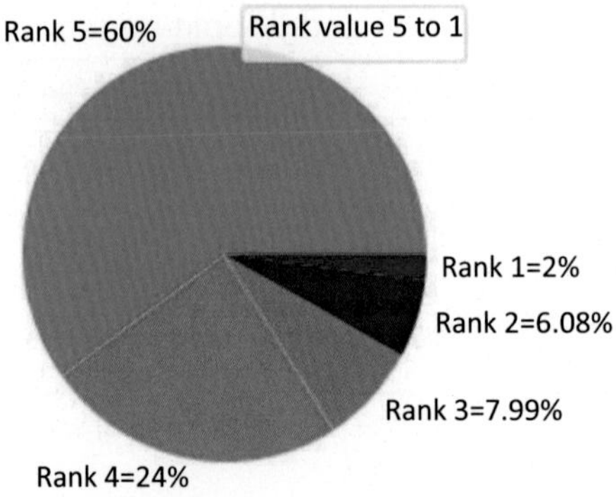

Rank 5=60%

Rank value 5 to 1

Rank 1=2%

Rank 2=6.08%

Rank 3=7.99%

Rank 4=24%

FIGURE 9–5 Rank value-wise distribution of reviews.

Table 9–4   Percentage reviews on different feedbacks.

Rank value	%age of review	Overall analysis
5	60%	Positive feedback = 84%
4	24%	
3	7.99%	Neutral feedback = 8%
2	6.08%	Negative feedback = 8%
1	2%	

FIGURE 9–6 WordCloud visualization of device feature words and feedback rank words.

visualization of relevant words has been provided. Using the same, we have targeted Flipkart reviews' analysis. Apart from the WordCloud as represented in Fig. 9−6, we have also worked on the most common positive and negative sentiment words as shown in Fig. 9−7.

During the analysis, each sentiment is partitioned based on a word-wise unique index number. For all input sentences, each review sentence is accessed in the loop. Here, we have covered a list of negative sentiment words, and when two negative words are present in any of the reviews and are at consecutive indexes then such reviews are restored for deep analysis. For deep analysis of various targeted reviews, we have calculated the total score count value of total reviews in terms of three categories that is, positive, negative, and neutral as shown in Table 9−5.

As shown in Table 9−5, out of 2304 reviews, it has been calculated that 924 reviews are already about positive feedback. The red highlighted cell indicates the total count of reviews

FIGURE 9–7 Most common positive and negative sentiment words.

Table 9–5   Category-wise reviews' score count value.

Review type	Total number of reviews
Positive	924
Negative	97
Neutral	1283

Table 9–6   Targeted negative reviews.

Review no.	Product_name	Negative review	Rank
12	iphone color	Not bad look	1
99	Laptop	Can't avoid to use it	2
156	Laptop monitor view	Not awkward	1
332	Mobile screen	No poor resolution	2
2002	Laptop weight	Not heavy	2

that reflect negative feedback about Flipkart products as already shown in the dataset. The last row indicates that 1283 reviews are neutral, which means neither positive nor negative feedback. For further classification, work is performed on those 97 reviews, which are giving negative feedback but a few or all of them could be positive feedback as the customer is free to comment on the form of feedback about a product and that could be a double negative remark. So, it depends on the customer how he or she posts the comment on the feedback form as shown in Table 9−6 in which a collection of online available negative reviews is provided.

9.4 Experimental results and discussion

Fig. 9−8 depicts a view of the first 20 reviews out of 2304 feedback reviews, which have been retrieved from the Flipkart dataset for the year 2022. It provides reviews with details in four different columns. Column 1 is the serial number (ascending order), and column 2 is the product name for which feedback has been submitted by its customer after buying it or after using it. Column 3 is the actual review posted and the last column is system generated rank value.

As shown in Fig. 9−9, it is depicted after analyzing the reviews that a negative rank (range 1−2) doesn't always mean dissatisfaction of the customer. Nevertheless, if a negative review includes two consecutive negative words, then it twists the meaning and rating of the review toward a higher rating.

It is visualized from Table 9−7 that the reviews which were negative but had a positive impact are automatically changed to higher revised ranks in our system. It has been found

	Product_name	Review	Rating
0	Lenovo Ideapad Gaming 3 Ryzen 5 Hexa Core 5600...	Best under 60k Great performance! got it for a...	5
1	Lenovo Ideapad Gaming 3 Ryzen 5 Hexa Core 5600...	Good perfomence...	5
2	Lenovo Ideapad Gaming 3 Ryzen 5 Hexa Core 5600...	Great performance but usually it has also that...	5
3	DELL Inspiron Athlon Dual Core 3050U - (4 GB/2...	My wife is so happy and best product 👍😊	5
4	DELL Inspiron Athlon Dual Core 3050U - (4 GB/2...	Light weight laptop with new amazing features,...	5
5	DELL Inspiron Athlon Dual Core 3050U - (4 GB/2...	Amazing laptop, am so much happy, thanks for F...	5
6	DELL Inspiron Athlon Dual Core 3050U - (4 GB/2...	Over all a good laptop for personal use	5
7	DELL Inspiron Athlon Dual Core 3050U - (4 GB/2...	Thank you so much Flipkart	4
8	DELL Inspiron Athlon Dual Core 3050U - (4 GB/2...	Amazing product	5
9	DELL Inspiron Athlon Dual Core 3050U - (4 GB/2...	Good for normal work , students, online classe...	3
10	DELL Inspiron Athlon Dual Core 3050U - (4 GB/2...	Laptop received was in good packaging and good...	5
11	DELL Inspiron Athlon Dual Core 3050U - (4 GB/2...	Very nice	5
12	DELL Inspiron Athlon Dual Core 3050U - (4 GB/2...	Good product but dilevary slow	4
13	ASUS VivoBook 15 (2021) Core i3 10th Gen - (8 ...	If you can affort few thousands extra you can ...	2
14	ASUS VivoBook 15 (2021) Core i3 10th Gen - (8 ...	Good	5
15	ASUS VivoBook 15 (2021) Core i3 10th Gen - (8 ...	All good but battery backup not good enough	3
16	ASUS VivoBook 15 (2021) Core i3 10th Gen - (8 ...	I'll update this review again after a month us...	5
17	ASUS VivoBook 15 (2021) Core i3 10th Gen - (8 ...	I love it ....🏆	5
18	ASUS VivoBook 15 (2021) Core i3 10th Gen - (8 ...	Good	4
19	ASUS VivoBook 15 (2021) Core i3 10th Gen - (8 ...	Best Laptop 💻 👍 in the segment. Classy perform...	4

FIGURE 9–8 Input reviews in serial order of submission taken from the link: <https://www.analyticsvidhya.com/blog/2022/09/sentiment-analysis-on-flipkart-dataset/>.

that out of 97 negative reviews, 5 reviews were showing positive interest. So, our system has updated the overall scenario of score count values as shown in Table 9–8.

From Table 9–8, it can be identified that the reputation of Flipkart products is successfully improved by 5%. For evaluating our model, we split all the data, with 0.8 for training and 0.2 for validating. For training and validating we used the CNN model, we did 5 epochs of training with 120 batch size. After each epoch of training, there will be 0.2 of a batch size of data used for validation. For the loss function, we used Mean Squared Error (MSE) as given in the equation [Eq. (9–1)]. The accuracy is calculated by Keras to estimate how many predictions match with the labels.

$$\text{MSE} = \frac{1}{n}\sum_{i=1}^{n}(y_i - y_i')^2 \tag{9-1}$$

Fig. 9–10 shows the training, and testing of the dataset with the target values.

Different deep learning models such as CNN, SVM, RNN, and LSTM are used for the experimentation. RNN is a kind of deep learning technique that deals with sentiment analysis of

Product_name	Review	Rating
ASUS VivoBook 15 (2021) Core i3 10th Gen - (8 GB/512 GB SSD/Windows 11 Home) X515JA-EJ362WS Thin and Light Laptop (15.6 inch, Transparent Silver, 1.80 kg, With MS Office)	Not Good	1
ASUS VivoBook 15 (2021) Core i3 10th Gen - (8 GB/512 GB SSD/Windows 11 Home) X515JA-EJ362WS Thin and Light Laptop (15.6 inch, Transparent Silver, 1.80 kg, With MS Office)	Not poor	1
DELL Inspiron Ryzen 3 Dual Core 3250U - (8 GB/256 GB SSD/Windows 11 Home) INSPIRON 3515 Thin and Light Laptop (15.6 Inch, Carbon Black, 1.8 Kgs, With MS Office)	cann't ignore	2
SAMSUNG Galaxy A12 (Black, 128 GB) (6 GB RAM)	Although the phone is good all over but the camera quality is pathetic	2
SAMSUNG Galaxy F12 (Sky Blue, 128 GB) (4 GB RAM)	look is not awkward	2
...	...	...
Whirlpool 7.5 kg Fully Automatic Top Load with In-built Heater Grey (SW Ultra 7.5 (SC) Grey 10YMW)	Worst product electric problem & Heavy vibrations too much sound .....I think reviews all not genuine	1
Xiaomi 11i Hypercharge 5G (Camo Green, 128 GB) (6 GB RAM)	Xiaomi 11i Hypercharge Camera not work properly camera quality is very poor camera not focus properly in camera take a picture is blurry. she does not return my order please don't order this mobile camera is not work properly	1
Xiaomi 11i Hypercharge 5G (Stealth Black, 128 GB) (6 GB RAM)	Xiaomi 11i Hypercharge Camera not work properly camera quality is very poor camera not focus properly in camera take a picture is blurry. she does not return my order please don't order this mobile camera is not work properly	1

FIGURE 9–9 Input reviews containing only negative customer reviews.

Table 9–7   Revised negative to positive rank value based on input customer reviews having double negation.

Before the application of deep learning technique		After the application of deep learning technique		
Negative review	Rank	Negative review	Double consecutive negation	Revised rank
Not bad look	1	Not bad look	Yes	5
Can't avoid to use it	2	Can't avoid to use it	Yes	5
Not awkward	1	Not awkward	Yes	5
No poor resolution	2	No poor resolution	Yes	5
Not heavy	2	Not heavy	Yes	5

Table 9–8   Updation of category-wise reviews' score count value.

Review type	Total number of reviews
Positive	929 (earlier was 924)
Negative	**92 (earlier was 97)**
Neutral	1283 (no change)

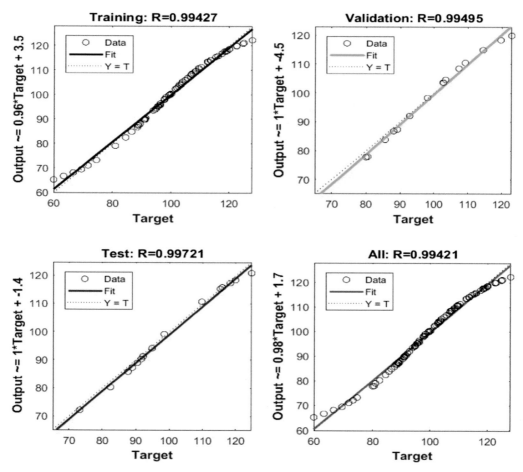

FIGURE 9–10 Training and testing with the target dataset.

time series-based data. LSTM network which is an extension of RNN is used for high memory. The LSTM model is used for time-series data processing, prediction, and classification. SVM is a deep learning algorithm that is used to classify data groups. CNN takes input and assigns weight to different input aspects. We have performed the simulation using various deep learning algorithms on the same collected dataset for double negative detection in textual data for customer feedback analysis on a product. The comparison between various deep learning models such as CNN, SVM, RNN, and LSTM is shown in Fig. 9–11.

A comparison of various deep learning models that are currently in use to address the double negative review detection on customer feedback on products is shown in Fig. 9–11. The key parameters for the comparative analysis are precision, recall, and F-Score. The comparison shows that the RNN model has offered better precision; the CNN model has provided better recall; and RNN and SVM have provided the highest F-score for double-negative

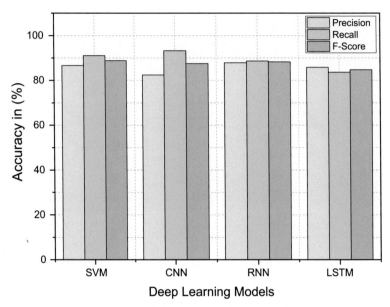

FIGURE 9–11 Comparative analysis of various deep learning models such as SVM, CNN, RNN, and LSTM for double-negative detection in textual data for customer feedback analysis on a product.

detection in textual data for customer feedback analysis on a product. Out of which, the performance of RNN is found to be the best among all.

9.5 Conclusion

In this study, we developed a more effective method for sentiment analysis that should make it easier to determine the positive rank of sentiments that are contained within negative sentiments. It is one of the powerful customer feedback-based sentiment analysis techniques to scale upbusiness and to provide deserved rank value to companies based on their product quality. In order to aid classifiers in recognizing statements with double negation, we have presented a double negation marking approach. To accomplish this, we did experiments on a dataset based on Flipkart Product Reviews to identify the sentiment rank within marked negative ranks. It has been concluded that RNN is the best among the other deep learning models such as SVM, CNN, and LSTM in terms of precision; CNN is the best among the other deep learning models such as SVM, RNN, and LSTM in terms of recall; and RNN and SVM are the best among the other deep learning models such as CNN and LSTM in terms of F-score for double-negative detection in textual data for customer feedback analysis on a product. It has been found that RNN technique supremes overall existing techniques. In future, the efficiency of RNN can be further enhanced by using: (1) AI-based fuzzy technique and (2) Hybrid approach (RNN + LSTM).

References

[1] S. Sohangir, D. Wang, A. Pomeranets, T.M. Khoshgoftaar, Big data: deep learning for financial sentiment analysis, J. Big Data 5 (2018) 1−25. Available from: https://doi.org/10.1186/s40537-017-0111-6. vol.

[2] D.M. Hussein, A survey on sentiment analysis challenges, J. King Saud. Univ.Eng Sci. 30 (2018) 330−338. Available from: https://doi.org/10.1016/j.jksues.2016.04.002. vol.

[3] Q.T. Ain, M. Ali, A. Riaz, A. Noureen, M. Kamran, B. Hayat, et al., Sentiment analysis using deep learning techniques: a review, Int. J. Adv. Comput Sci. Appl. 8 (2017) 424−433. Available from: https://doi.org/10.14569/IJACSA.2017.080657. vol.

[4] L. Li, T. Goh, D. Jin, How textual quality of online reviews affect classification performance: a case of deep learning sentiment analysis, Neural Comput. Appl. 32 (2020) 4387−4415. Available from: https://doi.org/10.1007/s00521-018-3865-7. vol.

[5] H.H. Do, P.W. Prasad, A. Maag, A. Alsadoon, Deep learning for aspect-based sentiment analysis: a comparative review, Expert. Syst. Appl. 118 (2019) 272−299. Available from: https://doi.org/10.1016/j.eswa.2018.10.003. vol.

[6] M. Faiz, A.K. Daniel, A multicriteria cloud selection model based on fuzzy logic technique for QoS, Int. J. Syst. Assur. Eng. Manag. (2022) 1−18. Available from: https://doi.org/10.1007/s13198-022-01723-0.

[7] M. Faiz, A.K. Daniel, Threats and challenges for security measures on the internet of things, Law, State Telecommun. Rev. 14 (2022) 71−97. Available from: https://doi.org/10.26512/lstr.v14i1.38843. vol.

[8] M. Faiz, A.K. Daniel, FCSM: fuzzy cloud selection model using QoS parameters, in: 2021 First International Conference on Advances in Computing and Future Communication Technologies (ICACFCT), Meerut, India, 2021, pp. 42−47. Available from: https://doi.org/10.1109/ICACFCT53978.2021.9837347.

[9] R.N. Laczniak, T.E. DeCarlo, S.N. Ramaswami, Consumers' responses to negative word-of-mouth communication: an attribution theory perspective, J. Consum. Psychol. 11 (2001) 57−73. Available from: https://doi.org/10.1207/S15327663JCP1101_5. vol.

[10] N.P. Cruz, M. Taboada, R. Mitkov, A machine-learning approach to negation and speculation detection for sentiment analysis, J. Assoc. Inf. Sci. Technol. 67 (2016) 2118−2136. Available from: https://doi.org/10.1002/asi.23533. vol.

[11] F.H. Khan, U. Qamar, S. Bashir, A semisupervised approach to sentiment analysis using revised sentiment strength based on SentiWordNet, Knowl. Inf. Syst. 51 (2017) 851−872. Available from: https://doi.org/10.1007/s10115-016-0993-1. vol.

[12] D. Ghai, H.K. Gianey, A. Jain, R.S. Uppal, Quantum and dual-tree complex wavelet transform-based image watermarking, Int. J. Mod. Phys. B 34 (2020). Available from: https://doi.org/10.1142/S0217979220500095. vol.

[13] D. Ghai, S. Tiwari, N.N. Das, Bottom-boosting differential evolution based digital image security analysis, J. Inf. Secur. Appl. 61 (2021). Available from: https://doi.org/10.1016/j.jisa.2021.102811. vol.

[14] D. Ghai, S.L. Tripathi, S. Saxena, M. Chanda, M. Alazab, Machine Learning Algorithms for Signal and Image Processing, first ed., Wiley-IEEE Press, 2022, pp. 1−512.

[15] D. Ghai, D. Gera, N. Jain, A new approach to extract text from images based on DWT and K-means clustering, Int. J. Comput. Intell. Syst. 9 (2016) 900−916. Available from: https://doi.org/10.1080/18756891.2016.1237189. vol.

[16] D. Ghai, N. Jain, Comparative analysis of multiscale wavelet decomposition and k-means clustering based text extraction, Wirel. Personal. Commun. 109 (2019) 455−490. Available from: https://doi.org/10.1007/s11277-019-06574-w. vol.

[17] D. Ghai, N. Jain, Comparison of different text extraction techniques for complex color images, Machine Learning Algorithms for Signal and Image Processing, Wiley-IEEE Press, 2022, pp. 139−160. Available from: https://doi.org/10.1002/9781119861850.ch9.

[18] T. Allard, L.H. Dunn, K. White, Negative reviews, positive impact: consumer empathetic responding to unfair word of mouth, J. Mark. 84 (2020) 86−108. Available from: https://doi.org/10.1177/0022242920924389. vol.

[19] Y. Azemi, W. Ozuem, K.E. Howell, The effects of online negative word-of-mouth on dissatisfied customers: a frustration−aggression perspective, Psychol. Mark. 37 (2020) 564−577. Available from: https://doi.org/10.1002/mar.21326. vol.

[20] N.C. Dang, M.N. Moreno-García, F. De la Prieta, Sentiment analysis based on deep learning: a comparative study, Electronics 9 (3) (2020) 483−512. Available from: https://doi.org/10.3390/electronics9030483. vol.

[21] P. Mukherjee, Y. Badr, S. Doppalapudi, S.M. Srinivasan, R.S. Sangwan, R. Sharma, Effect of negation in sentences on sentiment analysis and polarity detection, Procedia Comput Sci. 185 (2021) 370−379. Available from: https://doi.org/10.1016/j.procs.2021.05.038. vol.

[22] P.K. Singh, S. Paul, Deep learning approach for negation handling in sentiment analysis, IEEE Access. 9 (2021) 102579−102592. Available from: https://doi.org/10.1109/ACCESS.2021.3095412. vol.

[23] S. Mohapatra, Sentiment Analysis on Flipkart Dataset. <https://www.analyticsvidhya.com/blog/2022/09/sentiment-analysis-on-flipkart-dataset/> 2022.

10

Sarcasm detection using deep learning in natural language processing

S. Lakshmi

SRM INSTITUTE OF SCIENCE AND TECHNOLOGY, KATTANKULATHUR, CHENNAI, TAMIL NADU, INDIA

10.1 Introduction

Detection of a specific emotion or sarcasm is the minimum requirement in almost all social media. It can be used in chatbots, e-commerce, e-tourism, and other business to understand the customer expectations at the earliest to produce valuable products and to attract the clients to attain organizational goal. Automatic sarcasm detection is a challenging task. Some situations could be more difficult to human being for understanding the sarcasm.

10.1.1 What is sarcasm?

Sarcasm is defined as a sentiment in which trying to convey positive opinion instead of negative one. The Oxford online dictionary defines sarcasm as the use of irony to make or convey contempt. Mondher Bouazizi et al. defined the sarcasm as a sophisticated form of irony widely used in social networks and microblogging websites [1].

Some examples for sarcasm:

1. When you are recollecting and worrying about the incidents which has happened in the office, your friend asks you about the day, your response "great" when you really mean "terrible."
2. I like how loud you play piano.
3. Your best friend says that he is going to the gym, you say, "Good for you."
4. When someone sneezes and you say, "God Bless you."
5. I can't believe how successful you have become!
6. I can't imagine anything better than this!

Computational Intelligence Methods for Sentiment Analysis in Natural Language Processing Applications.
DOI: https://doi.org/10.1016/B978-0-443-22009-8.00013-6

10.1.2 Sentiment analysis

Sentiment analysis and opinion mining are purely depending on emotional words in the given context. Generally, emotions played a major role in analyzing the product reviews and sentiments of the human being. Fig. 10−1 shows the general emotions of human being as a wheel. The emotions such as happy, anger, fear, surprise, disgust, and sad are considered as basic emotions, and these emotions occupy the inner circle of the wheel. All other emotions are formed from these basic emotions.

According to Dr. Gloria Willcox, who was created the wheel of emotions, the inner ring represents the basic emotions such as mad, sad, scared, joyful, peaceful, and powerful and the outer ring words are created with the combinations of primary emotions. The wheel of emotion shows the various sentiments of human being, which identifies the mood of a person.

10.1.3 Sarcasm detection

Detection of sarcasm from the given text message or audio message, that is, speech will help us to make wise decision without hesitation. Analyzing the sarcasm is the need of the requirement in research such as opinion mining and sentiment analysis. Detection of sarcasm will also identify the psychology, mood, and health condition of the people, which will lead us to identify certain health issues at the earliest. Sarcasm is everywhere in social media that can be used for analyzing the sentiments of the people [2,3]. Companies are regularly doing data analysis for knowing the market position, power of social networks to acquire the higher market potential, reach the goals and move beyond the boundaries through this budding umbrella of sentiment analysis [4,5]. Detecting and handling sarcasm are a most challenging job in natural language processing since sarcasm can change the meaning of the sentence entirely [6,7].

Generally, to deal with text on social networks is a difficult task since it has some distinguishing features. People can use unstructured words, distorted language in a defensive way, misspelled words with different slang, etc. The limitation of twitter word count is 280. Detecting sarcasm from tweet messages can be done as a binary text classification method. The automatic sarcasm detection has got much attention from the natural language processing group [8]. The main issues arising during sarcasm detection are classification, disambiguated and sequence labeling. The classification problem may be a decision problem, which

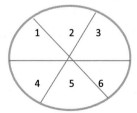

FIGURE 10−1 Wheel of emotion. 1. Happy; 2. Anger; 3. Fear; 4. Surprise; 5. Disgust; and 6. Sad.

returns true if given data has sarcastic information, otherwise false [9,10]. In the word disambiguation, sarcasm is detected by analyzing the word sense, which has sarcastic nature or literal sense [11].

The sarcasm can be identified by taking the hidden variables in the sequence of sentences. [12−14]. Rule-based sarcasm detection techniques used by Davidov et al. [15] and Ridloff et al. [16]. This method always looks for evidence and indicators of sarcasm that is in the form of rules. Hao et al. [17] applied rule-based technique by considering a 9-rule approach where each rule is verified based on the number of search results. Maynard et al. used rules for classification from the Hashtag analysis [8,9]. In more recent studies, sarcasm was detected by using machine learning and deep learning algorithms [18,19]. The twitter writers leave the contextual clues using hashtags and hyperboles. Sarcasm is detected by finding the clues in twitter [16].

A soft attention-based LSTM with convolution network model used by Kumar et al. [20] for working on Twitter dataset to detect sarcasm. The main drawback of this system is not being able to distinguish today's slang on social networks. Gao et al. [18] proposed a target-dependent sentimental analysis using BERT for categorizing the statements as positive, negative, neutral, and ironic. Ren et al. [19] used the context augmented convolutional neural network to predict sarcasm on Twitter dataset. Content-based feature technique using BERT on Twitter and IAC-v2 dataset by Eke et al. [21]. Hence, it is compulsory to have a relevant model for sarcasm detection. Hao et al. [22] applies rule-based technique by considering a 9-rule approach where at each rule is verified based on number of search results for simile fitting the form "* as *." Greenwood claims that hashtag sentiment is a key indicator of sarcasm.

Santosh Kumar et al. use an essential rule of sarcasm that a negative phrase occurs in a positive sentence than it could be sarcastic. To do so, they use parse trees to identify situation phrases that bear sentiment. Gupta et al. [23], in their initial stage of sarcasm detection, focused on extracting attributes regarding sentiments and punctuations. The Chi-square test was adopted to select the features. In the second stage, 200 TF-IDF attributes with sentiment and punctuation-related attributes for recognizing the sarcastic content in the tweet. Arifuddin et al. [24] developed a system for recognizing sarcastic sentences in the text. The 480-test data and 120 test data were taken from Twitter, and the features were extracted, then using SVM classifier, the sarcasm was detected.

10.2 Datasets

Collecting the dataset of detecting sarcasm is a challenging task even for humans when we don't have the exact understanding of people from various backgrounds. Two methods used to label texts for detecting sarcasm. They are distant supervision and manual labeling by human annotators. In a distinct supervision method, some predefined criteria such as hashtags can be used for detecting sarcasm. Manual labeling is collecting text and presenting them to human annotators. Based on the size of the data, the datasets can also be classified into three types. They are

Short text: Nowadays, there exists a huge amount of data in the form of text as the opinion of individuals in social media. Twitter messages come undershort messages due to this limitation of size that is, 280 characters. Twitter datasets are used for sarcasm detection.

Long text: Data from review sites including movie reviews, product reviews, hotel reviews and program reviews are considered as long text.

Transcripts: Transcripts and dialogs in the Review reports are considered as datasets for sarcasm detection.

In this work, the following four datasets were used for experimental purposes.

1. News Headline dataset for sarcasm detection.
2. Sarcasm Corpus V2
3. Sarcasm detection from Kaggle
4. iSarcasm Dataset

10.2.1 News headline dataset for sarcasm detection

This headline dataset for sarcasm detection is collected from two news websites. The sarcastic messages are collected about the events by TheOnion and nonsarcastic or real news headlines from HuffPost. The Sarcasm_Headlines_Dataset.json has high quality labels such as is sarcastic and headline. The is sarcastic is 1 if the record is sarcastic otherwise 0.

10.2.2 Sarcasm corpus V2

It is a subset of the Internet Argument Corpus (IAC) for sarcasm. It contains the data representing three categories of sarcasm:

- General sarcasm,
- Hyperbole sarcasm and
- Rhetorical sarcasm

This file has the following fields:

Corpus: represents the type of the corpus—
    GEN—General sarcasm
    HYP—Hyperbole sarcasm
    RQ—Rhetorical sarcasm
Label: based on response—"sarc" or "not saarc"
ID: unique ID for every post
Text: The text annotated for sarcasm

The GEN contains 3360 posts per class for a total of 6550 posts. The HYP and RQ contain 580 and 850 posts per class respectively.

10.2.3 Sarcasm detection from Kaggle

A balanced dataset has been created by taking sarcastic news headlines from http://www.theo-nion.com and the nonsarcastic headlines from http://www.bbc.com, http://www.foxnews.com and http://www.euronews.com. The dataset consists of text format headlines and Class labels. It has nearly 12,500 unique values in which 52% of nonsarcastic and 48% of sarcastic

10.2.4 iSarcasm dataset

Since sarcasm is ubiquitous in social network, it is very much essential to study the exact views of the public in sentimental analysis [8]. This iSarcasm dataset is created by not only collecting the sarcastic and nonsarcastic comments from twitter users but also collecting the valid reason with explanation for sarcasm and nonsarcasm on the request of the author. The collected twitter messages are verified by the expert linguist for categorizing sarcasm and nonsarcasm, which explained by Leggitt et al. [25]. State-of-the-art sarcasm detection models applied and tested on iSarcasm dataset to investigate the efficiency of sarcasm models. iSarcasm contains 4484 English tweets with sarcasm labels.

The main purpose of distinct supervision is to build large labeled datasets with no manual effort. The iSarcasm dataset contains 777 sarcastic and 3707 nonsarcastic tweets after applying the quality check process and the length of tweet message is on average 20 words. The main contributors were from the United Kingdom and USA and 51% were the female contributors. The two versions of the dataset are made publicly available for research purposes. The first version is available for direct download at https://bit.ly/iSarcasm along with the labels. It has tweet_id, sarcasm_label, and sarcasm_type. The second version is provided based on the request underthe agreement to protect the privacy of the author. This version gives the additional information about the tweet text so that the researchers can perform the sarcasm detection from the text directly without using labeled categorization.

10.3 Overall process of sarcasm detection

The problem of sarcasm detection can be handled in three ways. They are

 i. Classification—A decision problem returns true if the given data point is sarcastic or not [18,19].
 ii. Word sense disambiguation—a word is assumed to have either a sarcastic or literal sense [21] and
iii. Sequence labeling—each utterance in the given text is taken as unit of sequence the sarcasm is hidden. The prediction of sarcasm in the hidden value explained in [17].

The overall process of the sarcasm detection is shown in the Fig. 10−2.

Building an efficient sarcasm detection model depends on many aspects. Fig. 10−1 illustrates the overall process of the sarcasm detection using deep learning algorithms. The various stages can be explained in detail as follows:

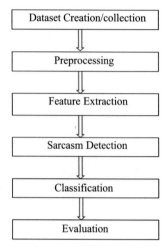

FIGURE 10–2 Overall process of sarcasm detection.

- Dataset Creation/collection

    Collecting the suitable data or acquisition of a dataset is the first and foremost step in any classification problem. Dataset is acquired from Twitter streaming API for both sarcasm and no sarcasm data. Every message contains the information of users including the user identification, URL and username of tweets. The key information is used to build a feature set which is used for classification.
- Data Preprocessing

    Generally, all real-world data contains some unwanted noisy information which should be removed before processing it to get accurate results. The tweet message consists of simple text, user details, URL references, content tags and hashtags. In this step, more than one operation is performed to wipe out the unwanted information like retweets, duplicates, numbers, different languages and URL. Fig. 10−3 depicts the preprocessing steps diagrammatically.

    The following preprocessing methods are implemented after converting the entire text into lower case.

- Tokenization: It is the process of breaking the words or sentences into small meaningful chunks known as tokens. The procedure for tokenization removes the whitespace, blank space which is present in the document. These tokens are fed as input for further investigation. Effective mechanisms are available in NLTK for performing tokenization [17].
- Stop word removal: The general words like articles and prepositions could be removed since it has no effect in analyzing the text. NLTK has special functions to remove the stop words.
- Spell Correction: All misspelled words are corrected in this step. (PyEnchant)
- Stemming: It is a process of removing the prefixes and suffixes from the word to find out the root word called stem. It improves the classification process when a word is derived from different kinds of keywords.
- Lemmatization: It is a text normalization technique used to find the meaningful root words.

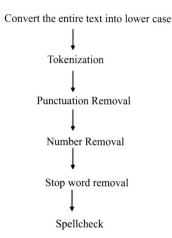

Convert the entire text into lower case

↓

Tokenization

↓

Punctuation Removal

↓

Number Removal

↓

Stop word removal

↓

Spellcheck

FIGURE 10–3 Preprocessing steps.

- Part-of-speech (POS-tagging): Some words can represent more than one POS at different times. Since the parts of speech are complex in nature, it is very difficult to find out the POS which leads to ambiguity. Hence, the correct POS tagging is essential in all computational methods.

Feature extraction: The extracted features played a major role for classifying sarcastic and nonsarcastic text messages. Certain attributes in social media posts are considered as key words for sarcasm detection [8]. Some of the features are listed below for identifying sarcasm. Context played a major role in categorizing sarcastic sentences easily. Conventional features like parts of speech tags (POS tagging), word unigrams and bigrams are helpful to understand the sarcasm in the given text but contextual features are mainly used to recognize sarcasm.

1. Pragmatic features

   Symbolic text attributes are common in tweets which are considered for text classification. Pragmatic features: symbolic and figurative texts correspond to practical attributes. The twitter message length is upto 240 letters, a limited one. These attributes are most common in tweets which acts as a strong sign of sarcasm detection. Many researchers turn towards the direction of these attributes to further sarcasm classification.

2. Sentiment related feature

   Whisper is the widely accepted sarcasm type. Sarcastic accents use negative emotions to define positive cases and vice versa. Sarcasm can also be identified by certain tone which is commonly used feature for recognizing sarcasm. [2,26,27].

3. Punctuation features

   Generally, product reviewers use exclamation marks to share their sarcastic nature while passing comments. Total number of punctuation marks, total number of exclamation marks are also used as a feature for detecting sarcasm [1].

   The total number of question marks(?),

   Total number of exclamation marks(!) and

   Total number of full stops(.) are taken as feature for passing their opinion.

4. TF-IDF (Term Frequency- Inverse Document Frequency)

TF represents the number of occurrences of a given word t in a document. IDF measures the rank of the specific word in the given text

TF = Number of times the word t occurs in the text/(Total number of words in the sentence)

IDF = total amount of documents/Number of documents with word t in it.

TF-IDF = TF $\times$ IDF

Thus, TF-IDF is the product of TF and IDF

This technique is widely used for text summarization and text classification applications.

5. Hashtag features

Generally, hashtags are used to express the emotions in social media effectively. These hashtag features can be positive or negative.

Liebrecht et al. [28] reported the reliability of the user-generated sarcastic hashtags as a golden label as twitter users cannot segregate what is sarcasm or not. The sample set of hashtags are "#not," "tweets," "#sarcasm," "#irony."

Hashtag features can be positive or negative but they want to convey their emotions "#I hate you" generally suggests that the user is expressing gratitude for nothing in fact in need, [26] but hating it for not helping on time.

6. Lexical features

The lexical features are unigrams, bigrams and the syntactic features are part of speech tags used for sarcasm detection, emotion mining and the level of emotion in the given text.

10.4 Sarcasm detection and classification

Feature extraction process is done by using six different deep learning algorithms, and the sarcasm detection and classification process is clearly shown in the Fig. 10−4.

10.4.1 Deep neural network

Deep Neural Network (DNN) is the first deep learning model with one input layer, three hidden layers, and one output layer with two neurons. The first hidden layer has 1024 neurons, second hidden layer has 512 neurons, and third hidden layer has 256 neurons. The term frequency−inverse document frequency, that is, TF-IDF encoding technique is used to find whether the given text is sarcasm or not. The results are tabulated.

10.4.2 Convolutional neural networks

Convolutional neural networks (CNN) are an advanced version of neural networks that play a major role for the sarcasm detection process in social networks. Fig. 10−5 shows the CNN model and CNN has the following multiple layers to extract features from the input.

1. Convolution layer: This layer acts as backbone of CNN and it has many filters to perform the convolution operation.

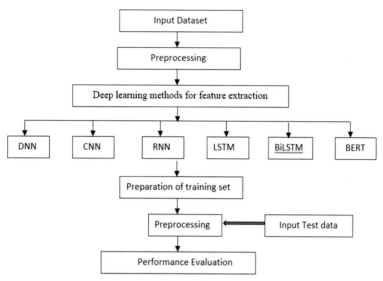

FIGURE 10–4 Sarcasm detection and classification.

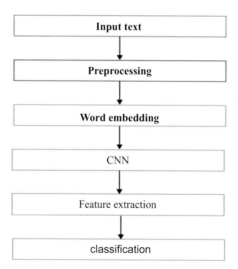

FIGURE 10–5 CNN model.

2. Rectified Linear Unit (ReLU): Here the operations are performed on elements and the output is a rectified feature map.
3. Pooling layer: This layer is used to minimize the computational power while having more data. That is, it reduces the dimensions of the feature map. There are three types of pooling. They are max pooling, average pooling and sum pooling.
4. Fully connected layer: This is used to classify the output.

The convolutional layer

- An input layer of size 1 × 100 × N where N is the number of instances from the dataset. Embedded words like Fast Text are used as an input.
- One convolution layer with 200 neurons with the filter 1 × 100 × N
- Two convolution layers with 200 neurons with 1 × 100 × 200 as filter size.
- Three ReLU activation layers are used.
- Three dropout layers with dropout
- A max pooling with stride.
- A fully connected layer with 10 neurons.

To avoid overfitting, the minimum 2% dropout layers are used. The max pooling layer is used for sarcasm detection, that is, final result. Word embedding can be done by FastText. The first group can be called unigram, second group as bigram, and third as trigram. In this method, a pure CNN classifier is used to extract the features.

10.4.3 BERT

Raising the processing speed and reducing the processing time are the requirement of today in deep learning applications. BERT is a Bidirectional Encoder representation from Transformers, which is a language model in natural language processing designed to make computers understand the ambiguity in text. In this deep learning model, every output element is connected to every input element and the weightings are dynamically calculated based on the connection. The process is called attention in natural language processing. Generally, the traditional language models are designed to read input sequentially but the BERT model is designed to read either from left to right or right to left. It uses bidirectional encoder representations from transformers to preprocess the text for sarcasm detection based on the contextual relationships between words in a text.

The language models were designed primarily using Recurrent Neural Network (RNN) and CNN. The transformers were introduced by Google in 2017. Since the transformers process the data in any direction, the greatest challenge of ambiguity in natural language processing is addressed efficiently in BERT. In Wikipedia nearly 2500 million words and in Google's book nearly 800 million words need to be processed in BERT efficiently. In BERT approach there are two main steps involved in

- Creating a language model by pretraining
- Fine-tune the model for specific NLP applications

This allows users to benefit from the vast knowledge the model has accumulated, without the need for excessive computing power. Some of the pretrained BERT models are

- BERT-Base, Uncased: It has 12 transformer blocks, 768 hidden layers and 12 attention heads.
- Bert-Large, uncased—24 layers,1024 hidden layers, 16 heads.

In the same way we have

- BERT -Base. Cased method with 12 transformer blocks,768 hidden layers, and 12 attention heads.

"CLS," "SEP' tokens are used for the separation of a sentence. "PAD" token is used to make a sentence of uniform length. Several BERT models in our experiments to validate the sarcasm detection. The accuracy of 99.63%, the precision of 99.33%, recall of 99.83% and a F1-score of 99.56% were achieved. The BERT-Base cased method with 12 transformer blocks is depicted in the Fig. 10−6.

10.4.4 Long short-term memory

Long Short-Term Memory (LSTM) uses the GloVe embedded input vectors which is an extension of RNN. All the memory cells are linked to one another and every memory cell is made upof an input gate, a forget gate, an output gate and a cell state. LSTM maintains the long dependencies by using gates. The architecture of LSTM model is displayed as follows in the Fig. 10−7.

10.4.5 Recurrent neural network

RNN automatically extracts features from the dataset and calculates the current state using a set of current input and previous output. RNN is trained by using two types of features, that

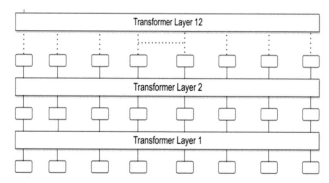

FIGURE 10–6 Bert base case: 12 transformer blocks.

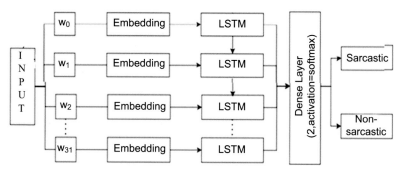

FIGURE 10–7 Architecture of LSTM.

is, Word to sentence and vector express the relations between role pairs. Porwel et al. stated a RNN to detect the sarcasm [27]. This technique was capable of extracting the features automatically and those features can be fed to machine learning methods.

10.4.6 BiLSTM

LSTM is a sequence-based model, the cell state is moved forward and backward. Really, two RNNS are connected. LSTM are more effective in this sarcasm detection because LSTM being sequence model, the cell state is moved forward and backward while in case of CNN each word is localized and independent of each other that is Sequence of words converted into sequence of vectors which are then fed into CNN like an image by reshaping the Input vector, which doesn't preserve the actual semantics. The weights of this embedding layer get trained after the training process. It uses Bidirectional LSTM because the later words might also affect the meaning of previous words in sarcastic sentences, so Bidirectional LSTM ensures that cell information flows in both directions.

10.5 Sarcasm detection: python code implementation

Sarcasm detection is the challenging problem in natural language processing. Detection of sarcasm is implemented in python by using libraries and tools such as NLTK and TEXTBlob which was used for extracting the features at the preprocessing stage. There is a scientific computing library named sklearn is used for splitting the training and testing the dataset. We need to train our model by using various machine learning algorithms like support vector machine, logistic regression, naive bayes, random forest and so on. This chapter deep learning methods and algorithms are used to extract the features from the dataset and Convolutional neural network, Recurrence neural network, Bidirectional encoder representation and LSTM and so on. Fig. 10−8 shows the accuracy and loss graphically.

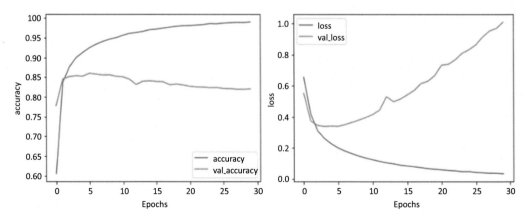

FIGURE 10–8 Accuracy and loss.

The train and test split is done as follows in python:

from sklearn. model_selection import train_test_split
X_train, X_test, y_train, y_test = train_test_split (sentences, labels, train_size = 0.8,
random_state = 42, shuffle = True)

Training and testing sets are created in the ratio of 80:20 by using the above code train_-
test_split method in python. Again, the training set split into 80:20 ratios of train and validation. Hence the entire dataset is divided into three parts as Train, test and validation sets in
the ratio of 64:16:20. The neural network was able to achieve 99% accuracy on the training
dataset and 81% accuracy on the test dataset.

10.6 Evaluation

After extracting the features, techniques can be applied to detect the sarcasm. Those techniques are evaluated by using the following metrics of measurement.

Precision = TP/TP + FP
Recall = TP/TP + FN
Accuracy = Correct predictions/Total predictions
F1-score = 2 × ((precision. recall)/(precision + recall))

Precision is the count of instances of true positive from the total of true positive and false
positive instances. If the prediction value is high, then we can very well conclude the system
works well. If the prediction is low, then the sarcasm detection technique's performance is
poor.

Recall is the count of instances which are true positive overthe total number of instances
of true positive and false negative. F1 measure is used to balance precision and recall.

10.7 Results and discussion

The LSTM method is a sequence method, the cell state is moved forward and backward easily. In CNN each word is localized and independent of each other. Sequence of vectors is
generated from the sequence of words and those vectors are fed into the CNN method. The
weights of this embedding layer get trained in the training process. In sarcasm detection, the
meaning of the current word affects the meaning of the previous word. In bidirectional
LSTM ensures that the cell information flows in both directions. that is from left to right and
right to left.

BERT represents input as subwords and learns embeddings for subwords. The BERT language model loads the vector in "gpu." Having a fixed size vocabulary like BERT has a practical advantage of being able to load the vectors in a GPU regardless of corpus size.

Bidirectional LSTM is implemented and the results are tabulated. This BiLSTM shows 1%
better accuracy than LSTM for this news headline dataset. While applying the BERT language

model, the results are outstanding and we are getting nearly 98.4% accuracy in BERT. The Precision, Recall, F1-Score values are calculated and tabulated subsequently. The performance of all six model results is shown graphically and the BERT model outperforms when compared with all models in the News Headline dataset.

The performance of the sarcasm detection algorithms results is shown in terms of precision, recall, F1-score and Accuracy for all four different datasets. While applying deep neural networks for News headline sarcasm detection, the accuracy is 88.57 for 20 epochs. Precision and recall are 89.34 and 89.12 respectively. The F1-score is 89.03.

The results are tabulated in Table 10−1. Then the results are taken after implementing the convolution neural network algorithm and getting better results when compared with normal deep learning algorithms. Nearly 4% better results in accuracy in CNN. RNN algorithms are implemented and the results are tabulated. LSTM is applied and the results are documented. LSTM gives better results than DNN and RNN.

In Table 10−2, the Sarcasm Corpus v2 dataset is taken and all the algorithms are implemented to find the sarcasm and the values are tabulated. In accuracy, BERT model shows 92.2% and stands first then Bi-LSTM shows 90%, then LSTM shows 89.7 CNN shows 89.3, the deep neural network shows 86, and RNN shows 82.8% The precision, recall, and F1-score values are calculated and showed in Table 10−2. The performance evaluation of this Sarcasm Corpus v2 dataset is shown graphically.

The Kaggle sarcasm dataset is downloaded and applied to all the algorithms and models to find the efficiency of them. The results are properly tabulated for DNN, CNN, RNN, LSTM, BiLSTM, and BERT methods. As usual the BERT model outperforms and the comparison results are graphically. In LSTM 89.9% accuracy and BILSTM shows 91.1% accuracy. But for this dataset, the BERT model got only 95% accuracy. (Table 10−3).

Taking iSarcasm dataset again repeated the same set of algorithms to check the results. The iSarcasm dataset contains three fields named twitter_id, sarcasm type and sarcasm label. In this dataset, I got the same accuracy level in CNN and LSTM techniques. For RNN got 86%, Bi_LSTM 92.9 and DNN got only 89.3. While applying BERT language model 97.8% accuracy acquired. The results are tabulated and the performance evaluated and shown graphically (Table 10−4).

Performance can be evaluated by taking accuracy for all datasets and the output is displayed as graph as follows: For news headline dataset (i.e.,-dataset1) and sarcasm dataset (dataset 4). Both are balanced datasets and the accuracy of this is 98% above. Fig. 10−9 shows the diagrammatic representation of performance evaluation of four datasets and its accuracy. The precision, recall and F1-score values of all four datasets were taken individually and the algorithm's performance could be analyzed accordingly. For data set 3- Kaggle sarcasm detection dataset is an unbalanced dataset. LSTM and BiLSTM both methods perform well and we are getting almost the same results with CNN. The language-based BERT model shows wonderful performance on any type of dataset. The performance is evaluated for all evaluation metrics that is, accuracy, F1-score, Precision and Recall for all four data sets and the results are diagrammatically represented in the Figs. 10−10−10−12.

Table 10–1   Performance comparison for news headline dataset- Dataset 1.

Algorithm	Accuracy	Precision	Recall	F1 -Score
DNN	88.57	89.34	89.12	89.03
CNN	92.65	93.12	93.35	93.23
RNN	83.91	84.22	84.77	84.87
LSTM	90.89	91.86	91.98	91.88
Bi-LSTM	91.17	93.08	93.50	94.35
BERT	98.43	98.44	98.21	98.33

Table 10–2   Performance comparison of Sarcasm Corpus v2—Dataset 2.

Algorithm	Accuracy	Precision	Recall	F1-Score
DNN	86.12	86.98	86.99	87.12
CNN	89.34	90.11	90.15	93.11
RNN	82.88	83.54	83.55	86.45
LSTM	89.76	90.11	90.45	90.67
Bi-LSTM	90.12	92.11	93.34	94.22
BERT	92.23	94.05	94.54	97.32

Table 10–3   Performance comparison for Sarcasm Detection from Kaggle—Dataset 3.

Algorithm	Accuracy	Precision	Recall	F1-Score
DNN	85.34	84.34	84.98	88.11
CNN	88.13	86.22	86.12	89.05
RNN	83.67	85.23	85.11	88.44
LSTM	89.97	90.33	90.68	90.65
Bi-LSTM	91.15	91.98	91.66	91.34
BERT	95.22	96.65	96.56	98.12

Table 10–4   Performance comparison for sarcasm—Dataset 4.

Algorithm	F1 -Score	Precision	Recall	Accuracy
DNN	88.65	89.33	89.56	89.30
CNN	91.21	92.11	91.54	91.88
RNN	85.44	86.11	86.43	86.43
LSTM	90.66	91.43	91.45	91.77
Bi-LSTM	92.34	92.56	92.34	92.98
BERT	96.77	97.87	97.96	97.98

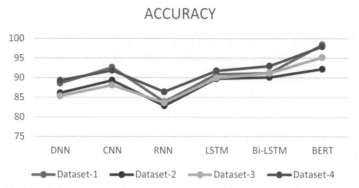

FIGURE 10–9 Performance evaluation of Accuracy the accuracy is 88.57 for 20 epochs. Precision and recall are 89.34 and 89.12 respectively. The F1-score is 89.03.

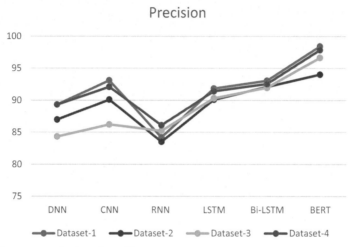

FIGURE 10–10 Performance evaluation of precision.

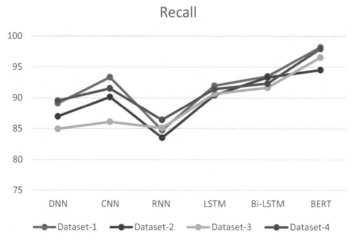

FIGURE 10–11 Performance evaluation of recall.

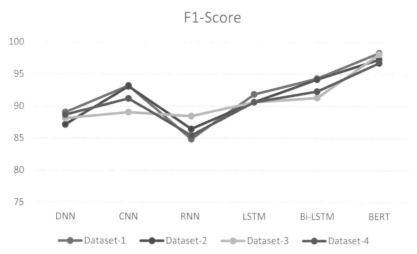

FIGURE 10–12 Performance evaluation of F1-Score.

10.8 Conclusion

The results of our experiments prove the efficiency of extracting various features from the sarcasm dataset. This work started with simple deep learning algorithms, moved on to various deep learning algorithms such as Convolutional neural network, RNN, LSTM and BiLSTM, then the well-known language model BERT discussed in detail. By taking four different sarcasm datasets and applying different deep learning algorithms for detecting sarcasm and the comparison of results were discussed in detail.

In this work, we have compared the effect of using BERT as the model for obtaining word embeddings of the social media post, since BERT captures both contexts and the semantics of the underlying text and hence, aided further in determining the sarcastic posts. We explored the use of deep learning networks for the detection of tweet sarcasm. More importantly, we discovered that the pretrained BERT classifier can achieve better performance as compared to state-of-the-art results for sarcasm detection. We have also compared the effect of introducing BERT with another embedding framework Word2Vec. The language model BERT can outperform when compared with other sarcasm detection methods.

References

[1] M. Bouazizi, T. Otsuki, A pattern -based approach for Sarcasm Detection on Twitter, (Senior member, IEEE) Graduate School of Science and Technology, Keio University, Yokohama 223−8522, Japan.

[2] C.-C. Peng, M. Lakis, J.W. Pan, Detecting Sarcasm in Text: An Obvious Solution to a Trivial Problem, 2015.

[3] D. Bamman, N.A. Smith, Contextualized sarcasm detection on Twitter, in: Proceedings of the Ninth International AAAI Conference on Web and social media.

[4] A. Ghosh, T. Veale, Magnets for sarcasm: making sarcasm detection timely, contextual and very personal, Proceeding of Conference on Empirical Methods in Natural Language Processing. (2017) 482−491.

[5] J. Aquino, "Transforming social media data into predictive analytics, CRM Magzine 16 (11) (2012) 38–42.

[6] B. Liu, L. Zhang, A survey of opinion mining and sentiment analysis, Mining Text Data, Springer, Boston, MA, 2012, pp. 415–463.

[7] A. Joshi, S. Agrawal, P. Bhattacharyya, M.J. Carman, Expect the unexpected: harnessing sentence completion for sarcasm detection, Proc. Int. Conf. Pacific Assoc. Computational Linguistics, Springer, Singapore, 2017, pp. 275–287.

[8] A. Srivastava, V. Singh, G. Singh, Sentiment analysis of Twitter data: sarcasm detection survey, 4th International Conference on "Computing for Sustainable Global Development", New Delhi, India, 2017.

[9] F.R. Francesco Barbieri, Italian irony detection in twitter: a first approach. in: The First Italian Conference on Computational Linguistics CLiC-it 2014 & the Fourth International Workshop EVALITA, 2014a, 28–32.

[10] P.R. Antonio Reyes, A multidimensional approach for detecting irony in twitter, Lang. Resour. Eval. 47 (1) (2013) 239–268.

[11] W.G. Debanjan Ghosh, Sarcastic or not: word embeddings to predict, EMNLP. Sarcasm Detection (2015).

[12] V.T. Aditya Joshi, Harnessing sequence labeling for sarcasm detection in dialogue from TV series friends, CoNLL 2016 (2016) (2016) 146.

[13] V.T. Aditya Joshi, Are word embedding-based features for Sarcasm detection? EMNLP (2016). 2016.

[14] V.S. Aditya Joshi, Harnessing context incongruity for sarcasm detection, Proc. 53rd Annu. Meet. Assoc. Computational Linguist. 7th Int. Jt. Conf. Nat. Lang. Process. 2 (2015) 757–762. Vol.

[15] D. Davidov, O. Tsur, A. Rappoport, Semi-supervised recognition of sarcasm in twitter and amazon, Proc. 14th Conference on Computational Natural Language (2010) 107–116.

[16] S. Poria, E. Cambria, D. Hazarika, P. Vij, A deeper look into sarcastic tweets using deep convolutional neural networks, 2016, arXiv:1610.08815. http://arxiv.org/abs/1610.08815.

[17] D.G. Maynard, M.A. Greenwood, Who cares about sarcastic tweets? Investigating the impact of sarcasm on sentiment analysis, in: LREC 2014 proceedings, ELRA, 2014.

[18] Z. Gao, A. Feng, X. Song, X. Wu, Target-dependent sentiment classification with BERT, IEEE Access. 7 (2019) 154290–154299.

[19] Y. Ren, D. Ji, H. Ren, Context-augmented convolutional neural networks for twitter sarcasm detection, Neurocomputing 308 (2018) 1–7.

[20] A. Kumar, S.R. Sangwan, A. Arora, A. Nayyar, M. Abdel-Basset, Sarcasm detection using soft attention-based bidirectional long short-term memory model with convolution network, IEEE Access. 7 (2019) 23319–23328.

[21] C.I. Eke, A.A. Norman, L. Shuib, Context-based feature technique for sarcasm identification in benchmark datasets using deep learning and BERT model, IEEE Access. 9 (2021) 48501–48518. Available from: https://doi.org/10.1109/ACCESS.2021.3068323.

[22] T.V. Hao, Detecting ironic intent in creative comparisons, ECAI 215 (2010) 765–770. Vol.

[23] R. Gupta, J. Kumar, H. Agrawal, A statistical approach for sarcasm detection using Twitter data, in: 2020 4th International Conference on Intelligent Computing and Control Systems (ICICCS), Madurai, India, 2020.

[24] N.A. Arifuddin, I.S.A. Indrabayu, Comparison of feature extraction for sarcasm on Twitter in Bahasa, in: 2019 Fourth International Conference on Informatics and Computing (ICICI), Semarang, Indonesia, 2019.

[25] J.S. Leggitt, R.W. Gibbs Jr. 2000. Emotional reactions to verbal irony.

[26] D. Bamman, N.A. Smith, Contextualized Sarcasm detection on twitter, in: Proceedings of the Ninth International AAAI Conference on Web and Social Media.

[27] S.A. Jodi Eisterhold, Reactions to irony in discourse: evidence for the least disruption principle, J. Pragmat. 38 (8) (2006) 1239–1256.

[28] T. Ahmad, H. Akhtar, A. Chopra, M.W. Akhtar, Satire detection from web documents using machine learning methods, 2014 International Conference on Soft Computing and Machine Intelligence, New Delhi, India, 2014, pp. 102−105.

Further reading

M. Abulaish, A. Kamal, M.J. Zaki, A survey of figurative language and its computational detection in online social networks, ACM Trans. Web 14 (1) (2020) 1−52. Feb.

M. Khokhlova, V. Patti, P. Rosso, Distinguishing between irony and sarcasm in social media texts: linguistic observations, in: 2016 International FRUCT Conference on Intelligence, Social Media and Web (ISMW FRUCT), St. Petersburg, Russia, 2016, pp. 1−6.

C. Liebrecht, F. Kunneman, A. Van den Bosch, The perfect solution for detecting sarcasm in tweets #not, Proc. 4th Workshop Computational Approaches Subjectivity, Sentim. Soc. Media Anal. (2013) 29−37.

N. Majumder, S. Poria, H. Peng, N. Chhaya, E. Cambria, A. Gelbukh, Sentiment and sarcasm classification with multitask learning, IEEE Intell. Syst. 34 (3) (2019) 38−43. May/Jun.

S. Porwal, G. Ostwal, A. Phadtare, M. Pandey, M.V. Marathe, Sarcasm detection using recurrent neural network, in: 2018 Second International Conference on Intelligent Computing and Control Systems (ICICCS), Madurai, India, 2018.

D.K. Tayal, S. Yadav, K. Gupta, B. Rajput, K. Kumari, Polarity detection of sarcastic political tweets, 2014 International Conference on Computing for Sustainable Global Development (INDIACom), New Delhi, India, 2014, pp. 625−628.

11

Abusive comment detection in Tamil using deep learning

Deepawali Sharma[1], Vedika Gupta[2], Vivek Kumar Singh[1]

[1]DEPARTMENT OF COMPUTER SCIENCE, BANARAS HINDU UNIVERSITY, VARANASI, UTTAR PRADESH, INDIA [2]JINDAL GLOBAL BUSINESS SCHOOL, O.P. JINDAL GLOBAL UNIVERSITY, SONIPAT, HARYANA, INDIA

11.1 Introduction

In the present-day world, social media plays a crucial role in our lives where people share their thoughts, opinions and thus communicate with each other using social media platforms. Sometimes, people find mental and emotional support and motivation through social media content. However, the freedom of creating content and posting on social media often leads to generating displeasing content that might cause discomfort to some users. Mostly, it has been observed that the users share the content in their regional languages or code-mixed languages. The identification and analysis of the content in low-resourced languages are challenging and have drawn considerable attention from the research community. In many instances, social media has witnessed the acts of using content that is hostile, profane, discriminating, abusive, and/or violent against an individual or targeted community on the basis of gender, religion, and ethnicity. Such content comes under the umbrella term Hate Speech [1]. Fig. 11−1 depicts the most popular categories of hate speech researched in existing literature.

Several studies have been performed on abusive language detection on social media in the English language [2−5]. Similarly, different studies have been conducted on hate speech and cyberbullying detection in the English language [6−9]. As compared with the English language, there are comparatively fewer studies in low-resourced languages. Tamil, Malayalam, Telugu, Kannada, and many other Dravidian languages are under- or low-resourced languages specific to India. These languages have relatively less data available for training purposes.

In this chapter, we focus on one of the low-resource languages—Tamil. Tamil is a Dravidian language and is natively spoken by people of South Asia. Abusive comments in Tamil and code-mixed Tamil−English language are classified. Those comments that defame, agitate, or bully someone have been considered abusive for the task of classification. This chapter thus focusses on the low-resource Tamil language and code-mixed Tamil−English language for detection of comments in social media as abusive or otherwise.

Computational Intelligence Methods for Sentiment Analysis in Natural Language Processing Applications.
DOI: https://doi.org/10.1016/B978-0-443-22009-8.00001-X

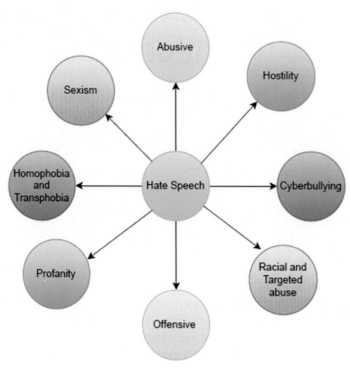

FIGURE 11–1 Popular categories of hate speech.

The dataset used in this study is provided by DravidianLangTech@ACL 2022. The comments in the dataset are classified into eight categories: hope speech, homophobia, misandry, misogyny, counter-speech, xenophobia, transphobic, and none of the above. Deep learning models (SimpleRNN, LSTM, and Bi-LSTM) using GloVe embedding are deployed to detect the abusive comments.

The rest of the chapter is organized as follows: Section 11.2 discusses the related work for abusive comment detection in Tamil, hate speech and offensive comment identification, sentiment analysis for Dravidian languages in code-mixed text, and homophobia and transphobia detection in social media comments. Section 11.3 describes the dataset and its dimensions. Section 11.4 presents the methodology. Results are presented in Section 11.5. The chapter concludes in Section 11.6 with a summary of the results obtained and the major conclusions drawn.

11.2 Related work

Hate speech includes abusive, offensive content, homophobia, transphobia, and many more. In the English language, a lot of studies have been done on hate speech and related termi-nologies. However, Tamil is a low-resource language, and the availability of datasets is a challenging task here. Some datasets are available on hate speech in Dravidian languages mainly in Tamil, Malayalam, and Kannada languages. Major datasets that are available in Tamil and code-mixed Tamil−English are given in Table 11−1. This table describes four datasets and also provides the previously existing studies on these datasets in Tamil language (Refer to Section 11.2.1−11.2.4). Fig. 11−2 shows the different approaches implemented on described datasets (Table 11−1) in Tamil.

11.2.1 Abusive comment detection in Tamil

There are also initial studies on hate speech detection in Tamil. Some studies have used the conventional machine learning approaches to classify abusive comments in Tamil and code-mixed language. One of them implemented the Random Kitchen Sink (RKS) algorithm with a Support Vector Machine (SVM) classifier and reported the weighted average F1-score for Tamil and Tamil−English code-mixed as 0.32 and 0.25, respectively [14]. Similarly, another

Table 11–1   Datasets available in Tamil and code-mixed Tamil−English.

Dataset	Description	Link
Abusive comment detection in Tamil [10]	To detect abusive comments in Tamil and code-mixed Tamil−English languages. The comments classify into eight categories: hope speech, homophobia, misogyny, misandry, counter-speech, xenophobia, transphobic and none of the above.	https://competitions.codalab.org/competitions/36403#participate
Hate speech and offensive content identification (HASOC) in Dravidian languages [11]	To identify offensive language content of the code-mixed dataset of comments in Dravidian Languages (Tamil−English, Malayalam−English, and Kannada−English). The comments classify into six categories: Not-offensive, offensive-untargeted, offensive-targeted-individual, offensive-targeted-group, offensive-targeted-other and not-in-indented-language	https://competitions.codalab.org/competitions/27654#participate
Sentiment analysis for Dravidian language in code-mixed text [12]	To identify sentiment polarity in code-mixed text in Dravidian languages (Tamil−English, Malayalam−English, and Kannada−English). The comments classify into five categories: Positive, negative, neutral, mixed-emotions and not in the intended languages.	https://competitions.codalab.org/competitions/30642#participate
Homophobia and transphobia detection in social media comments [13]	To detect homophobia and transphobia in Dravidian languages (Tamil, Malayalam) and English. The comments classify into three categories: Homophobic, transphobic, and non-anti-LGBT + content.	https://competitions.codalab.org/competitions/36394#participate

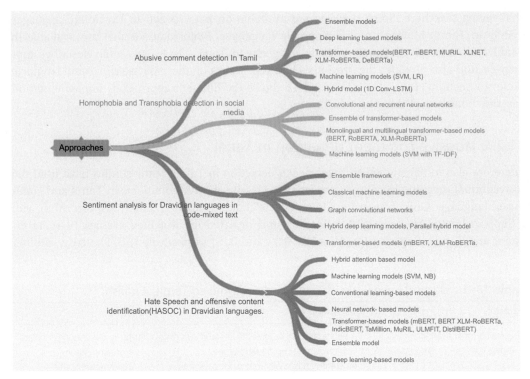

FIGURE 11–2 Approaches implemented on different datasets in Tamil.

study experimented with custom embedding with an SVM classifier for the Tamil dataset and achieved the macro F1-score of 0.54 [15]. Several studies [16—19] experimented with the deep learning models and the transformer-based models to classify the comments in the given categories for both Tamil and code-mixed languages. One study experimented with different machine learning models [Random Forest (RF), SVM, Logistic Regression, Decision tree], deep learning models (BiLSTM-M1, BiLSTM-M2), and transformer-based models (mBERT, IndicBERT) to classify the comments. For the Tamil dataset, BiLSTM-M2 performed the best and reported a weighted average F1-score of 0.7, and for code-mixed Tamil—English, RF outperformed the other models and achieved an F1-score of 0.78 [16]. Similarly, another study also used machine learning, deep learning, and transformer-based models to classify the comments in the Tamil dataset and obtained an F1-score of 0.39 [19]. The authors in [17] focused on the transformer model and reported weighted average F1-scores of 0.52 and 0.56 for Tamil and code-mixed, respectively. Another study experimented with transformer-based models (BERT, mBERT, XLNET) for two different datasets [20]. Quite identically, the authors in [18] used the transformer models for both datasets and achieved an accuracy of 0.66 and 0.72 for Tamil and code-mixed Tamil—English. One more study implemented the transformer-based model for Tamil and reported an F1-score of 0.62 [21].

Some studies also focused on ensemble models. One of these studies ensembles the machine learning models and also experiments with deep learning and transformer-based models [22]. Another study implemented the ensemble model using different transformer-based models and reported the weighted average F1-score of 67.46 and 71.61 for Tamil and Tamil−English languages, respectively [23]. Hybrid model (1D Conv-LSTM) is also used in a different study achieving a weighted F1-score of 0.43 and 0.56 for Tamil and Tamil−English, respectively [24]. The summarized form of the previous related work to classify the abusive comments in given categories is reported in Table 11−2.

Table 11–2 Tabular representation of the previous work for abusive comment detection in Tamil.

S. No.	Authors	Approach	Results
1.	Prasanth, S. N., Raj, R. A., Adhithan, P., Premjith, B., & Kp, S. (2022, May) [14]	RKS algorithm and SVM classifier	F1-score Tamil—0.32 Tamil−English—0.25
2	Bharathi, B., & Varsha, J. (2022, May) [20]	Transformer models (BERT, mBERT, XLNET)	Weighted average F1-score Tamil—0.59 Tamil−English—0.96
3.	Rajalakshmi, R., Duraphe, A., & Shibani, A. (2022, May) [16]	Machine learning, Deep learning and transformer-based models.	Weighted average F1-score Tamil—0.7 Tamil−English—0.78
4.	Patankar, S., Gokhale, O., Litake, O., Mandke, A., & Kadam, D. (2022) [22]	Ensemble models	Macro averaged F1-score Tamil—0.43 Tamil−English—0.45
5.	Balouchzahi, F., Gowda, A., Shashirekha, H., & Sidorov, G. (2022, May) [24]	n-gram-MLP, 1D Conv-LSTM models	Weighted F1-score Tamil—0.43 Tamil−English-0.56
6.	Swaminathan, K., Divyasri, K., Gayathri, G. L., Durairaj, T., & Bharathi, B. (2022, May) [15]	Custom embedding with SVM classifier	Macro F1-score—0.54
7.	Bhattacharyya, A. (2022, May) [21]	Machine Learning and Transformer based model (MuRIL)	F1-score Tamil—0.62
8.	Pahwa, B. (2022, May) [17]	Transformer models	Weighted average F1-scoreTamil-0.52Tamil−English-0.56
9.	García-Díaz, J., Valencia-Garcia, M., & Valencia-García, R. (2022, May) [23]	Ensemble model	Weighted average F1-score Tamil-67.46 Tamil−English-71.61
10.	Prasad, G., Prasad, J., & Gunavathi, C. (2022, May) [18]	Transformer models (XLM-RoBERTa, DeBERTa)	Accuracy Tamil—0.66 Tamil−English-0.72
11.	Hossain, A., Bishal, M., Hossain, E., Sharif, O., & Hoque, M. M. (2022, May) [19]	Machine learning, deep learning and transformer-based model	F1-score Tamil—0.39

11.2.2 Hate speech and offensive content identification

The identification of offensive content is important to minimize its presence on social media. Many studies have been carried out to detect Hate Speech and offensive content identification in Dravidian languages. Many of these studies experimented with traditional machine learning models, deep learning models, transformer-based models, and ensemble approaches. Some studies used the machine learning approach along with deep learning and transformer models [25–27]. Another set of studies focused on neural networks or deep learning models [28–30]. To detect hate speech and offensive content, many studies experimented with the transformer-based learning approach. Some of them implemented the transformer-based model (mBERT) [31,32]. Similarly, some studies experimented with another transformer-based model (MuRIL) to detect hate speech and offensive content identification in Dravidian languages [33,34]. Another group of studies implemented the language-specific models, multilingual models, and IndicBERT model [35–37]. Many studies used the hybrid and ensemble approach to detect hate speech in Dravidian languages [38–42]. Table 11–3 shows the tabular representation of previous works to detect hate speech and offensive content identification.

11.2.3 Sentiment analysis for Dravidian languages in code-mixed text

Through sentiment analysis from social media comments, we can find out whether the polarity of the online posted content is positive, negative, or neutral. Several studies have been conducted to analyze the sentiment for the Dravidian language in code-mixed scenario. While machine learning and deep learning remain the most popularly adopted choices of approaches for sentiment analysis [43–45], transformer-based models have been making rounds in the past few years. Some of the existing articles implemented the LSTM and Bi-LSTM models for sentiment analysis [46–48]. Another set deployed different deep learning models and hybrid deep learning models [49–51]. This trend has been followed by a new trend of adopting transformer-based models as the state of the art for several tasks. For sentiment analysis in Dravidian code-mixed language, BERT, mBERT, and various BERT-based multilingual transformer (XLM-RoBERTa) models have been implemented [52–57]. Some studies also implemented other different transformer models (DistilBERT) and many other variants [58,59]. The authors in [60], [61] experimented with an ensemble approach. Table 11–4 shows the summarized description of previous works for sentiment analysis.

11.2.4 Homophobia and transphobia detection in social media comments

The LGBTIQA + community is sometimes targeted in negative light on social media. The detection of homophobia and transphobia in social media comments becomes important to safeguard the mental and emotional health of this community that is frequently harmed through social media. There are a few studies [65,66] on the detection of Homophobia and

Table 11–3 Tabular representation of previous work to detect the hate speech and offensive content identification.

S. No.	Authors	Approach
1.	Rajalakshmi, R., Selvaraj, S., & Vasudevan, P. (2023) [35]	TF-IDF and transformer-based models like BERT, XLM-RoBERTa, IndicBERT, mBERT, TaMillion, and MuRIL
2.	Roy, P. K., Bhawal, S., & Subalalitha, C. N. (2022) [38]	Ensemble model
3.	Vasantharajan, C., & Thayasivam, U. (2022) [37]	Transformer based models (XLM-RoBERTa. ULMFiT, DistilBERT) and hybrid models (mBERT-BiLSTM, CNN-BiLSTM)
4.	Saumya, S., Kumar, A., & Singh, J. P. (2021, April) [25]	Conventional learning-based models, neural network-based models and transfer learning—based models.
5.	Dowlagar, S., & Mamidi, R. (2021, April) [31]	Transformer model (multilingual BERT)
6.	Pathak, V., Joshi, M., Joshi, P., Mundada, M., & Joshi, T. (2021) [39]	Machine learning models (SVM, MNB) and ensemble approach
7.	Vasantharajan, C., & Thayasivam, U. (2021, April) [32]	Transformer model (mBERT)
8.	Zhao, Y., & Tao, X. (2021, April) [36]	XLM-RoBERTa with DPCNN
9.	Ganganwar, V., & Rajalakshmi, R. (2022) [33]	Tranformer-based model (MuRIL)
10.	Subramanian, M., Ponnusamy, R., Benhur, S., Shanmugavadivel, K., Ganesan, A., Ravi, D.,. . . & Chakravarthi, B. R. (2022) [26]	Machine learning models, transformer-based models.
11.	Priya, A., & Kumar, A. (2021) [28]	Dense Neural Network (CNN)-based mode
12	Tripathy, S., Pathak, A., & Sharma, Y. (2021) [30]	Deep learning-based approach
13.	Basava, S. N. V. C., & Karri, A. P. (2021) [40]	Ensemble approach
14.	Bhawal, S., Roy, P., & Kumar, A. (2021) [27]	Conventional machine learning based models, neural network based models, transfer learning based models
15.	Kumar, A., Saumya, S., & Singh, J. P. (2020) [41]	Hybrid attention based model
16.	Benhur, S., & Sivanraju, K. (2021) [34]	Transformer-based model (MuRIL)
17	Chen, S., & Kong, B. (2021, April) [29]	Deep learning-based models
18.	Kumari, J., & Kumar, A. (2021) [42]	Ensemble-based method

Transphobia in the Dravidian language. To detect homophobia and transphobia in comments, the machine learning approach (SVM with TF-IDF) is implemented in [65], and another study experimented with SVM and BERT-based transformer approach [66]. Convolutional and recurrent neural networks have also been implemented using word and sentence embeddings to classify the comments as homophobia and transphobic [67]. Another group of studies experimented with transformer-based models (BERT, XLM-RoBERTa, Roberta) and various monolingual and multilingual transformer-based models [68−70]. An interesting study focused on deploying an ensemble approach using transformer-based models [71]. Table 11−5 shows the tabular representation of the previous related work to detect homophobia and transphobia in social media comments.

Table 11–4   Tabular representation of previous work on sentiment analysis in the Dravidian languages.

S. No.	Author	Approach
1.	Mandalam, A. V., & Sharma, Y. (2021, April) [43]	Machine learning models
2.	Dowlagar, S., & Mamidi, R. (2021, April) [62]	Graph convolutional networks
3.	Balouchzahi, F., Shashirekha, H. L., & Sidorov, G. (2021) [44]	Machine learning models
4.	Sun, R., & Zhou, X. (2020) [52]	Transformer model (XLM-RoBERTa)
5.	Sharma, D. (2020) [45]	Classic machine learning algorithms
6.	Kumar, A., Saumya, S., & Singh, J. P. (2020) [49]	Hybrid deep learning model.
7.	Chanda, S., & Pal, S. (2020) [58]	Pretrained models (BERT, DistilBERT, fastText)
8.	Sharma, Y., & Mandalam, A. V. (2020) [46]	Deep learning model (LSTM)
9.	Zhu, Y., & Dong, K. (2020) [53]	Transformer-based model (mBERT)
10.	Anusha, M. D., & Shashirekha, H. L. (2021) [47]	Deep learning—based model (Bi-LSTM)
11.	Bai, Y., Zhang, B., Gu, Y., Guan, T., & Shi, Q. (2021) [56]	Transformer-based model (XLM-RoBERTa)
12.	Mishra, A. K., Saumya, S., & Kumar, A. (2021) [63]	Machine learning, deep learning and parallel hybrid deep learning
13.	Kumar, A., Saumya, S., & Singh, J. P. (2021) [60]	Ensemble model
14.	Kumari, J., & Kumar, A. (2021) [50]	Deep neural network—based model
15.	Kannan, R. R., Rajalakshmi, R., & Kumar, L. (2021). [59]	Transformer-based model
16.	Kalaivani, A., & Thenmozhi, D. (2020) [54]	Transformer-based model (mBERT)
17.	Prasannakumaran, D., Sideshwar, J. B., & Thenmozhi, D. (2021) [61]	Ensemble framework
18.	Babu, Y. P., & Eswari, R. (2021) [55]	Transformer model (XLM-RoBERTa)
19.	Shanmugavadivel, K., Sampath, S. H., Nandhakumar, P., Mahalingam, P., Subramanian, M., Kumaresan, P. K., & Priyadharshini, R. (2022) [64]	Machine learning, deep learning, transfer learning approach, and hybrid model
20.	Sa, A., & Sb, V. (2020) [48]	Deep learning—based model (Bi-LSTM)
21.	Roy, P. K., & Kumar, A. (2021) [51]	Deep learning approach
22.	Sun, H., Gao, J., & Sun, F. (2020) [57]	Transformer-based model (BERT)

Table 11–5   Tabular form of previous work on detection of homophobia and transphobia.

S. No.	Authors	Approach
1.	Upadhyay, I. S., Srivatsa, K. A., & Mamidi, R. (2022, May) [71]	Ensemble of transformer-based models
2.	Nozza, D. (2022, May) [68]	Transformer-based models (BERT, RoBERTa, XLM-RoBERTa)
3.	Ashraf, N., Taha, M., Abd Elfattah, A., & Nayel, H. (2022, May) [65]	Machine learning model (SVM with TF-IDF)
4.	García-Díaz, J., Caparrós-Laiz, C., & Valencia-García, R. (2022, May). [67]	Convolutional and recurrent neural networks using word and sentence embeddings.
5.	Maimaitituoheti, A. (2022, May) [69]	Transformer-based model (RoBERTa)
6.	Swaminathan, K., Bharathi, B., Gayathri, G. L., & Sampath, H. (2022, May) [66]	SVM and BERT-based transformers
7.	Bhandari, V., & Goyal, P. (2022) [70]	Monolingual and multilingual transformer-based models.

11.3 Dataset description

The dataset used in this chapter is provided by DravidianLangTech@ACL 2022 and is available at https://competitions.codalab.org/competitions/36403#participate. The dataset contains YouTube comments in Tamil and code-mixed languages. The two datasets are provided—one contains the comments in Tamil language and the other contains the comments in code-mixed Tamil-English language [10]. The task is to classify these comments into eight given categories: Hope Speech, Homophobia, Misandry, Misogyny, Counter-speech, Xenophobia, Transphobic and None of the above. This is a multiclass classification problem in which the comment belongs to any one of the given categories. There are 2,240 comments in Tamil language dataset and 5,943 comments in code-mixed dataset. Table 11−6 and Table 11−7 show the distribution of comment categories in the Tamil and Tamil−English languages.

Table 11–6   Distribution of comment categories in the tamil dataset.

Category	No. of comments
Hope speech	86
Homophobia	35
Misandry	446
Misogyny	125
Counter-speech	149
Xenophobia	95
Transphobic	6
None of the above	1296
Not-tamil	2

Table 11–7   Distribution of comment categories in Tamil−English dataset.

Category	No. of comments
Hope-speech	213
Homophobia	172
Misandry	830
Misogyny	211
Counter-speech	348
Xenophobia	297
Transphobic	157
None of the above	3715

11.4 Methodology

This section presents the details of the adopted methodology for the abusive comment detection task. Fig. 11−3 provides a diagrammatic representation of the adopted methodology.

The methodology proceeds in the following steps:

i. *Data preprocessing*: Firstly, data cleaning and preprocessing are performed on the dataset. It involves the removal of punctuations, special characters, URLs, and blank spaces.

ii. *Tokenization and padding*: The preprocessed data are tokenized, and word_index is built from it. These tokens are covered into the list of sequences. The text_to_sequences() method is used for this purpose. Now, to make the data uniform, padding is performed using pad_sequences() function in Keras.

iii. *GloVe embedding*: To read the contents of the GloVe Vector file, a function is used that returns a dictionary that maps the words to their respective word embeddings. Zero vector is assigned to those words that are not in the GloVe dictionary. The tokenized data are fed into the embedding layer. It maps the words to their respective embedding vectors from the embedding matrix.

iv. *Deep learning model*: In this chapter, three deep learning models are deployed— SimpleRNN, LSTM, and Bi-LSTM (Refer Section 11.4.1−11.4.3).

11.4.1 SimpleRNN

SimpleRNN is a neural network that has a memory containing already processed information and learns from previous iterations during the training. Recurrent Neural Network (RNN) is the first algorithm that memorizes the input due to the presence of its memory component

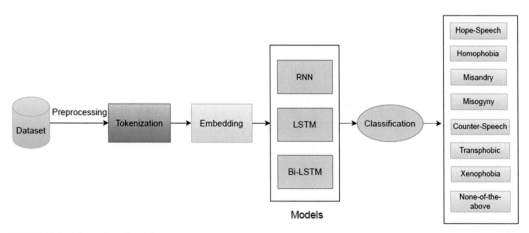

FIGURE 11–3 Adopted methodology.

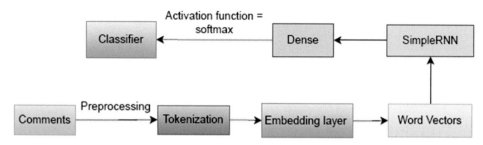

FIGURE 11–4 Block diagram to show the implementation of SimpleRNN.

[72]. RNN has short-term memory that allows to retain the previous information and expose the relationships between data points that are far from each other. RNNs can perform the same task for every element of a sequence, with the output being dependent on the previous iterations. This is the reason that RNN is called recurrent. After preprocessing the data, the tokens are passed to the embedding layer, which represents each token in vector form. Fig. 11−4 shows the implementation of the SimpleRNN. SimpleRNN is the next layer with the rectified linear unit as an activation function. The last layer is the dense layer. The model is trained on 100 epochs with a batch size of 32 for the Tamil dataset and for the code-mixed, the model is trained on 100 epochs with a batch size of 64. *"Adam"* is used as an optimizer with *"categorical cross-entropy"* as a loss function with softmax as activation is used for both datasets to classify the comments into given categories.

11.4.2 LSTM

LSTM is a special kind of RNN. The LSTM model has some layers like other neural networks that help the model to learn and recognize the patterns. LSTM holds the required information and discards the irrelevant information or which is not useful for future predictions. Firstly, the data are preprocessed, followed by tokenization and padding of the sequences. The first layer is the embedding layer in which the tokens are passed. The tokens are converted into word vectors. The obtained embedded vectors are fed to the LSTM modelLSTM is the next layer with 128 neurons, which works as the memory unit of the model. After that, dense layer is added, which is an output or final layer with softmax as an activation function, which helps in classification. For the Tamil dataset, the model is trained on 100 epochs with a batch size of 32, and for the Tamil−English code-mixed, the model is trained on 100 epochs with a batch size of 64. Fig. 11−5 shows the LSTM approach with GloVe embedding to classify the comments in given categories.

11.4.3 Bi-LSTM

A bidirectional LSTM consists of two LSTMs in which one works in the forward direction and the other works in the backward direction to take the input [73]. In Bi-LSTM, the input

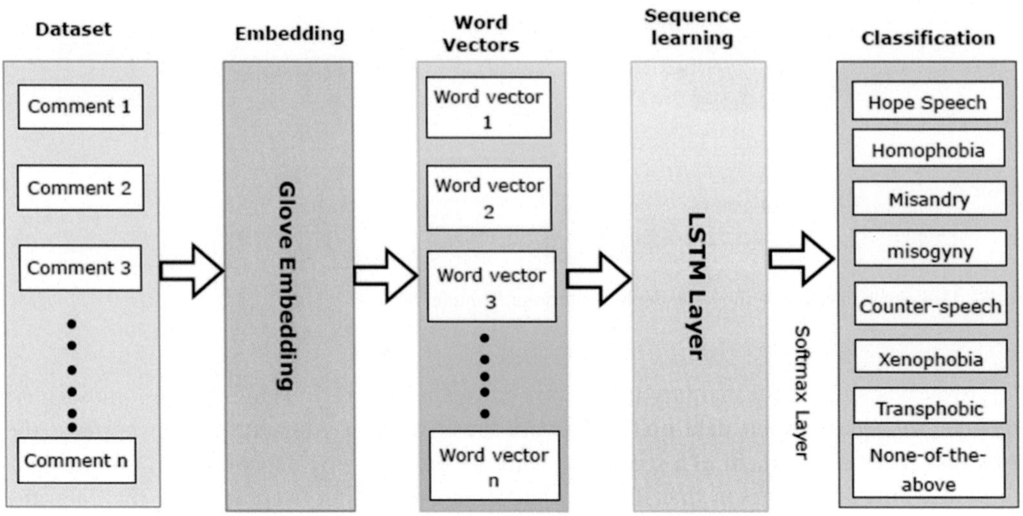

Dataset   **Embedding**   **Word Vectors**   **Sequence learning**   **Classification**

Comment 1

Comment 2

Comment 3

•
•
•
•

Comment n

Glove Embedding

Word vector 1

Word vector 2

Word vector 3

•
•
•
•

Word vector n

LSTM Layer

Softmax Layer

Hope Speech

Homophobia

Misandry

misogyny

Counter-speech

Xenophobia

Transphobic

None-of-the-above

FIGURE 11–5 Implementation of LSTM to classify the abusive comments.

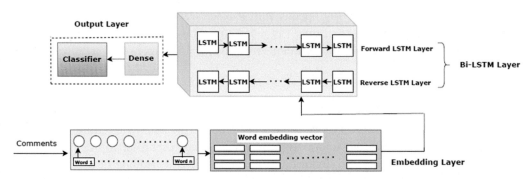

FIGURE 11–6 Bi-LSTM approach to classify the abusive comments in Tamil and code-mixed.

flows in both directions and makes use of information from both sides that makes the Bi-LSTM different from LSTM. The inputs can flow only in one direction either in forward or backward direction with LSTM. The preprocessed data are tokenized and fed into the embedding layer, that is, the first layer in which tokens are represented using vectors. Fig. 11–6 shows the implementation of BiLSTM. After that, embedded vectors are passed to the Bi-LSTM layer as input. The last and final layer is a dense layer with an activation function. The classifier classifies the text into predefined categories: hope speech, homophobia, misogyny, misandry, counter-speech, xenophobia, transphobic, and none of these. For both datasets, softmax is used as an activation function to classify the comments, and the model is trained on 100 epochs.

11.5 Results

This section presents the results of the deep learning models implemented on both Tamil and Tamil−English datasets. Figs. 11−7 and 11−8 present the confusion matrix of three implemented models for Tamil and code-mixed Tamil−English languages, respectively.

The metrics (precision, recall, F1-score) are computed independently for each category of both datasets and then the weighted average of them is reported. Table 11−8 shows the performance evaluation of SimpleRNN on both datasets.

Tables 11−9 and 11−10 shows the values of precision, recall, and F1-score of each category of two deep learning models, LSTM and Bi-LSTM for both Tamil and code-mixed Tamil−English, languages.

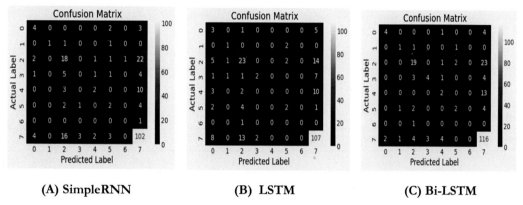

(A) SimpleRNN   **(B) LSTM**   **(C) Bi-LSTM**

FIGURE 11–7 Confusion matrix of three implemented models for Tamil dataset. (A) SimpleRNN, (B) LSTM, (C) Bi-LSTM.

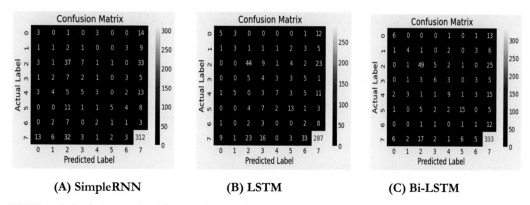

(A) SimpleRNN   **(B) LSTM**   **(C) Bi-LSTM**

FIGURE 11–8 Confusion matrix of three implemented models for Tamil−English dataset. (A) SimpleRNN, (B) LSTM, (C) Bi-LSTM.

Table 11–8   Results for SimpleRNN on Tamil and code-mixed dataset.

Language	Category	Precision	Recall	F1-score
Tamil	Hope speech	0.36	0.44	0.40
	Homophobia	1.00	0.33	0.50
	Misandry	0.40	0.40	0.40
	Misogyny	0.10	0.12	0.10
	Counter-speech	0.33	0.13	0.19
	Xenophobia	0.20	0.22	0.21
	Transphobic	0.00	0.00	0.00
	None of the above	0.70	0.78	0.74
Tamil–English	Hope speech	0.12	0.14	0.13
	Homophobia	0.06	0.06	0.06
	Misandry	0.36	0.45	0.40
	Misogyny	0.11	0.10	0.10
	Counter-speech	0.25	0.09	0.13
	Xenophobia	0.56	0.17	0.26
	Transphobic	0.06	0.06	0.06
	None of the above	0.79	0.84	0.81

Table 11–9   Results for LSTM on Tamil and code-mixed dataset.

Language	Category	Precision	Recall	F1-score
Tamil	Hope speech	0.14	0.33	0.19
	Homophobia	0.33	0.33	0.30
	Misandry	0.51	0.51	0.51
	Misogyny	0.50	0.17	0.25
	Counter-speech	0.10	0.12	0.10
	Xenophobia	0.33	0.22	0.27
	Transphobic	0.08	0.10	0.08
	None of the above	0.74	0.82	0.78
Tamil–English	Hope speech	0.29	0.24	0.26
	Homophobia	0.25	0.18	0.21
	Misandry	0.56	0.53	0.54
	Misogyny	0.09	0.19	0.12
	Counter-speech	0.50	0.20	0.29
	Xenophobia	0.46	0.43	0.45
	Transphobic	0.04	0.12	0.06
	None of the above	0.82	0.77	0.80

Table 11−11 shows the weighted average F1-score and macro average F1-score of implemented models on both datasets. For Tamil dataset, the weighted average F1-score for SimpleRNN is 0.55 and 0.59 for LSTM. Similarly, for the code-mixed English−Tamil dataset, the weighted average F1-score for SimpleRNN and LSTM is 0.60 and 0.63, respectively.

Table 11–10   Results for Bi-LSTM on Tamil and code-mixed dataset.

Language	Category	Precision	Recall	F1-score
Tamil	Hope speech	0.67	0.44	0.53
	Homophobia	0.33	0.33	0.33
	Misandry	0.63	0.42	0.51
	Misogyny	0.57	0.33	0.42
	Counter-speech	0.22	0.13	0.17
	Xenophobia	0.40	0.22	0.29
	Transphobic	0.10	0.12	0.10
	None of the above	0.71	0.89	0.79
Tamil–English	Hope speech	0.38	0.29	0.32
	Homophobia	0.36	0.24	0.29
	Misandry	0.64	0.59	0.61
	Misogyny	0.35	0.29	0.32
	Counter-speech	0.45	0.26	0.33
	Xenophobia	0.62	0.50	0.56
	Transphobic	0.06	0.06	0.06
	None of the above	0.80	0.90	0.85

Table 11–11   Weighted and macro average F1-score of all implemented models on both datasets.

Model	Language	Weighted average F1-score	Macro average F1-score
SimpleRNN	Tamil	0.55	0.31
	Tamil–English	0.60	0.24
LSTM	Tamil	0.59	0.29
	Tamil–English	0.63	0.34
Bi-LSTM	Tamil	0.63	0.38
	Tamil–English	0.69	0.42

The deep learning model, Bi-LSTM outperformed the SimpleRNN and LSTM for both Tamil and Tamil–English languages and reported a weighted average F1-score of 0.63 for Tamil and 0.69 for Tamil–English.

The comparison of the metric values for different implemented models shows that the Bi-LSTM outperformed the SimpleRNN and LSTM. It is possibly due to the reason that Bi-LSTM implements two LSTMs to the input data. Firstly, an LSTM is used on the input sequence (i.e., forward layer). Secondly, another LSTM is used to reverse the form of the input sequence (i.e., backward layer). Applying the LSTM twice leads to improving the learning of long-term dependencies and thereby improving the overall performance of the model. It also observed that input data transverse twice that enables BiLSTM to capture the underlying context better (from left to right and then from right to left).

11.6 Conclusion

The rapid and phenomenal development of online social media platforms and social networks has led to significant growth of information and entertainment for every age group. Online content makes a considerable impression on the minds of online users. An inevitable consequence is when users start posting and spreading hate and abusive comments. These posts/comments might be targeting an individual or a community and has a negative impact on them psychologically. The abusive content found on online social media networks might constitute a mixture of languages or the native language. This chapter detected abusive comments in different categories: Homophobia, Xenophobia, Transphobic, Misandry, Misogyny, Counter-speech, and Hope speech from Tamil and Tamil−English code-mixed language. This chapter presented the deep learning models SimpleRNN and their variants (LSTM, Bi-LSTM) with glove embedding for classifying the abusive comments in the chosen language set. Results obtained show that the Bidirectional LSTM outperformed the SimpleRNN and LSTM.

References

[1] R.K. Whillock, D. Slayden, Hate Speech. SAGE Publications, Inc., Thousand Oaks, CA, 1995 (paperback: ISBN-0-8039-7209-1, $22.95; clothbound: ISBN-0-8039-7208-3, $54).

[2] A. Koufakou, E.W. Pamungkas, V. Basile, V. Patti, HurtBERT: incorporating lexical features with BERT for the detection of abusive language, Fourth Workshop on Online Abuse and Harms, Association for Computational Linguistics, 2020, pp. 34−43.

[3] A.S. Uban, L.P. Dinu, On transfer learning for detecting abusive language online, International Work-Conference on Artificial Neural Networks, Springer, Cham, 2019, pp. 688−700. June.

[4] K.B. Nelatoori, H.B. Kommanti, Attention-based Bi-LSTM network for abusive language detection, IETE J. Res. (2022) 1−9.

[5] M. Wich, E. Mosca, A. Gorniak, J. Hingerl, G. Groh, Explainable abusive language classification leveraging user and network data, Joint European Conference on Machine Learning and Knowledge Discovery in Databases, Springer, Cham, 2021, pp. 481−496. September.

[6] D. Nozza, Exposing the limits of zero-shot cross-lingual hate speech detection, in: Proceedings of the 59th Annual Meeting of the Association for Computational Linguistics and the 11th International Joint Conference on Natural Language Processing (Volume 2: Short Papers), 2021, August, pp. 907−914.

[7] M. Mozafari, R. Farahbakhsh, N. Crespi, Hate speech detection and racial bias mitigation in social media based on BERT model, PLoS One 15 (8) (2020) e0237861.

[8] R. Bayari, A. Bensefia, Text mining techniques for cyberbullying detection: state of the art, Adv. Sci. Technol. Eng. Syst. J. 6 (2021) 783−790.

[9] A. Ali, A.M. Syed, Cyberbullying detection using machine learning, Pak. J. Eng. Technol. 3 (2) (2020) 45−50.

[10] R. Priyadharshini, B.R. Chakravarthi, S. Cn, T. Durairaj, M. Subramanian, K. Shanmugavadivel, et al., Overview of abusive comment detection in Tamil-ACL 2022, in: Proceedings of the Second Workshop on Speech and Language Technologies for Dravidian Languages, 2022, May, pp. 292−298.

[11] B.R. Chakravarthi, M. Anand Kumar, J.P. McCrae, B. Premjith, K.P. Soman, T. Mandl, Overview of the track on HASOC-offensive language identification-DravidianCodeMixDecember FIRE (Working Notes) (2020) 112−120.

[12] B.R. Chakravarthi, R. Priyadharshini, V. Muralidaran, S. Suryawanshi, N. Jose, E. Sherly, et al., Overview of the track on sentiment analysis for dravidian languages in code-mixed textDecember Forum Inf. Retr. Eval. (2020) 21−24.

[13] B.R. Chakravarthi, R. Priyadharshini, T. Durairaj, J.P. McCrae, P. Buitelaar, P. Kumaresan, et al., Overview of the shared task on homophobia and transphobia detection in social media comments, in: Proceedings of the Second Workshop on Language Technology for Equality, Diversity and Inclusion, 2022, May, pp. 369−377.

[14] S.N. Prasanth, R.A. Raj, P. Adhithan, B. Premjith, S. Kp, CEN-Tamil@ DravidianLangTech-ACL2022: abusive comment detection in Tamil using TF-IDF and random kitchen sink algorithmMay Proc. Second. Workshop Speech Lang. Technol. Dravidian Lang. (2022) 70−74.

[15] K. Swaminathan, K. Divyasri, G.L. Gayathri, T. Durairaj, B. Bharathi, PANDAS@ abusive comment detection in tamil code-mixed data using custom embeddings with LaBSE, in: Proceedings of the Second Workshop on Speech and Language Technologies for Dravidian Languages, 2022, May, pp. 112−119.

[16] R. Rajalakshmi, A. Duraphe, A. Shibani, DLRG@ DravidianLangTech-ACL2022: abusive comment detection in tamil using multilingual transformer modelsMay Proc. Second. Workshop Speech Lang. Technol. Dravidian Lang. (2022) 207−213.

[17] B. Pahwa, BpHigh@ TamilNLP-ACL2022: effects of data augmentation on indic-transformer based classifier for abusive comments detection in Tamil, in: Proceedings of the Second Workshop on Speech and Language Technologies for Dravidian Languages, 2022, May, pp. 138−144.

[18] G. Prasad, J. Prasad, C. Gunavathi, GJG@ TamilNLP-ACL2022: using transformers for abusive comment classification in Tamil, in: Proceedings of the Second Workshop on Speech and Language Technologies for Dravidian Languages, 2022, May, pp. 93−99.

[19] A. Hossain, M. Bishal, E. Hossain, O. Sharif, M.M. Hoque, COMBATANT@ TamilNLP-ACL2022: fine-grained categorization of abusive comments using logistic regression, in: Proceedings of the Second Workshop on Speech and Language Technologies for Dravidian Languages, 2022, May, pp. 221−228.

[20] B. Bharathi, J. Varsha, SSNCSE NLP@ TamilNLP-ACL2022: Transformer based approach for detection of abusive comment for Tamil languageMay Proc. Second. Workshop Speech Lang. Technol. Dravidian Lang. (2022) 158−164.

[21] A. Bhattacharyya, Aanisha@ TamilNLP-ACL2022: abusive detection in Tamil, in: Proceedings of the Second Workshop on Speech and Language Technologies for Dravidian Languages, 2022, May, pp. 214−220.

[22] S. Patankar, O. Gokhale, O. Litake, A. Mandke, D. Kadam, Optimize_Prime@ DravidianLangTech-ACL2022: abusive comment detection in tamil, arXiv preprint arXiv:2204.09675 (2022).

[23] J. García-Díaz, M. Valencia-Garcia, R. Valencia-García, UMUTeam@ TamilNLP-ACL2022: abusive detection in tamil using linguistic features and transformers, in: Proceedings of the Second Workshop on Speech and Language Technologies for Dravidian Languages, 2022, May, pp. 45−50.

[24] F. Balouchzahi, A. Gowda, H. Shashirekha, G. Sidorov, MUCIC@ TamilNLP-ACL2022: abusive comment detection in Tamil language using 1D Conv-LSTM, in: Proceedings of the Second Workshop on Speech and Language Technologies for Dravidian Languages, 2022, May, pp. 64−69.

[25] S. Saumya, A. Kumar, J.P. Singh, Offensive language identification in Dravidian code mixed social media text, in: Proceedings of the first workshop on speech and language technologies for Dravidian languages, 2021, April, pp. 36−45.

[26] M. Subramanian, R. Ponnusamy, S. Benhur, K. Shanmugavadivel, A. Ganesan, D. Ravi, et al., Offensive language detection in Tamil YouTube comments by adapters and cross-domain knowledge transfer, Comput. Speech Lang. 76 (2022) 101404.

[27] S. Bhawal, P. Roy, A. Kumar, Hate speech and offensive language identification on multilingual code mixed text using BERT, in: Working Notes of FIRE 2021-Forum for Information Retrieval Evaluation (Online). CEUR, 2021.

[28] A. Priya, A. Kumar, Hate and offensive content identification from Dravidian social media posts: a deep learning approach, 2021.

[29] S. Chen, B. Kong, cs@ DravidianLangTech-EACL2021: offensive language identification based on multilingual BERT model, in: Proceedings of the First Workshop on Speech and Language Technologies for Dravidian Languages, 2021, April, pp. 230−235.

[30] S. Tripathy, A. Pathak, Y. Sharma, Offensive language classification of code-mixed Tamil with Keras, in: Working Notes of FIRE 2021-Forum for Information Retrieval Evaluation (Online). CEUR, 2021.

[31] S. Dowlagar, R. Mamidi, OFFLangOne@ DravidianLangTech-EACL2021: transformers with the class balanced loss for offensive language identification in Dravidian code-mixed text, in: Proceedings of the First Workshop on Speech and Language Technologies for Dravidian Languages, 2021, April, pp. 154−159.

[32] C. Vasantharajan, U. Thayasivam, Hypers@ DravidianLangTech-EACL2021: Offensive language identification in Dravidian code-mixed YouTube comments and posts, in: Proceedings of the First Workshop on Speech and Language Technologies for Dravidian Languages, 2021, April, pp. 195−202.

[33] V. Ganganwar, R. Rajalakshmi, MTDOT: a multilingual translation-based data augmentation technique for offensive content identification in Tamil text data, Electronics 11 (21) (2022) 3574.

[34] S. Benhur, K. Sivanraju, Pretrained transformers for offensive language identification in Tanglish, arXiv preprint arXiv:2110.02852 (2021).

[35] R. Rajalakshmi, S. Selvaraj, P. Vasudevan, HOTTEST: hate and offensive content identification in Tamil using transformers and enhanced STemming, Comput. Speech Lang. 78 (2023) 101464.

[36] Y. Zhao, X. Tao, ZYJ123@ DravidianLangTech-EACL2021: offensive language identification based on XLM-RoBERTa with DPCNN, in: Proceedings of the First Workshop on Speech and Language Technologies for Dravidian Languages, 2021, April, pp. 216−221.

[37] C. Vasantharajan, U. Thayasivam, Towards offensive language identification for tamil code-mixed youtube comments and posts, SN Comput. Sci. 3 (1) (2022) 1−13.

[38] P.K. Roy, S. Bhawal, C.N. Subalalitha, Hate speech and offensive language detection in Dravidian languages using deep ensemble framework, Comput. Speech Lang. 75 (2022) 101386.

[39] V. Pathak, M. Joshi, P. Joshi, M. Mundada, T. Joshi, Kbcnmujal@ hasoc-dravidian-codemix-fire2020: using machine learning for detection of hate speech and offensive code-mixed social media text. arXiv preprint arXiv:2102.09866 (2021).

[40] S.N.V.C. Basava, A.P. Karri, Transformer ensemble system for detection of offensive content in Dravidian languages, in: Working Notes of FIRE 2021-Forum for Information Retrieval Evaluation (Online), CEUR, 2021.

[41] A. Kumar, S. Saumya, J.P. Singh, NITP-AI-NLP@ HASOC-Dravidian-CodeMix-FIRE2020: a machine learning approach to identify offensive languages from Dravidian code-mixed text, in: FIRE (Working Notes), 2020, pp. 384−390.

[42] J. Kumari, A. Kumar, Offensive language identification on multilingual code mixing text, in: Working Notes of FIRE 2021-Forum for Information Retrieval Evaluation (Online). CEUR, 2021.

[43] A.V. Mandalam, Y. Sharma, Sentiment analysis of Dravidian code mixed data, in: Proceedings of the First Workshop on Speech and Language Technologies for Dravidian Languages, 2021, April, pp. 46−54.

[44] F. Balouchzahi, H.L. Shashirekha, G. Sidorov, CoSaD-code-mixed sentiments analysis for Dravidian languages, in: CEUR Workshop Proceedings, vol. 3159. CEUR-WS, 2021, pp. 887−898.

[45] D. Sharma, TADS@ Dravidian-CodeMix-FIRE2020: sentiment analysis on codemix dravidian language, in: FIRE (Working Notes), 2020, pp. 615−619.

[46] Y. Sharma, A.V. Mandalam, Bits2020@ Dravidian-CodeMix-FIRE2020: sub-word level sentiment analysis of dravidian code mixed data, in: FIRE (Working Notes), 2020, pp. 503−509.

[47] M.D. Anusha, H.L. Shashirekha, BiLSTM-sentiments analysis in code-mixed Dravidian languages (2021).

[48] A. Sa, V. Sb, SA-SVG@ Dravidian-CodeMix-FIRE2020: deep learning based sentiment analysis in code-mixed Tamil-English text (2020).

[49] A. Kumar, S. Saumya, J.P. Singh, NITP-AI-NLP@ Dravidian-CodeMix-FIRE2020: a hybrid CNN and Bi-LSTM network for sentiment analysis of dravidian code-mixed social media posts, in: FIRE (Working Notes), 2020, pp. 582−590.

[50] J. Kumari, A. Kumar, A deep neural network-based model for the sentiment analysis of Dravidian code-mixed social media posts, Management 5 (6) (2021).

[51] P.K. Roy, A. Kumar, Sentiment analysis on tamil code-mixed text using Bi-LSTM, in: Working Notes of FIRE 2021-Forum for Information Retrieval Evaluation (Online). CEUR, 2021.

[52] SRJ @ Dravidian-CodeMix-FIRE, Automatic Classification and Identification Sentiment in Code-Mixed Text, 2020.

[53] Y. Zhu, K. Dong, YUN111@ Dravidian-CodeMix-FIRE2020: sentiment analysis of Dravidian code mixed text, in: FIRE (Working Notes), 2020, pp. 628−634.

[54] A. Kalaivani, D. Thenmozhi, Multilingual sentiment analysis in Tamil, Malayalam, and Kannada code-mixed social media posts using MBERT, in: FIRE (Working Notes), 2020.

[55] Y.P. Babu, R. Eswari, Sentiment analysis on dravidian code-mixed YouTube comments using paraphrase XLM-RoBERTa model, in: Working Notes of FIRE, 2021.

[56] Y. Bai, B. Zhang, Y. Gu, T. Guan, Q. Shi, Automatic detecting the sentiment of code-mixed text by pre-training model, in: Working Notes of FIRE, 2021.

[57] H. Sun, J. Gao, F. Sun, HIT_SUN@ Dravidian-CodeMix-FIRE2020: sentiment analysis on multilingual code-mixing text base on BERT, in: FIRE (Working Notes), 2020, pp. 517−521.

[58] S. Chanda, S. Pal. IRLab@ IITBHU@ Dravidian-CodeMix-FIRE2020: sentiment analysis for dravidian languages in code-mixed text, in: FIRE (Working Notes), 2020, pp. 535−540.

[59] R.R. Kannan, R. Rajalakshmi, L. Kumar, IndicBERT based approach for sentiment analysis on code-mixed tamil tweets (2021).

[60] A. Kumar, S. Saumya, J.P. Singh, An ensemble-based model for sentiment analysis of Dravidian code-mixed social media posts, in: Working Notes of FIRE 2021-Forum for Information Retrieval Evaluation (Online). CEUR, 2021.

[61] D. Prasannakumaran, J.B. Sideshwar, D. Thenmozhi, ECMAG-ensemble of CNN and multi-head attention with Bi-GRU for sentiment analysis in code-mixed data (2021).

[62] S. Dowlagar, R. Mamidi. Graph convolutional networks with multi-headed attention for code-mixed sentiment analysis, in: Proceedings of the First Workshop on Speech and Language Technologies for Dravidian Languages, 2021, April, pp. 65−72.

[63] A.K. Mishra, S. Saumya, A. Kumar, Sentiment analysis of Dravidian-CodeMix language, in: Working Notes of FIRE 2021-Forum for Information Retrieval Evaluation (Online), CEUR, 2021.

[64] K. Shanmugavadivel, S.H. Sampath, P. Nandhakumar, P. Mahalingam, M. Subramanian, P.K. Kumaresan, et al., An analysis of machine learning models for sentiment analysis of Tamil code-mixed data, Computer Speech Lang. (2022) 101407.

[65] D. Nozza, Nozza@ LT-EDI-ACL2022: ensemble modeling for homophobia and transphobia detection, in: Proceedings of the Second Workshop on Language Technology for Equality, Diversity and Inclusion, 2022, May, pp. 258−264.

[66] V. Bhandari, P. Goyal, bitsa_nlp@ lt-edi-acl2022: leveraging pretrained language models for detecting homophobia and transphobia in social media comments, arXiv preprint arXiv:2203.14267 (2022).

[67] M. Singh, P. Motlicek, IDIAP submission@ LT-EDI-ACL2022: homophobia/transphobia detection in social media comments, in: Proceedings of the Second Workshop on Language Technology for Equality, Diversity and Inclusion, 2022, May, pp. 356−361.

[68] K. Swaminathan, B. Bharathi, G.L. Gayathri, H. Sampath, Ssncse_nlp@ lt-edi-acl2022: homophobia/ transphobia detection in multiple languages using SVM classifiers and Bert-based transformers, in: Proceedings of the Second Workshop on Language Technology for Equality, Diversity and Inclusion, 2022, May, pp. 239–244.

[69] A. Maimaitituoheti, ABLIMET@ LT-EDI-ACL2022: A RoBERTa based approach for homophobia/ transphobia detection in social media, in: Proceedings of the Second Workshop on Language Technology for Equality, Diversity and Inclusion, 2022, May, pp. 155–160.

[70] J. García-Díaz, C. Caparrós-Laiz, R. Valencia-García, UMUTeam@ LT-EDI-ACL2022: detecting homophobic and transphobic comments in Tamil, in: Proceedings of the Second Workshop on Language Technology for Equality, Diversity and Inclusion, 2022, May, pp. 140–144.

[71] N. Ashraf, M. Taha, A. Abd Elfattah, H. Nayel, Nayel@ LT-EDI-ACL2022: homophobia/transphobia detection for equality, diversity, and inclusion using SVM, in: Proceedings of the Second Workshop on Language Technology for Equality, Diversity and Inclusion, 2022, May, pp. 287–290.

[72] A. Sherstinsky, Fundamentals of recurrent neural network (RNN) and long short-term memory (LSTM) network, Phys. D: Nonlinear Phenom. 404 (2020) 132306.

[73] Z. Cui, R. Ke, Z. Pu, Y. Wang, Deep bidirectional and unidirectional LSTM recurrent neural network for network-wide traffic speed prediction, arXiv Prepr. arXiv 1801 (2018) 02143.

12

Implementation of sentiment analysis in stock market prediction using variants of GARCH models

V. Vijayalakshmi

DEPARTMENT OF DSBS, FACULTY OF ENGINEERING AND TECHNOLOGY, SRM INSTITUTE OF SCIENCE AND TECHNOLOGY, KATTANKULATHUR, TAMIL NADU, INDIA

12.1 Introduction

GARCH models are very popular techniques in time series forecasting using stock market financial data. The GARCH model was invented by Bollerslev in 1986 [1] and used by many. Andersen and Bollerslev explained about ARCH models [2]. Bollerslev et al.described the different variants of GARCH models [3]. The standard ARCH model developed by Engle [4], Mhmoud and Dawalbait used three GARCH models such as GARCH(1,1), EGARCH(1,1) and GRJ-GARCH(1,1) to forecast and estimate Saudi stock market with different distributions such as Normal, student-t and GED. They used metrices such as Mean Absolute Errors (MAE), Root Mean Squared Errors (RMSE), Theil Inequality Coefficient, and Mean Absolute Percentage Errors. They found that GRJ-GARCH(1,1) was best model [5]. Sentiment analysis identifies the emotions of customers or users by analyzing or reviewing their suggestions, comments, feedbacks, or tweets. Many researchers applied sentiment analysis concept for stock market forecasting using time series data. Jishag et al. [6] predicted stock market behavior with both financial news and historic financial data by applying sentiment analysis in news. They collected stock data for 11 companies. They got prediction accuracy of 67.14% with sentiment analysis and then combined with ARIMA functions reached accuracy of 89.80%.

Mehta et al. [7] enhanced stock market prediction with sentiment analysis on social media data using deep learning. They collected share opinion from Facebook, Twitter, and Google + and applied machine learning and deep learning algorithms. Ko and Chang [8] used sentiment analysis based on LSTM for forecasting the stock price. They have done fundamental analysis using forum post or news article and technical analysis using stock historical stock data. They used BERT tool for sentiment analysis and LSTM for forecasting stock information with 12.05 RMSE. Wu et al. [9] built stock price prediction model by generating technical indicator from historical stock data and sentiment index from stock financial news. They used CNN-based sentiment analysis and applied LSTM for prediction system.

Gondaliya et al. [10] predicted Indian stock market during the pandemic period using sentiment analysis. They collected social media from forum, Twitter, news, RSS feed and applied sentiment analysis and then six machine learning algorithms were used for creating prediction model, in which Logistic Regression and Support Vector Machine outperformed with TF-IDF and bag-of-words techniques.

Thormann et al. [11] built stock price predictions model using LSTM by analyzing Twitter sentiments. They collected stock data from Yahoo finance and Twitter data using Twitter API with AAPL ticker, using TextBlob polarity and sentiment score generated and classified as neutral, positive, and negative. Finally, LSTM was applied for stock price prediction. Manogna [12] used sentiment analysis for stock price prediction on financial news. They proved that news creates impact in the change of stock. They used machine learning algorithms on NIFTY50 data, economical news in which Random Forest outperformed. Koukaras et al. [13] predicted stock market using sentiment analysis and machine learning. They collected Twitter, stocktwist data and applied sentiment analysis as well as financial data from Yahoo finance about Microsoft company. Seven machine learning algorithms were applied in which SVM with VADER outperformed other algorithms. Darapaneni et al. [14] built stock price prediction model using deep learning and sentiment analysis. They applied LSTM on four company stocks. Mendoza-Urdiales et al. [15] scrapped social media data from Twitter on 24 companies and generated sentiment index. Then, transfer entropy and EGARCH methods were used for projecting the impact on stock performance.

12.2 Literature review

Many researchers have done research using GARCH model in time series financial data. Koima et al. used GARCH (1, 1) to estimate the volatility of Kenyan stock markets [16]. Vasudevan and Vetrivel used data from 1997 to 2015 of BSE-SENSEX for forecasting and modeling the Indian stock market using asymmetric GARCH model [17]. Tran et al. [18] proposed multiplicative seasonal ARIMA/GARCH model to show that volatility effect occurred in mobile traffic series [18]. Costa used different GARCH models to forecast volatility of financial data from 1986 to 2016 [19]. Hasan studied three major indexes and used the ICSS (Iterated Cumulative Sums of Squares) algorithm to gather time periods of rapid changes in volatility. The perseverance of volatility decreases meaningfully when regime shifts are joined with a GARCH model [20]. Abdullah et al. utilized different GARCH models in daily exchange data from 2008 to 2015 with both normal and student's t-distribution of errors [21]. Maqsood et al. used GARCH models for the volatility estimation of Kenyan stock market daily returns in NSE (Nairobi Securities Exchange) from 2013 to 2016. They concluded that asymmetric GARCH model is better than symmetric models [22]. Shbier et al. proposed SWGARCH (Sliding Window GARCH) model to forecast to estimate the variance in time series data [23]. Virginia, Erica predicted the share price and forecast the volatility of Adaro energy Tbk, Indonesia, for 2 years with window dressing. They identified AR(1)-GARCH(1,1) as best model with 2.16% as percentage error [24]. Ghani and Rahim modeled an approach using ARMA-GARCH model for rubber price data to forecast 20 days ahead of daily price data. They found that ARMA(1,0)-GARCH(1,2) was the best model [25].

Adenomon investigated backtesting approach in financial data using nine GARCH models. The eGARCH(1,1) model with student distribution was the best model for (Nigeria Zenith Bank stock returns) [26]. Naik et al. proposed a model with correlation of mean, median, and GARCH. They used stocks of Infosys and sbi companies [27]. Ravikumar and Saraf used both the classification and regression algorithms to predict the stock prices. Regression algorithm predicted the final price of stock of an organization, and the classification algorithm predicted that whether the closing price of stock will decrease or increase for the next day [28]. Vijh et al. used machine learning techniques such as ANN and RF to predict the next day closing price for different companies [29]. Gao created a model using ARIMA-GARCH to predict the trend and law of stock price exchange financial data of China from 2017 to 2019 [30].

Nybo compared the instability forecast performance of GARCH and Artificial Neural Network model using US stock price data from 2005 to 2020. They concluded that ANN model is useful when predicting the volatility of resources with less volatility profiles and GARCH model is useful when predicting the volatility with high- and medium-volatility assets [31]. Meshal Harbi Odah has done a comparison between ARMA and GARCH models with the metrices MAE, MASE. They proved that GARCH(1,1) model is best forecasting time series for financial data [32]. Li and Zhang created GARCH model for short-term forecasting using CYTS stock price [33]. Payal Yogya, and Krishnan have done a methodical survey on machine learning methods in prediction of stock price [34].

12.3 Methodology

The overall process of the work is demonstrated as visual representation in Fig. 12−1 with two phases.

These two phases are (1) Sentiment Analysis on Twitter data and (2) Forecast on Financial Stock data; in first phase, Twitter data were collected using Twitter API with $aapl ticker, preprocessed the data by applying procedures such as converting into lower case, removal of numbers, whitespace, punctuations, hyperlink, and stop words, then applied sentiment analysis to find the emotions of people by generating sentiment score using Term Document Matrix (TDM) and get_nrc_sentiment(). Then in second phase, financial stock data were collected from Apple company using getSymbols() by passing the parameter "AAPL," daily return is the extracted feature from the financial dataset, and applied different types of GARCH models to forecast the future stock predictions. At last, both processes gave the positive perspective of Apple stock company for upcoming days. Sentiment analysis gives the impact of the progress of the stock market forecasting by analyzing the social media emotions of the people.

12.4 Sentiment analysis on twitter data

Sentiment analysis is playing major role in stock market forecasting and prediction. Based on the sentiment emotion of the user, the value of the stock market values changes.

Data Collection: Social media data were collected about Apple company from Twitter using Twitter API. Approximately 10,000 tweets were collected. The libraries such as Twitter, ROAuth,

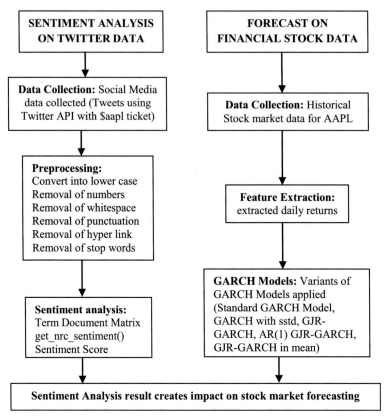

FIGURE 12–1 Overall stock market prediction model.

openssl, and httpuv were used to authenticate and collect the tweets based on the ticker $aapl. The api_key, api_secret, access_token, access_secret parameters, and its corresponding values were passed to setup_twitter_oauth() method. The searchTwitter() was used to specify the ticker name, number of tweets to extract, language of the tweets. The tweets successfully were extracted with 16 columns such as latitude, longitude, retweeted, isRetweet, retweetCount, screenname, statusSource, replyToUID, id, replyToSID, truncated, created, favoriteCount, replyToSN, favorited, and text. Sample text tweets are shown in Fig. 12–2. The twListToDF() method was used to convert tweets into data frame; then it can be converted into apple.csv file.

Preprocessing: There were many steps involved to preprocess the tweets using Text mining library "tm" and tm_map() method. The csv file was first loaded and then corpus created from the file. Then corpus was converted into lower case; numbers, punctuations, URL, whitespace, and stopwords were removed by using parameter tolower, removeNumbers, removePunctuation, removeURL, stripWhitespace, and stopwords ("english"), respectively.

Sentiment analysis: After preprocessing the data, TDM was created using TermDocumentMatrix() method. The barplot() method was used to display the plot for all terms with their frequencies as shown in Fig. 12–3.

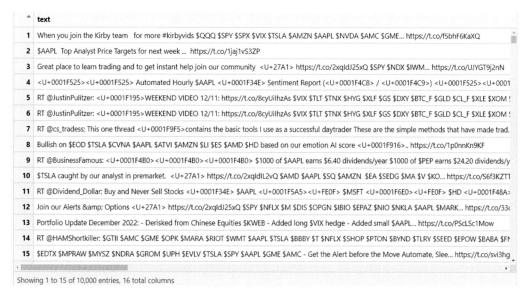

	text
1	When you join the Kirby team for more #kirbyvids $QQQ $SPY $SPX $VIX $TSLA $AMZN $AAPL $NVDA $AMC $GME... https://t.co/f5bhF6KaXQ
2	$AAPL Top Analyst Price Targets for next week ... https://t.co/1jaj1vS3ZP
3	Great place to learn trading and to get instant help join our community <U+27A1> https://t.co/2xqIdJ25xQ $SPY $NDX $IWM... https://t.co/UJYGT9j2nN
4	<U+0001F525><U+0001F525> Automated Hourly $AAPL <U+0001F34E> Sentiment Report (<U+0001F4C8> / <U+0001F4C9>) <U+0001F525><U+0001
5	RT @JustinPulitzer: <U+0001F195>WEEKEND VIDEO 12/11: https://t.co/8cyUilhzAs $VIX $TLT $TNX $HYG $XLF $GS $DXY $BTC_F $GLD $CL_F $XLE $XOM !
6	RT @JustinPulitzer: <U+0001F195>WEEKEND VIDEO 12/11: https://t.co/8cyUilhzAs $VIX $TLT $TNX $HYG $XLF $GS $DXY $BTC_F $GLD $CL_F $XLE $XOM !
7	RT @cs_tradess: This one thread <U+0001F9F5>contains the basic tools I use as a successful daytrader These are the simple methods that have made trad.
8	Bullish on $EOD $TSLA $CVNA $AAPL $ATVI $AMZN $LI $ES $AMD $HD based on our emotion AI score <U+0001F916>.. https://t.co/1p0nnKn9KF
9	RT @BusinessFamous: <U+0001F4B0><U+0001F4B0><U+0001F4B0> $1000 of $AAPL earns $6.40 dividends/year $1000 of $PEP earns $24.20 dividends/y
10	$TSLA caught by our analyst in premarket. <U+27A1> https://t.co/2xqIdIL2vQ $AMD $AAPL $SQ $AMZN $EA $SEDG $MA $V $KO... https://t.co/S6f3KZT1
11	RT @Dividend_Dollar: Buy and Never Sell Stocks <U+0001F34E> $AAPL <U+0001F5A5><U+FE0F> $MSFT <U+0001F6E0><U+FE0F> $HD <U+0001F48A>
12	Join our Alerts & Options <U+27A1> https://t.co/2xqIdJ25xQ $SPY $NFLX $M $DIS $OPGN $IBIO $EPAZ $NIO $NKLA $AAPL $MARK... https://t.co/33c
13	Portfolio Update December 2022: - Derisked from Chinese Equities $KWEB - Added long $VIX hedge - Added small $AAPL... https://t.co/PScLSc1Mow
14	RT @HAMShortkiller: $GTII $AMC $GME $OPK $MARA $RIOT $WMT $AAPL $TSLA $BBBY $T $NFLX $SHOP $PTON $BYND $TLRY $SEED $EPOW $BABA $FM
15	$EDTX $MPRAW $MYSZ $NDRA $GROM $UPH $EVLV $TSLA $SPY $AAPL $GME $AMC - Get the Alert before the Move Automate, Slee... https://t.co/svi3hg

Showing 1 to 15 of 10,000 entries, 16 total columns

FIGURE 12–2 Sample tweets.

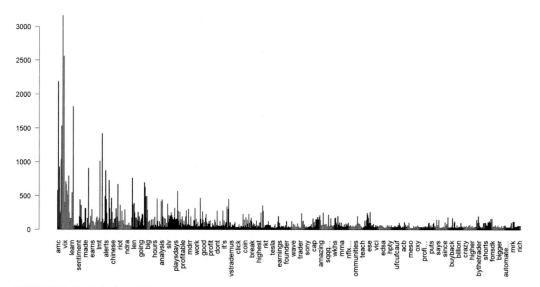

FIGURE 12–3 Barplot of tweets.

Each word is considered as tag, that is, representing with different font and color based on the number of frequencies. Wordcloud and wordcloud2 are two packages available in R Programming to create interactive wordclouds. Using this visual representation of tweets, we can clearly understand that few words with more frequencies available about Apple company. Few words with high frequencies are aapl, amzn, tsla, spy, trading, stock, price, etc., as shown in Figs. 12−4 and 12−5.

FIGURE 12–4 WordCloud of tweets.

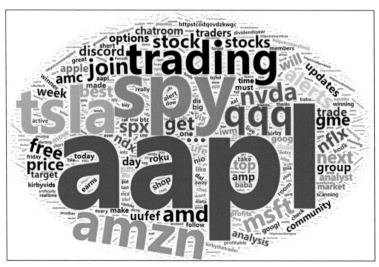

FIGURE 12–5 WordCloud2 of tweets.

The libraries required for sentiment score calculation are syuzhet, lubridate, ggplot2, scales, reshape2, and dplyr. The nrc sentiments were generated using get_nrc_sentiment() method by passing the tweets data. As a result, sentiment scores were generated for 10 emotions such as positive, negative, trust, surprise, sadness, joy, fear, disgust, anticipation, and anger with corresponding values as shown in Fig. 12–6, and the visual representation of sentiment scores of Apple tweets is displayed as shown in Fig. 12–7.

Sentiment scores are categorized into three types based on sentiment values. If sentiment value is equal to zero, it is "neutral," greater than zero, it is "positive" and less than zero, it is "negative." Sentiment categories and its corresponding values are shown in Fig. 12–8.

```
> s <- get_nrc_sentiment(tweets)
> head(s)
  anger anticipation disgust fear joy sadness surprise trust negative positive
1     0            0       0    0   0       0        0     1        0        1
2     0            2       0    0   0       0        0     2        0        2
3     0            0       0    0   0       0        0     0        0        3
4     0            0       0    0   0       0        0     1        0        0
5     0            0       0    0   0       0        0     0        0        0
6     0            0       0    0   0       0        0     0        0        0
```

FIGURE 12–6 nrc sentiments of tweets with 10 emotions.

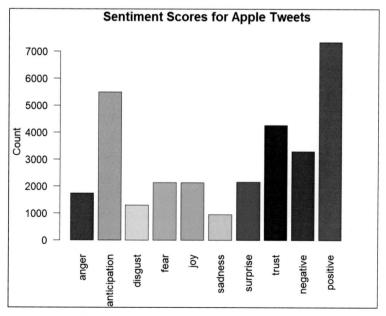

FIGURE 12–7 Sentiment scores of tweets.

```
> table(category_senti)
category_senti
Negative  Neutral Positive
    1952     2648     5400
```

FIGURE 12-8 Sentiment categories of tweets.

	AAPL.Open	AAPL.High	AAPL.Low	AAPL.Close	AAPL.Volume	AAPL.Adjusted
2008-01-02	7.116786	7.152143	6.876786	6.958571	1079178800	5.941449
2008-01-03	6.978929	7.049643	6.881786	6.961786	842066400	5.944194
2008-01-04	6.837500	6.892857	6.388929	6.430357	1455832000	5.490445
2008-01-07	6.473214	6.557143	6.079643	6.344286	2072193200	5.416954
2008-01-08	6.433571	6.516429	6.100000	6.116071	1523816000	5.222096
2008-01-09	6.117857	6.410714	6.010714	6.407143	1813882000	5.470623
2008-01-10	6.342143	6.464286	6.264643	6.357857	1482975200	5.428541
2008-01-11	6.285714	6.351786	6.071429	6.167500	1232285600	5.266009
2008-01-14	6.340000	6.407857	6.256071	6.385000	1100450400	5.451717
2008-01-15	6.347143	6.400714	5.880714	6.037143	2343278000	5.154707
2008-01-16	5.901071	6.036071	5.596429	5.701429	2213845200	4.868062
2008-01-17	5.768214	5.905714	5.657857	5.746071	1757859600	4.906178
2008-01-18	5.775357	5.919643	5.700357	5.762857	1724343600	4.920512
2008-01-22	5.287857	5.713571	5.214286	5.558571	2434754000	4.746086
2008-01-23	4.863929	5.000000	4.505000	4.966786	3372969600	4.240801
2008-01-24	4.999643	5.025000	4.714643	4.842857	2005866800	4.134986
2008-01-25	4.963929	4.967500	4.628929	4.643214	1554739200	3.964524
2008-01-28	4.577143	4.757143	4.516071	4.643214	1474844000	3.964524
2008-01-29	4.683929	4.742500	4.608929	4.697857	1099982800	4.011180
2008-01-30	4.691786	4.837500	4.642857	4.720714	1243051600	4.030697

Showing 1 to 20 of 3,728 entries, 6 total columns

FIGURE 12-9 Dataset snippet.

12.5 Forecasting on financial stock data

There are four libraries needed to import, such as quantmod, xts, PerformanceAnalytics, and rugarch. Apple stock prices data were loaded using getSymbols("AAPL") duration from January 2nd, 2008 to October 20th, 2022. There are 3728 records and six columns in these data, namely AAPL opening price, low of the day, high of the day, AAPL closing price, adjusted prices, and also volume as shown in Fig. 12−9.

The chart was created using chartSeries() for 2022−10. This chart is in candle stick format. The first candles stick for October 3rd, 2022. In each candle, the top one is high of the day and

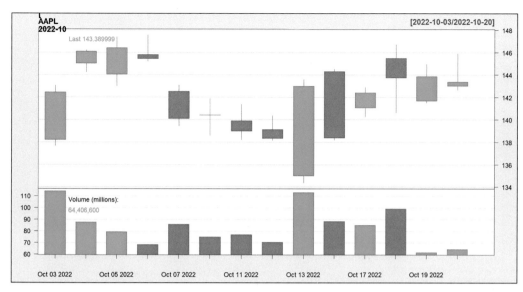

FIGURE 12–10 Candle stick format of data.

lower one is for low of the day. If the candle is green, the bottom line (opening price) was lower than top line (closing price) of the day. If the candle is orange, the bottom line (closing price) was lower than top line (opening price) of the day as shown in Fig. 12−10.

The entire data can be displayed as a chart in which, there is lot of fluctuations as shown in Fig. 12−11. This type of time series data is difficult to model to analyze using standard time series methods.

For analyzing we do not use these data directly, need to convert into daily return data. The CalculateReturns() is used to calculate daily returns by using closing price. Return value calculated as taking second value subtracted by first value and divided by first value. The histogram of return looks like symmetric distribution as shown in Fig. 12−12 (*left*).

The chart histogram was created by adding density curve in green color, normal curve in red color, and histogram in blue color as shown in Fig. 12−12 (*right*). The curve for return is taller, and there are days having very high and very low return values. Fig. 12−13 depicts the chart series of return with white theme. Even with a lot of fluctuations or volatility, but this plot depicts that there are stationary time series data without any trend or seasonal component.

The monthly volatility was created using chart.RollingPerformance() by passing the following parameters such as return (2008−22), width = 22 (trading days in month), sd.annualized, scale = 252 (trading days in year) as shown in Fig. 12−14. In October 2008, it went very high and back very down, and again in October 2020, it went very high and back very down. This figure clearly gives the high and low volatility of data.

The yearly volatility was created using chart.RollingPerformance() by passing the following parameters such as return (2008−22), width = 252 (trading days in month),

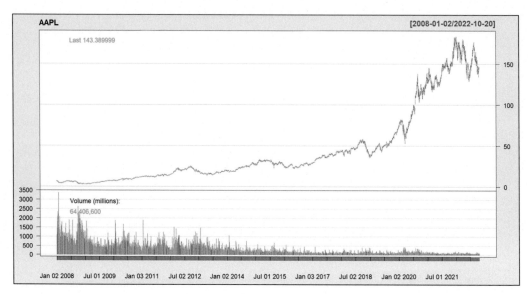

FIGURE 12–11 Chart representation of data.

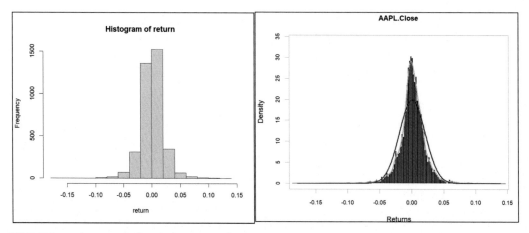

FIGURE 12–12 Histogram (*left*) and Distribution of data (*right*).

sd.annualized, scale = 252 (trading days in year) as shown in Fig. 12−15. This figure more clearly gives the high and low volatility of data. In 2022, the volatility increased.

12.6 Implementation of GARCH models

The implementation was done using R Programming [35]. GARCH models are very well suited for time series data that are highly volatile. GARCH stands for Generalized AutoRegressive Conditional Heteroskedasticity. Heteroskedasticity means that variances do

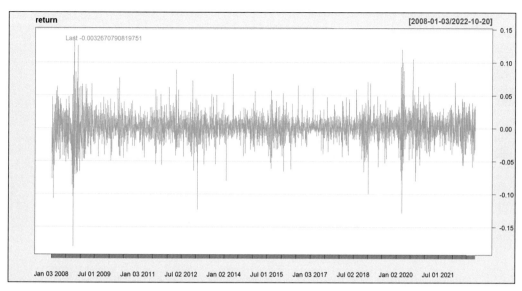

FIGURE 12–13 Chart series of return values.

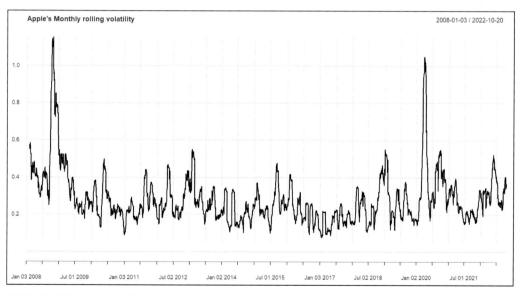

FIGURE 12–14 Monthly volatility.

not remain the same, but they vary with time. Apple stock prices data are highly volatile. The variants of GARCH Model is as follows: Standard GARCH Model, GJR-GARCH, GARCH with sstd, GJR-GARCH in mean, AR(1) GJR-GARCH, and Stimulating stock prices.

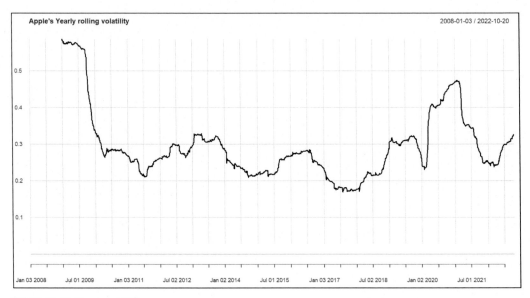

FIGURE 12–15 Yearly volatility.

12.6.1 Standard GARCH model

The standard GARCH model was created with constant mean. The specification was created using ugarchspec() with three things as follows:

- Mean model (armaOrder = c(0,0))—AutoRegressive Moving Average
- Variance model (sGARCH)—Standard GARCH model
- Distribution model (norm)—Normal Distribution

The model was created by using ugarchfit() by passing return and specification. The following Fig. 12−16 shows the result of standard GARCH model.

This model has four parameters such as mu, omega, alpha1, and beta1 with standard error, estimated value, p value, and the t value. The p values are very low, almost 0; that means all four parameters are statistically significant. Eq. (12−1) has Returns of the model R_t, average μ, and the error term e_t. This error term follows the normal distribution with means 0 and variance σ_t^2. The μ value of 0.001860 is substituted in Eq. (12−2). Eq. (12−3) gives the variability at time t and αe_{t-1}^2—prediction error for the previous time period. The ω, α, and β values are substituted in Eq. (12−4).

$$R_t = \mu + e_t \qquad\qquad (12-1)$$

$$R_t = 0.001860 + e_t \qquad\qquad (12-2)$$

$$\sigma_t^2 = \omega + \alpha e_{t-1}^2 + \beta \sigma_{t-1}^2 \qquad\qquad (12-3)$$

```
R 4.1.2 · ~/
*          GARCH Model Fit          *
*-----------------------------------*

Conditional Variance Dynamics
-----------------------------------
GARCH Model      : sGARCH(1,1)
Mean Model       : ARFIMA(0,0,0)
Distribution     : norm

Optimal Parameters
------------------------------------
        Estimate  Std. Error  t value Pr(>|t|)
mu      0.001860    0.000231   8.0449  0.00000
omega   0.000015    0.000004   3.8681  0.00011
alpha1  0.110692    0.015874   6.9730  0.00000
beta1   0.851391    0.007979 106.7027  0.00000

Robust Standard Errors:
        Estimate  Std. Error  t value Pr(>|t|)
mu      0.001860    0.000797  2.33286 0.019655
omega   0.000015    0.000022  0.65779 0.510674
alpha1  0.110692    0.099309  1.11462 0.265013
beta1   0.851391    0.035806 23.77757 0.000000

LogLikelihood : 9739.421

Information Criteria
------------------------------------

Akaike       -5.2243
Bayes        -5.2176
Shibata      -5.2243
Hannan-Quinn -5.2219
```

```
R 4.1.2 · ~/
Weighted Ljung-Box Test on Standardized Residuals
------------------------------------
                        statistic p-value
Lag[1]                     0.3849  0.5350
Lag[2*(p+q)+(p+q)-1][2]    0.5574  0.6673
Lag[4*(p+q)+(p+q)-1][5]    3.3841  0.3414
d.o.f=0
H0 : No serial correlation

Weighted Ljung-Box Test on Standardized Squared Residuals
------------------------------------
                        statistic p-value
Lag[1]                     0.3552  0.5512
Lag[2*(p+q)+(p+q)-1][5]    1.8340  0.6581
Lag[4*(p+q)+(p+q)-1][9]    3.1700  0.7306
d.o.f=2

Weighted ARCH LM Tests
------------------------------------
            Statistic Shape Scale P-Value
ARCH Lag[3]    0.7384 0.500 2.000  0.3902
ARCH Lag[5]    2.3486 1.440 1.667  0.3992
ARCH Lag[7]    2.5283 2.315 1.543  0.6066

Nyblom stability test
------------------------------------
Joint Statistic:  15.5251
Individual Statistics:
mu     0.1035
omega  2.4064
alpha1 0.2903
beta1  0.3128
```

```
R 4.1.2 · ~/
Asymptotic Critical Values (10% 5% 1%)
Joint Statistic:          1.07 1.24 1.6
Individual Statistic:     0.35 0.47 0.75

Sign Bias Test
------------------------------------
                   t-value   prob sig
Sign Bias           1.0874 0.27694
Negative Sign Bias  0.7918 0.42856
Positive Sign Bias  0.5525 0.58063
Joint Effect        6.8369 0.07728    *


Adjusted Pearson Goodness-of-Fit Test:
------------------------------------
  group statistic p-value(g-1)
1    20     126.9    5.738e-18
2    30     139.5    2.144e-16
3    40     156.6    4.934e-16
4    50     165.2    1.667e-14


Elapsed time : 0.2048872

>
```

FIGURE 12–16 Result of standard GARCH model.

$$\sigma_t{}^2 = 0.000015 + 0.110692e_{t-1}^2 + 0.851391\sigma_{t-1}^2 \qquad (12-4)$$

if we do not have beta term in the variance, then it reduces to $\text{ARCH}(1) = \omega + \alpha e_{t-1}{}^2$.

12.6.1.1 Model output

The information criteria are useful to avoid unnecessarily choosing very complex model. It is based on four different methods such as Akaike, Bayes, Shibata, and Hannan-Quinn. The simpler model has very low information criteria, and this model is very useful for returns as shown in Fig. 12–8. The elapsed time is 0.2048872. Another output is *L* junk Box Test on Standardized Residuals. Null Hypothesis H0 is no serial correlation because *p* value of Lag [1] is more than *p* value of Lag$[2 \times (p+q) + (p+q) - 1]$ [2]. We cannot reject null hypothesis. Next output is Standardized Squared Residuals, there is no evidence of serial correlation, and also it behaves like white noise process. Therefore, this GARCH model is valid. Another test is Goodness-of-Fit Test, in which all the p values are quite smaller than 0.5. That means that we can reject null hypothesis and conclude for residuals that we used, in this case, normal distribution is not really a good choice.

If the distribution for the residuals is good fit, then this Goodness-of-Fit Test should give the p value greater than 0.5, and there is a scope to improve this model. There are 12 different plots generated when plotting. These are News-Impact Curve, ACF of Squared Standardized Residuals, ACF of Standardized Residuals, QQ-Plot of Standardized Residuals, Empirical Density of Standardized Residuals, Cross Correlation, ACF of absolute observations, ACF of squared observations, ACF of observations, Conditional SD, Series with 1% VaR Limits, and Series with 2 conditional SD superimposed. These 12 plots can be displayed as single plot as shown in Fig. 12–17.

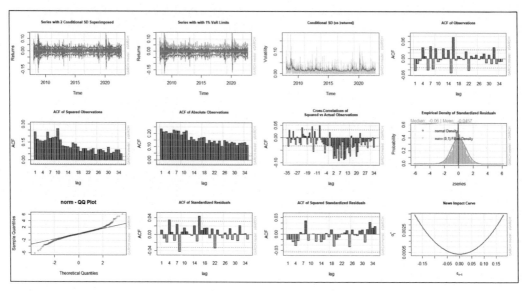

FIGURE 12–17 Plots of standard GARCH model.

The series with 2 conditional standard deviation superimposed is the first plot. The red lines are at 2 SD. Almost 95% of the data values on returns. The next chart is series with 1% value at risk limits. The next plot is for conditional SD versus returns. Returns are absolute value, and blue lines are SD, and next plot is for autocorrelations for the observations. These are 4 squared observations, and almost all lines are above red lines, which indicate the presence of significant autocorrelations. Plots 5 and 6 represent the squared and absolute observations. The next plot is for cross-correlation of squared and actual observations, and next one is histogram for residuals or errors, which is slightly different from normal distributions. The next one is QQ-Plot in which the tails digress from the ordinary appropriation fundamentally both for lower values and higher qualities. The next plot refers to the autocorrelations for normalized residuals improving altogether and four squared normalized residuals, and all the values are within the red line, and this curve indicates whether we have news that has positive or negative impact on returns.

12.6.1.2 Forecasting

The ugarchforecast() with two parameters such as model and next 30 trading, then the fitted values plot will be generated as shown in Fig. 12−18 (*left*).

This is constant mean model, so all the predictions are also constant. The variability can be plotted using sigma values as shown in Fig. 12−18 (*right*). The model expects that for the next 30 days, the volatility is going to decrease. Analyze the volatility (v) with sqrt(252) × sigma(model). The w is weight assigned to risky asset. 5% of risk assign to the volatility. Then the plot shown in Fig. 12−19 represents the merging of v and w. The top plot is for v or volatility, and bottom plot is for weight value and is assigned to danger or risky asset.

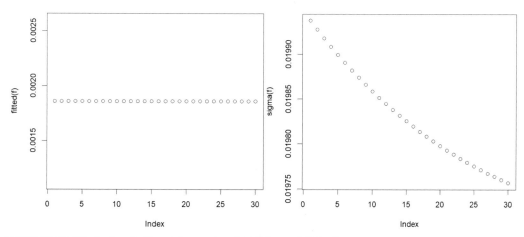

FIGURE 12–18 Fitted values (*left*) and sigma values (*right*) for next 30 trading.

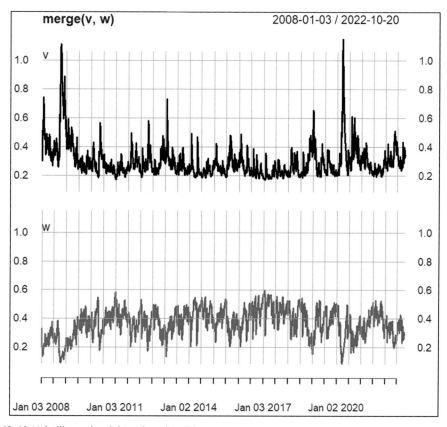

FIGURE 12–19 Volatility and weight assigned to risky asset.

```
R 4.1.2 · ~/
*---------------------------------------*
*          GARCH Model Fit              *
*---------------------------------------*

Conditional Variance Dynamics
-----------------------------------
GARCH Model    : sGARCH(1,1)
Mean Model     : ARFIMA(0,0,0)
Distribution   : sstd

Optimal Parameters
------------------------------------
        Estimate  Std. Error  t value  Pr(>|t|)
mu      0.001531   0.000258   5.9242   0.000000
omega   0.000000   0.000000   2.0154   0.043864
alpha1  0.099977   0.014099   7.0909   0.000000
beta1   0.885072   0.014213  62.2713   0.000000
skew    1.003438   0.022615  44.3697   0.000000
shape   5.112057   0.521230   9.8077   0.000000

Robust Standard Errors:
        Estimate  Std. Error  t value  Pr(>|t|)
mu      0.001531   0.000260   5.88774  0.000000
omega   0.000008   0.000011   0.72495  0.468485
alpha1  0.099977   0.029031   3.44375  0.000574
beta1   0.885072   0.024580  36.00792  0.000000
skew    1.003438   0.022737  44.13335  0.000000
shape   5.112057   1.047114   4.88204  0.000001

LogLikelihood : 9886.915
```

```
R 4.1.2 · ~/
Information Criteria
------------------------------------
Akaike        -5.3023
Bayes         -5.2923
Shibata       -5.3023
Hannan-Quinn  -5.2988

Weighted Ljung-Box Test on Standardized Residuals
------------------------------------
                            statistic  p-value
Lag[1]                        0.4123   0.5208
Lag[2*(p+q)+(p+q)-1][2]       0.5717   0.6609
Lag[4*(p+q)+(p+q)-1][5]       3.5795   0.3113
d.o.f=0
H0 : No serial correlation

Weighted Ljung-Box Test on Standardized Squared Residuals
------------------------------------
                            statistic  p-value
Lag[1]                        0.09807  0.7542
Lag[2*(p+q)+(p+q)-1][5]       1.34545  0.7778
Lag[4*(p+q)+(p+q)-1][9]       2.41332  0.8504
d.o.f=2

Weighted ARCH LM Tests
------------------------------------
            Statistic  Shape  Scale  P-Value
ARCH Lag[3]    0.6717  0.500  2.000  0.4125
ARCH Lag[5]    2.0241  1.440  1.667  0.4659
ARCH Lag[7]    2.2189  2.315  1.543  0.6710

Nyblom stability test
```

```
R 4.1.2 · ~/
------------------------------------
Joint Statistic:  5.3218
Individual Statistics:
mu      0.10819
omega   0.93968
alpha1  0.72297
beta1   0.81349
skew    0.04757
shape   1.11570

Asymptotic Critical Values (10% 5% 1%)
Joint Statistic:        1.49 1.68 2.12
Individual Statistic:   0.35 0.47 0.75

Sign Bias Test
------------------------------------
                    t-value   prob  sig
Sign Bias           1.3335  0.18245
Negative Sign Bias  0.5067  0.61239
Positive Sign Bias  0.6741  0.50028
Joint Effect        7.8456  0.04931  **

Adjusted Pearson Goodness-of-Fit Test:
------------------------------------
    group  statistic  p-value(g-1)
1    20      25.33      0.14991
2    30      43.25      0.04314
3    40      52.11      0.07799
4    50      53.67      0.30005

Elapsed time : 0.6121881
```

FIGURE 12–20 Results of GARCH with skewed student t-distribution.

Once the volatility is increased, the weight value is assigned to danger or risky asset and is bit lower and vice versa.

12.6.2 GARCH with skewed student t-distribution

In the standard GARCH model, normal distribution is not really good model for residuals. To overcome this drawback, the GARCH with skewed student t-distribution model applied to captures this distribution more accurately. This model was created using sstd instead of norm as shown in Fig. 12–20. This model has six parameters: mu, omega, alpha1, beta1, skew, and shape.

The skew value is greater than 1 and shape, that is, degrees of freedom, is 5. The elapsed time is 0.6121881. This GARCH with skewed t-distribution is the better choice compared with standard GARCH model.

The plot of this model is shown in Fig. 12–21. From the plot the tail now aligned with the straight line in much better way for sstd-QQ Plot and also information criteria are improved, that means these values are lower than those of the previous model.

12.6.3 GJR-GARCH

GJR-GARCH model was developed by Glosten–Jagannathan–Runkle. The GJR-GARCH model was created by passing gjrGARCH. This output of the model is shown in Fig. 12–22.

Fig. 12–23 clearly shows the plot of GJR-GARCH Model. There is big change in 12th plot. As per this model, when news has positive impact on stock price, the increase in prices is gradual. It is not getting huge jumps. But when the impact of certain news on the market is negative, the impact is significantly higher. So as per this model, the news impact is not symmetric, but it is much higher for negative news comparing to positive. This model has seven parameters: mu,

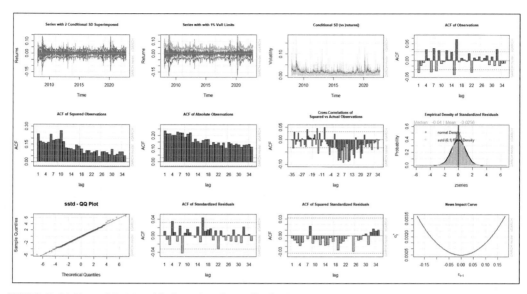

FIGURE 12–21 Plots of GARCH with skewed student *t*-distribution.

FIGURE 12–22 Results of GJR-GARCH.

omega, alpha1, beta1, gamma1, skew, and shape. The symmetric skew value is 1, and shape (degrees of freedom) is 5. The elapsed time is 0.933548. The μ value of 0.001305 is substituted in Eq. (12−5). Eq. (12−6) gives ω, α, γ, and β values, which are substituted in Eq. (12−7). The information criteria of this model are even lower; this model is better than the previous two models.

$$R_t = 0.001305 + e_t \qquad (12-5)$$

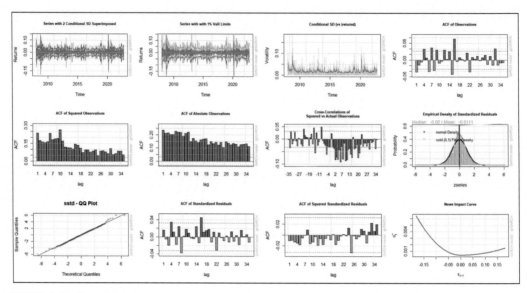

FIGURE 12–23 Plots of GJR-GARCH.

$$\sigma_t^2 = \omega + (\alpha + \gamma)e_{t-1}^2 + \beta\sigma_{t-1}^2 \qquad (12-6)$$

$$\sigma_t^2 = 0.000011 + (0.033037 + 0.151718)e_{t-1}^2 + 0.868844\sigma_{t-1}^2 \qquad (12-7)$$

12.6.4 AR(1) GJR-GARCH

To create AR(1) GJR-GARCH model, the parameter need to change as $c(1,0)$. The plot of this model is shown in Fig. 12–24.

This model has eight parameters such as mu, ar1, omega, alpha1, beta1, gamma1, skew, and shape. The ar1 value is not statistically significant. So, adding this term is not really helping our model. This model is not good as the previous three models.

12.6.5 GJR-GARCH in mean

To create GJR-GARCH in mean model, the parameter needs to change as $c(0,0)$, and two more parameters need to be specified such as archm = T and archpow = 2. The plot of this model is shown in Fig. 12–25.

This model has eight parameters such as mu, archm, omega, alpha1, beta1, gamma1, skew, and shape. The archm value is not statistically significant. So, adding this term is not really helping our model. This model is also not good as the first three models.

```
*          GARCH Model Fit          *
*---------------------------------------*

Conditional Variance Dynamics
---------------------------------------
GARCH Model    : gjrGARCH(1,1)
Mean Model     : ARFIMA(1,0,0)
Distribution   : sstd

Optimal Parameters
---------------------------------------
        Estimate  Std. Error  t value   Pr(>|t|)
mu      0.001295  0.000250    5.17462   0.00000
ar1     0.008621  0.016532    0.52148   0.60203
omega   0.000011  0.000001   10.98138   0.00000
alpha1  0.032520  0.003325    9.77894   0.00000
beta1   0.868714  0.009851   88.18765   0.00000
gamma1  0.153055  0.021150    7.23652   0.00000
skew    0.998317  0.022374   44.61973   0.00000
shape   5.506537  0.431265   12.76833   0.00000

Robust Standard Errors:
        Estimate  Std. Error  t value   Pr(>|t|)
mu      0.001295  0.000268    4.83625   0.000001
ar1     0.008621  0.015241    0.56564   0.571636
omega   0.000011  0.000001    8.20275   0.000000
alpha1  0.032520  0.008723    3.72792   0.000193
beta1   0.868714  0.010646   81.59840   0.000000
gamma1  0.153055  0.025495    6.00335   0.000000
skew    0.998317  0.021739   45.92357   0.000000
shape   5.506537  0.519896   10.59161   0.000000

LogLikelihood : 9917.92
```

```
Information Criteria
---------------------------------------
Akaike       -5.3179
Bayes        -5.3045
Shibata      -5.3179
Hannan-Quinn -5.3132

Weighted Ljung-Box Test on Standardized Residuals
---------------------------------------
                          statistic p-value
Lag[1]                     0.2539   0.6143
Lag[2*(p+q)+(p+q)-1][2]    0.2950   0.9946
Lag[4*(p+q)+(p+q)-1][5]    3.0334   0.4229
d.o.f=1
H0 : No serial correlation

Weighted Ljung-Box Test on Standardized Squared Residuals
---------------------------------------
                          statistic p-value
Lag[1]                     0.4614   0.4970
Lag[2*(p+q)+(p+q)-1][5]    1.7264   0.6843
Lag[4*(p+q)+(p+q)-1][9]    2.7673   0.7967
d.o.f=2

Weighted ARCH LM Tests
---------------------------------------
              Statistic Shape Scale P-Value
ARCH Lag[3]   0.6447    0.500 2.000 0.4220
ARCH Lag[5]   2.0368    1.440 1.667 0.4632
ARCH Lag[7]   2.3001    2.315 1.543 0.6539

Nyblom stability test
```

```
Individual Statistics:
mu      0.27876
ar1     0.29292
omega   5.77849
alpha1  1.12858
beta1   1.14651
gamma1  0.90037
skew    0.03951
shape   1.44517

Asymptotic Critical Values (10% 5% 1%)
Joint Statistic:       1.89 2.11 2.59
Individual Statistic:  0.35 0.47 0.75

Sign Bias Test
---------------------------------------
                     t-value  prob sig
Sign Bias            1.38151  0.1672
Negative Sign Bias   1.08651  0.2773
Positive Sign Bias   0.05871  0.9532
Joint Effect         2.54185  0.4678

Adjusted Pearson Goodness-of-Fit Test:
---------------------------------------
    group statistic p-value(g-1)
1   20    26.27     0.1230
2   30    34.14     0.2342
3   40    41.30     0.3706
4   50    53.13     0.3181

Elapsed time : 1.228885
```

FIGURE 12–24 Results of AR(1) GJR-GARCH.

```
*          GARCH Model Fit          *
*---------------------------------------*

Conditional Variance Dynamics
---------------------------------------
GARCH Model    : gjrGARCH(1,1)
Mean Model     : ARFIMA(0,0,0)
Distribution   : sstd

Optimal Parameters
---------------------------------------
        Estimate   Std. Error  t value    Pr(>|t|)
mu       0.001327  0.000329     4.038301  0.000054
archm   -0.088257  0.986858    -0.089432  0.928739
omega    0.000011  0.000001    11.478626  0.000000
alpha1   0.032987  0.005499     5.998831  0.000000
beta1    0.869095  0.009872    88.040251  0.000000
gamma1   0.151724  0.021421     7.082836  0.000000
skew     0.998092  0.022531    44.298086  0.000000
shape    5.494897  0.437802    12.551105  0.000000

Robust Standard Errors:
        Estimate   Std. Error  t value    Pr(>|t|)
mu       0.001327  0.000369     3.597492  0.000321
archm   -0.088257  0.987515    -0.089372  0.928786
omega    0.000011  0.000001     9.241079  0.000000
alpha1   0.032987  0.008720     3.782725  0.000155
beta1    0.869095  0.010808    80.413042  0.000000
gamma1   0.151724  0.025719     5.899202  0.000000
skew     0.998092  0.021494    46.436621  0.000000
shape    5.494897  0.504717    10.887074  0.000000

LogLikelihood : 9917.787
```

```
Information Criteria
---------------------------------------
Akaike       -5.3178
Bayes        -5.3045
Shibata      -5.3178
Hannan-Quinn -5.3131

Weighted Ljung-Box Test on Standardized Residuals
---------------------------------------
                          statistic p-value
Lag[1]                     0.9014   0.3424
Lag[2*(p+q)+(p+q)-1][2]    0.9463   0.5160
Lag[4*(p+q)+(p+q)-1][5]    3.6741   0.2976
d.o.f=0
H0 : No serial correlation

Weighted Ljung-Box Test on Standardized Squared Residuals
---------------------------------------
                          statistic p-value
Lag[1]                     0.4238   0.5150
Lag[2*(p+q)+(p+q)-1][5]    1.7108   0.6881
Lag[4*(p+q)+(p+q)-1][9]    2.7705   0.7962
d.o.f=2

Weighted ARCH LM Tests
---------------------------------------
              Statistic Shape Scale P-Value
ARCH Lag[3]   0.6484    0.500 2.000 0.4207
ARCH Lag[5]   2.0812    1.440 1.667 0.4536
ARCH Lag[7]   2.3436    2.315 1.543 0.6448

Nyblom stability test
```

```
Individual Statistics:
mu      0.28413
archm   0.18866
omega   5.61232
alpha1  1.13422
beta1   1.14941
gamma1  0.90083
skew    0.03874
shape   1.45016

Asymptotic Critical Values (10% 5% 1%)
Joint Statistic:       1.89 2.11 2.59
Individual Statistic:  0.35 0.47 0.75

Sign Bias Test
---------------------------------------
                     t-value  prob sig
Sign Bias            1.44921  0.1474
Negative Sign Bias   1.09581  0.2732
Positive Sign Bias   0.08107  0.9354
Joint Effect         2.74543  0.4326

Adjusted Pearson Goodness-of-Fit Test:
---------------------------------------
    group statistic p-value(g-1)
1   20    24.98     0.1613
2   30    31.50     0.3422
3   40    42.91     0.3074
4   50    54.12     0.2852

Elapsed time : 1.740633
```

FIGURE 12–25 Results of GJR-GARCH in mean.

12.7 Stimulating stock prices

The GJR-GARCH model is best one to consider for simulation. Now 1-year forecast is obtained for two different years. To create forecast, ugarchforecast() method is used with parameters such as data, fitORspec, and n.ahead = 12 (1 year). Two forecasts are created for 2008 and 2022. Then plot of the forecast for 2008 and 2022 is shown in Fig. 12–26.

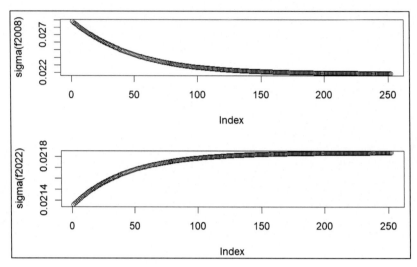

FIGURE 12–26 Forecasting values for next one year of 2018 and 2022.

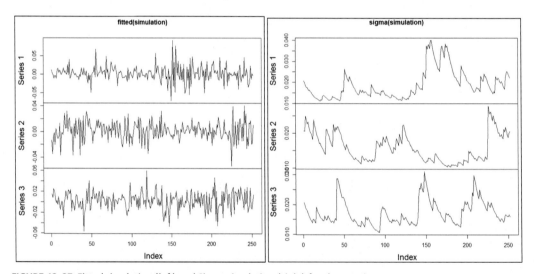

FIGURE 12–27 Fitted simulation (*left*) and Sigma simulation (*right*) for three series.

In 2008, we have very high volatility. So, it was forecasted after 2008 for next 1 year, the volatility is likely to fall. At the end of October of 2022, the volatility was low, so based on the forecast, it is expected that the volatility is going to increase in 2023. Basically, for the long run, the volatility is expected to go toward average. The ugarchpath() is used to create a simulation with specification, number of time series simulator return we want (3), 1 year of trading days, and random seed as 123. Using plot.zoo(fitted(simulation)) method, the simulation output with three simulated returns values based on our model are shown in Fig. 12−27

```
> tail(AAPL)
           AAPL.Open AAPL.High AAPL.Low AAPL.Close AAPL.Volume AAPL.Adjusted
2022-10-13    134.99    143.59   134.37     142.99   113224000        142.99
2022-10-14    144.31    144.52   138.19     138.38    88512300        138.38
2022-10-17    141.07    142.90   140.27     142.41    85250900        142.41
2022-10-18    145.49    146.70   140.61     143.75    99136600        143.75
2022-10-19    141.69    144.95   141.50     143.86    61758300        143.86
2022-10-20    143.02    145.89   142.65     143.39    64522000        143.39
```

FIGURE 12–28 Last six records of dataset using tail().

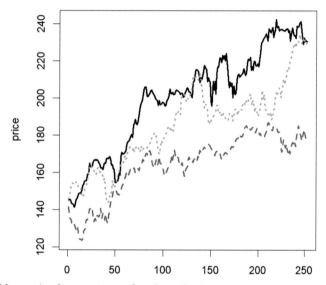

FIGURE 12–29 Plot of forecasting for next 1 year of apple stock price.

(*left*). Similarly, plot.zoo(sigma(simulation)) is used to display the simulation output with three simulated variability for 252 days in 2023 as shown in Fig. 12−27 (*right*).

Now instead of using the returns and the sigma, the actual Apple share prices are used. The tail(AAPL) is used to get the actual values as shown in Fig. 12−28.

The closing value of October 20th, 2022 is 143.39. The price of Apple stock formed using closing price as starting price is price <- 143.39 × apply(fitted(simulation), 2, "cumsum") + 143.39. Then, this price is plotted with line type of width 3 using matplot().

Apple stock price for next 1 year with three different simulated lines is shown in Fig. 12−29. Red simulated series line reached around 180$ maximum, and green series line continued to rise and reached around 220$ maximum, then fell back toward 190$, and finally, black simulated series line provided the best result out of three. As per black simulated line, Apple will have the stock price of 240$ before end of 2023.

12.8 Conclusion

This chapter attempts to forecast the Apple stock market financial data from January 2008 to October 2022. Sentiment analysis technique was applied on the data collected from Twitter about Apple company. Based on the emotions of the user or customer, the sentiment score was generated and categorized as neutral, positive, and negative. Then, the GARCH (Generalized AutoRegressive Conditional Heteroskedasticity) is one of the best models to work with heteroskedasticity issues. The different types of GARCH models were created for forecasting the apple stock market financial data in R Programming. The variants of GARCH Model used are as follows: Standard GARCH Model, GARCH with skewed student t-distribution, GJR-GARCH (Glosten−Jagannathan−Runkle-GARCH), GJR-GARCH in mean, AR(1) GJR-GARCH. Information criteria are calculated and compared with all the models. The results showed that GJR-GARCH model outperformed other models. Finally, simulation was created to forecast for next 1 year for two different years, 2008 and 2022. The volatility decreased after 2008 and increased after 2022 for next 1 year. Finally, the sentiment analysis gives the pathway based on those discussions and emotions of the people and makes the changes in the stock market.

References

[1] T. Bollerslev, Generalized autoregressive conditional heteroskedasticity, J. Econom. 31 (3) (1986) 307−327.

[2] T.G. Andersen, T. Bollerslev, Answering the skeptics: yes, standard volatility models do provide accurate forecasts, Int. Econ. Rev. (1998) 885−905.

[3] T. Bollerslev, R.Y. Chou, K.F. Kroner, ARCH modeling in finance: a review of the theory and empirical evidence, J. Econom. 52 (1-2) (1992) 5−59.

[4] R.F. Engle, Autoregressive conditional heteroscedasticity with estimates of the variance of United Kingdom inflation, Econometrica (1982) 987−1007.

[5] A.S. Mhmoud, F.M. Dawalbait, Estimating and forecasting stock market volatility using GARCH models: empirical evidence from Saudi Arabia, Int. J. Eng. Res. Technol. 4 (2) (2015) 464−471.

[6] A.C. Jishag, et al., Predicting the stock market behavior using historic data analysis and news sentiment analysis in R, First International Conference on Sustainable Technologies for Computational Intelligence, Springer, Singapore, 2020.

[7] P. Mehta, S. Pandya, K. Kotecha, Harvesting social media sentiment analysis to enhance stock market prediction using deep learning, PeerJ Comput. Sci. 7 (2021) e476.

[8] C.-R. Ko, H.-T. Chang, LSTM-based sentiment analysis for stock price forecast, PeerJ Comput. Sci. 7 (2021) e408.

[9] S. Wu, et al., S_I_LSTM: stock price prediction based on multiple data sources and sentiment analysis, Connect. Sci. 34 (1) (2022) 44−62.

[10] C. Gondaliya, A. Patel, T. Shah, Sentiment analysis and prediction of Indian stock market amid Covid-19 pandemic. IOP Conference Series: Materials Science and Engineering. Vol. 1020. No. 1. IOP Publishing, 2021.

[11] M.-L. Thormann, et al., Stock price predictions with LSTM neural networks and Twitter sentiment, Statist. Optim. Inf. Comput. 9 (2) (2021) 268−287.

[12] R.L. Manogna, Sentiment analysis of financial news for stock price prediction: empirical evidence from India. (2022).

[13] P. Koukaras, C. Nousi, C. Tjortjis, Stock market prediction using microblogging sentiment analysis and machine learning, Telecom. 3 (2) (2022). MDPI.

[14] N. Darapaneni, et al. Stock price prediction using sentiment analysis and deep learning for indian markets. arXiv preprint arXiv:2204.05783 (2022).

[15] R.A. Mendoza-Urdiales, et al., Twitter sentiment analysis and influence on stock performance using transfer entropy and EGARCH methods, Entropy 24 (7) (2022) 874.

[16] J.K. Koima, P.N. Mwita, D.K. Nassiuma. Volatility estimation of stock prices using Garch method. (2015).

[17] R.D. Vasudevan, S.C. Vetrivel, Forecasting stock market volatility using GARCH models: evidence from the Indian stock market, Asian J. Res. Soc. Sci. Humanit. 6 (8) (2016) 1565−1574.

[18] Q.T. Tran, L. Hao, Q.K. Trinh, A novel procedure to model and forecast mobile communication traffic by ARIMA/GARCH combination models, in: 2016 International Conference on Modeling, Simulation and Optimization Technologies and Applications (MSOTA2016). Atlantis Press, 2016.

[19] F.J.M. Costa, Forecasting volatility using GARCH models. Diss. Universidade do Minho (Portugal), 2017.

[20] S.A. Hassan, A time series analysis of major indexes using GARCH model with regime shifts, Int. J. Financ. Res. 8 (4) (2017) 127−133.

[21] S.M. Abdullah, et al., Modeling and forecasting exchange rate volatility in Bangladesh using GARCH models: a comparison based on normal and Student's t-error distribution, Financ. Innov. 3 (1) (2017) 1−19.

[22] A. Maqsood, et al., Modeling stock market volatility using GARCH models: a case study of Nairobi Securities Exchange (NSE), Open. J. Stat. 7 (2) (2017) 369−381.

[23] M.Z. Shbier, K.-M. Ku Ruhana, O. Mahmod, SWGARCH model for time series forecasting, Proc. 1st Int. Conf. Internet Things Mach. Learn. (2017).

[24] E. Virginia, Application of GARCH model to forecast data and volatility of share price of energy (Study on Adaro Energy Tbk, LQ45). (2018).

[25] I.M.Md Ghani, H.A. Rahim, Modeling and forecasting of volatility using arma-garch: case study on malaysia natural rubber pricesNo. 1 IOP Conference Series: Materials Science and Engineering, Vol. 548, IOP Publishing, 2019.

[26] M.O. Adenomon, Financial time series analysis via backtesting approach, Linked Open Data-Applications, Trends and Future Developments, IntechOpen, 2020.

[27] N. Naik, B.R. Mohan, R.A. Jha, GARCH model identification for stock crises events, Procedia Computer Sci. 171 (2020) 1742−1749.

[28] S. Ravikumar, P. Saraf, Prediction of stock prices using machine learning (regression, classification) Algorithms. 2020 International Conference for Emerging Technology (INCET). IEEE, 2020.

[29] M. Vijh, et al., Stock closing price prediction using machine learning techniques, Procedia Comput. Sci. 167 (2020) 599−606.

[30] J. Gao, Research on stock price forecast based on ARIMA-GARCH model. E3S Web of Conferences. Vol. 292. EDP Sciences, 2021.

[31] C. Nybo, Sector volatility prediction performance using GARCH models and artificial neural networks. arXiv preprint arXiv:2110.09489 (2021).

[32] M.H. Odah, Comparison of GARCH & ARMA models to forecasting exchange rate, Math. Model. Eng. Probl. (2021).

[33] Y. Li, L. Zhang, Modelling and forecasting cyts stock prices using garch model, Front. Econ. Manag. Res. 2 (1) (2021) 32−37.

[34] P. Soni, Y. Tewari, D. Krishnan, Machine learning approaches in stock price prediction: a systematic reviewNo. 1 J. Phys.: Conf. Ser., 2161, IOP Publishing, 2022.

[35] R Programming <https://www.r-project.org>.

13

A metaheuristic harmony search optimization—based approach for hateful and offensive speech detection in social media

S. Saroja[1], S. Haseena[2]

[1]DEPARTMENT OF COMPUTER APPLICATIONS, NATIONAL INSTITUTE OF TECHNOLOGY, TRICHY, TAMIL NADU, INDIA [2]DEPARTMENT OF INFORMATION TECHNOLOGY, MEPCO SCHLENK ENGINEERING COLLEGE, SIVAKASI, TAMIL NADU, INDIA

13.1 Introduction

Everyone in the universe has the right to express themselves through speech. However, in the name of free speech, people are frequently mistreated and have backstabbed others, either verbally or physically. This is referred to as "hate speech." Hate speech (HS) is speech used to express hatred toward an individual or group of individuals based on characteristics such as race, religion, ethnicity, gender, country of origin, impairment, and gender preference. HS can be expressed in a variety of ways, not just through speech. Individuals or groups can also be targeted using written articles, blogs, stories, and posters.

There were over five billion users reaping the benefits of the internet worldwide as of April 2022, accounting for 63.1% of the total strength. Out of this, 4.7 billion people or 59% were using social media [1]. This indicates that life is inactive in the absence of the Internet. The current information society is based on the Internet, which connects billions of people globally. China, India, and the United States have more Internet users than any other nation. China had over a billion Internet users as of February 2022, while India had approximately 658 million. Both nations still have massive populations that are not connected to the Internet.

Due to the extensive use of the Internet, a large number of users are having accounts on social media platforms such as Facebook, Twitter, Instagram, WhatsApp, Snapchat, Line, Quora, and YouTube. Also, there exists a great chance for the users to express their opinion on hot topics via blogs and discussion forums. Social media platforms are a great way for anyone to express themselves and have a big impact. This has the unintended consequence of increasing HS.

Computational Intelligence Methods for Sentiment Analysis in Natural Language Processing Applications.
DOI: https://doi.org/10.1016/B978-0-443-22009-8.00009-4

HS on social media can take various forms depending on the media. Examples include posts and reels in Facebook, tweets in Twitter, videos and comments in YouTube, and so on. Anonymity allows users to create fake profiles and pseudonyms without revealing any personal information.

In India, the Supreme Court, on October 2022, directed three state governments to promptly register criminal cases against the perpetrators without waiting for a complaint to be filed, describing HSes as a "very serious issue" [2]. There are numerous active HS cases involving discrimination issues involving politics, education, culture, and so on. Social media platforms such as YouTube and Twitter are constantly updating their policies to deal with HS cases, such as locking and suspending user accounts. To combat HS issues, these platforms have utilized machine learning algorithms and frameworks for the detection of HS. However, HS is still a problem on the internet, and it appears to be getting worse day by day. As a result, there is a growing need to find better solutions to this problem.

The proposed work will provide a suitable solution for classifying HS from offensive speech by utilizing metaheuristics and the LSTM method. Researchers primarily used two methodologies to detect HS on social media platforms: (1) the traditional machine learning approach and (2) the deep learning–based approach.

Algorithms that learn from examples are the core of the artificial intelligence subfield known as machine learning [3]. Machine learning techniques must be used for the process of classification in order to learn how to categorize instances from problem domains [4]. Classifying speech as "hate speech" or "agreeable speech" is a simple example. There are many different types of classification tasks that you may encounter in machine learning, as well as specialized modeling approaches for each. Classification is a supervised learning strategy used in machine learning and statistics, where a computer software learns from data and creates new observations or categorization.

Deep learning is a machine learning technique that teaches computers to do what humans do instinctively: learn by doing [5]. A deep learning model is intended to examine data indefinitely using a logical structure similar to how a human would draw conclusions. Deep learning applications use a layered structure of algorithms known as an artificial neural network, and its design is inspired by the biological network of neurons in the human brain, resulting in a learning system far more capable than standard machine learning models. It is achieving results that were previously unthinkable. In deep learning, a computer model learns to carry out classification tasks directly from images, text, or sound. In some cases, deep learning algorithms can even exceed humans in terms of accuracy.

The next section gives a detailed description about the research works related to HS detection using machine learning and deep learning techniques.

13.2 Literature survey

The problem of finding Internet movies that unintentionally provoke angry remarks from viewers while lacking any hateful content is addressed in VulnerCheck [6]. Simply labeling videos that promote hatred as such and taking them off from sharing websites is insufficient. VulnerCheck is an end-to-end supervised learning strategy that investigates the structure and semantics properties of audience comment networks in order to accurately distinguish between hateful and hate-free videos and those that are prone to inciting hatred. It uses logistic regression, support vector machines, multilayer perceptrons, boosting, and ensemble approaches for classification. VulnerCheck is resistant to skilled content producers who make unpleasant movies in order to get around current content regulation since it is content-agnostic in the sense that it does not assess the substance of the video.

To identify HS from Twitter data, Soumitra Goush [7] presented a stacked ensemble-based hate speech classifier (SEHC). They created and trained three basic and two stacked deep learning—based models, namely CNN, BiLSTM network, BiGRU network, stacked CNN BiGRU, and stacked CNN BiLSTM. Classification results for HS detection are obtained using an ensemble system comprised of the five models mentioned above, outperforming existing techniques. However, SEHC is not dynamic and cannot be applied to real-world scenarios. The method outlined in [8] employs emotive and semantic factors, as well as the most prevalent unigrams and HS patterns, to classify tweets as hateful, offensive, or clean.

To identify the existence of HS, a pattern-based Deep HS [9] detection model with a dual-level attention mechanism was presented. To improve representation by deleting unnecessary features, the model computes dot product attention rather than concatenating the features. By associating them with specific portions of speech, aspect terms are extracted at the first level of attention. Extraction of sentiment polarity for the purpose of pattern creation is part of the second degree of attention. This pattern serves as a vital tool in HS detection.

In the multimodal approach [10], classical machine learning algorithms such as Support Vector Machine, Random Forest, Logistic Regression, AdaBoost Classifier, K-nearest neighbor, Nave Bayes Classifier, and Decision Tree were used. Following the execution of all individual classification algorithms, a multimodal approach employs an ensemble learning hard voting method or majority voting to obtain the final classification output combining the individual detections.

The eXtreme Gradient Boosting learning algorithm was chosen for the MetaHate model's HS detection process [11]. HCovBi-Caps is a deep neural network model for HS detection that integrates the convolutional, BiGRU, and capsule network layers [12]. Input, embedding, and convolutional layers are combined with BiGRU and capsule networks, followed by dense and output layers.

A metaheuristic algorithm [13] is a search procedure that seeks a good solution to a complex and difficult-to-solve optimization problem. In this world of limited resources, finding a near-optimal solution based on imperfect or incomplete information is critical (e.g., computational power and time). Metaheuristics, unlike optimization algorithms, iterative methods, and simple greedy heuristics, can frequently find good solutions with less computational effort. There are numerous problems that are impractical to solve using an optimization algorithm to achieve global optimality.

In the solution proposed by [14], for preprocessing, the basic natural language processing (NLP) steps were followed. Bag of Words (BoW), Term Frequency (TF), and document vector were used to extract features (Word2Vec). For the classification task, ecology-based meta-heuristic algorithms such as Ant line Optimization and Moth Flame Optimization were used. The ALO and MFO algorithms outperformed machine learning methods in terms of accuracy, sensitivity, precision, and f-score. To address the conventional machine learning and deep learning–based models, researchers created a variety of models. [15–22].

Harmony Search Algorithm (HSA) [23] is a kind of metaheuristic search algorithm that attempts to mimic musicians' improvisation process in order to find a pleasing harmony. The three operators of the HSA—random search, harmony memory (HM) considering rule, and pitch adjusting rule—were drawn from the musical performance process. The exploration and exploitation strategies used by the three operators set the HSA apart as a unique metaheuristic algorithm.

13.3 Methodology

In this section, the proposed work for HSD is discussed in detail with its modules. Fig. 13–1 shows the framework of the HSD system. The data given to the proposed system perform a binary classification problem where tweets are classified as either HS or Non-Hate Speech (NHS). The HSD problem can be stated as follows: Suppose there are N tweets such as $\{A_1, A_2, \ldots, A_N\}$ with M categories such that $\{B_1, B_2, \ldots, B_M\}$. Then the tweets can be categories as B_1 or B_2 where B_1 represents HS and B_2 represents NHS. The modules in the proposed work are discussed as follows:

13.3.1 Data preprocessing and feature engineering

The main goal of preprocessing is to construct a document vector by convert textual data to numerical form. Many preprocessing techniques such as Tokenization, Removing

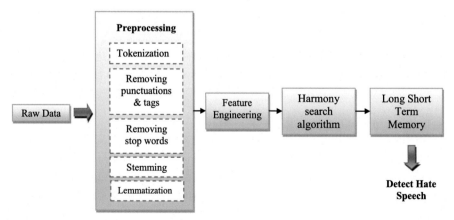

FIGURE 13–1 Proposed hate speech detection framework.

unnecessary punctuations and tags, removing stop words, stemming, Lemmatization are performed to the input data. To effectively anticipate the HS, robust feature engineering is used, which includes TF weighting, Bag of Word, TF-IDF, word embedding, and construction of document matrix. By using the TF value, the most repeating terms were determined, thus producing a document vector. An NLP technique called BoW retrieves all word roots from each piece of data. Word origins in each phrase were recorded. The procedure of extracting features from datasets was thus finished. The HSD problem is then treated as a classification problem to detect for HS or NHS.

13.3.2 Harmony search algorithm

Metaheuristic optimization algorithms can be effective tools for overcoming the difficulties of complex optimization problems. The improvisation process, which was first devised in [24], served as inspiration for the metaheuristic optimizer known as HS. A fixed number of musicians attempt to tune the pitch of their instruments to achieve pleasing harmony during the music improvisation process (best state). A unique relationship between many sound waves with different frequencies characterizes a harmony in nature.

Esthetic evaluation can help to raise the harmony's quality. Continuous practice and efforts of musicians play a vital role in the improvisation step of finding the best harmony process. There lies a good correlation between this process with the optimization processes. Finding the global optimum of the objective function (maximization or minimization) within a set of design constraints is the ultimate objective of an optimization problem. A solution vector corresponds to the choice variables in an optimization problem. The solution vector is updated during each iteration until the overall optimum is attained.

Harmony denotes a feasible solution in the HSA, and the decision variable of the solution corresponds to a note. HSA includes a HM that stores a fixed number of harmonies (N).

The definition of this optimization problem is as follows:

$$\text{Minimize or Maximize } f(x_1, x_2, \ldots, x_d)$$

where "f" is the fitness function, $x_i (i = 1,2,\ldots,d)$ is decision variable i and d denotes the problem dimensions.

In order to implement HS algorithm for optimization, the following steps should be used and it is illustrated in Fig. 13−2:

Step 1: Initialize the HM.
Step 2: Improve the HM
Step 3: Include/exclude the improved harmony in the HM.
Step 4: Repeat Steps 2 and 3 until the stopping criterion is met.
Step 5: The best harmony stored in HM is returned as the optimum solution.

Step 1: Initialize harmony memory
In HSA, N harmonies are produced randomly and stored in HM. The value of "N" depends on the number of features we are interested in for the process of HS detection.

Each harmony in the memory can be specified by a vector, utilizing the decision variable $HM_i = [h_{i,1}, \; h_{i,2} \ldots \; h_{i,d}]$. Then the fitness function is calculated for each harmony. Mathematically, harmony in the HM can be represented using the following equation:

$$h_{i,j} = l_j + \text{rand} \times (u_j - l_j) \, i = 1, 2, \ldots, N, \text{and} \, j = 1, 2, \ldots, d \qquad (13-1)$$

where l_j and u_j are the lower and upper bounds of decision variable j, respectively, and rand is a random number with uniform distribution from [0 1].

Step 2: Improve the Harmony Memory

Utilizing every harmony already in existence, a new harmony is created. It is actually a two-stage process. In stage 1, a random number (r) is generated in the range 0 and 1 by following the uniform distribution, and if $(r > \text{HMCR})$, then the decision variable for the new harmony is generated by following Eq. (13−1). Else, the decision variable for the new harmony will copy a value from the harmonies already available as part of the HM. Here, HMCR denotes HM Considering Rate, and it lies between 0 and 1.

In stage 2, the pitch adjustment technique is used to eliminate local optimum issues. A random number (r) is generated in the range 0 and 1 by following the uniform distribution, and if $(r = \text{PAR})$, then the decision variable for the new harmony is generated by following Eq. (13−2). Otherwise, nothing would change. Here, PAR denotes Pitch Adjusting Rate, and it lies between 0 and 1.

$$h_{new,j} = h_{new j} + bw \times (\text{rand} - 0.5) \times |u_j - l_j| \qquad (13-2)$$

The bandwidth is denoted by bw, which is between 0 and 1. It regulates the size of the movement's steps. Using large bw values increases the distance between the new value and the value in the HM. As such, we can customize the global and local searches based on the bw value.

Step 3: Include/Exclude the improved harmony in the harmony memory.

At the end of step 2, a new feasible harmony is available as part of the HM. The fitness function is calculated for the newly generated harmony, and if it is better than the worst harmony available as part of the HM, then the newly generated harmony will be included in the HM by replacing the worst. Otherwise, it will be discarded.

According to the fitness score assigned to the features, features will be selected. The selected features from this stage will serve as input to the LSTM network for the purpose of detecting HS.

13.3.3 LSTM

Long-Short Term Memory is abbreviated as LSTM. LSTM is a type of recurrent neural network that outperforms traditional recurrent neural networks in terms of memory [25]. LSTMs perform far better when it comes to learning specific patterns. Like any other neural network, LSTM contains a number of hidden levels, and when each layer is traversed, each cell retains information that is pertinent while discarding information that is not.

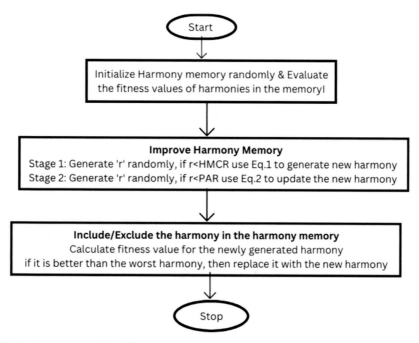

FIGURE 13–2 Flowchart representing HSA.

Unlike traditional feed-forward neural networks, LSTM has feedback connections. It can not only handle single data points (such as images), but also entire data streams (such as speech or video). LSTM can be used for tasks such as text classification including character recognition, handwriting recognition, and speech recognition.

13.3.3.1 LSTM organization structure
Four neural networks, as well as a large number of memory cells connected in a chain topology, make up the LSTM. A cell, an input gate, an output gate, and a forget gate make up a standard LSTM unit. The cell remembers values across arbitrary time intervals, and three gates regulate the flow of information into and out of the cell and it is shown in Fig. 13–3.

The gates control memory, whereas the cells store information. Three entries are included:

- **Input Gate:** Which input values are used to modify the memory is decided by this gate. It is decided by the sigmoid function whether 0 or 1 values are allowed. Additionally, the data are given weight using the tanh function, which rates its significance on a scale of -1 to 1.

$$i_t = \sigma(W_i.[h_{t-1}, x_t] + b_i) \qquad (13-3)$$

$$C_t = \tanh(W_c.[h_{t-1}, x_t] + b_c) \qquad (13-4)$$

- **Forget Gate:** Sigmoid function is used by the forget gate. It is used to filter the details that should be omitted from the block. For each number in the cell state C_{t-1}, it looks at the preceding state (h_{t-1}) and the content input (X_t) and produces a number between 0 (for omission) and 1 (for preserving).

$$f_t = \sigma\left(W_f.[h_{t-1}, x_t] + b_f\right) \tag{13-5}$$

- **Output Gate:** The input and memory of the block determine the output. The sigmoid function decides which values, 0 or 1, are permitted to pass. The tanh function additionally establishes which values can pass through 0 and 1. Additionally, the tanh function gives the provided values weight by multiplying their significance on a scale of -1 to 1 and the result of the sigmoid.

$$O_t = \sigma(W_o[h_{t-1}, x_t] + b_o) \tag{13-6}$$

$$h_t = O_t \times \tanh(C_t) \tag{13-7}$$

13.3.3.2 LSTM steps
The working of LSTM consists of four steps:

- Information from a prior time step that has to be forgotten is identified using the forget gate.
- New information is sought for updating cell state using the input gate and tanh.
- The data from the two gates mentioned above are used to update the cell state.
- Informational elements include the output gate and the squashing process.

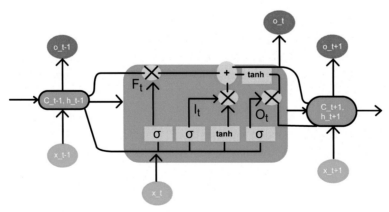

FIGURE 13–3 LSTM network.

13.4 Experiments and results

13.4.1 Datasets used

Three separate real-world datasets were utilized as shown in Table 13−1 for classifying the speech as HS or NHS. 70% of the dataset was utilized for training in each experiment, and 30% was used for testing. The circumstances for running each algorithm were identical. Dataset1 comprises tweets from Twitter that contain roughly 25K instances of HS and foul language. This dataset has three classes. These include offensive language, HS, and neither [26]. The dataset is written in English.

The dataset2 contains about 4K comments that are rude to other people. These opinions were gathered from online discussion forum pages. There are two classes in this dataset: insult and noninsult [27]. The information gathered from open web forum pages is in English.

About 13K tweets make up Dataset 3 contents. There are two classes in this dataset, which also contains HS directed against migrants and women. One of the most well-known online social networks, Twitter, serves as the primary source of this data [28]. If there was hatred for immigrants and women in these tweets, they would be classified as hateful. They were classified as not-hate-full if not. There are tweets in both English and Spanish in this collection. The Spanish comments were not included in BoW, which was only conducted in line with English.

13.4.2 Model performance measure

To measure the success of the proposed model various classification metrics such as precision, recall, F1- score, accuracy, and sensitivity are used, and it is given in Table 13−2.

Table 13–1   Datasets used.

Name of dataset	Source of dataset	Contents	Size of dataset	Classes
Dataset 1	Twitter	Hate speech and offensive language	25,000	3
Dataset 2	Web Forum	Community directed personal insults	4000	2
Dataset 3	Twitter	Hate speech against immigrants and Women	13,000	2

Table 13–2   Performance measures used.

Performance measures used	Complexity metrics
$\text{Precision} = \frac{TP}{TP+FP} \times 100$	TP: True positive
$\text{Recall} = \frac{TP}{TP+FN} \times 100$	TN: True negative
$\text{F1} - \text{score} = 2 \times \frac{\text{Precison} \times \text{Recall}}{\text{Precison} + \text{Recall}} \times 100$	FP: False positive
	FN: False negative
$\text{Accuracy} = \frac{TP+TN}{TP+TN+FP+FN} \times 100$	

13.4.3 Results for hate speech and offensive language in Twitter dataset 1

The performance of the proposed method is assessed by comparing the simulation results of the existing optimization algorithms such as Particle Swarm Optimization (PSO), Ant Colony optimization (ACO), Bee Colony optimization (BCO) with our proposed method (HSA) in dataset1. Table 13−3 shows experimental results obtained using four optimization algorithms, and the proposed method achieves best precision, recall, F1-score, and accuracy. Table 13−4 shows the experimental results obtained using four classification techniques, and the proposed method achieves best precision, recall, F1-score, and accuracy.

13.4.4 Results for community-directed personal insult

Table 13−5 shows experimental results obtained using four optimization algorithms in dataset 2, and the proposed method achieves best precision, recall, F1-score, and accuracy. Table 13−6 shows the experimental results obtained using four classification techniques in dataset 2, and the proposed method achieves best precision, recall, F1-score, and accuracy.

Table 13–3 Experimental results of various optimization algorithms on dataset 1.

Method	Precision (%)	Recall (%)	F1-Score (%)	Accuracy (%)
PSO	92	94	93	95
ACO	91	92	93	94
BCO	92	91	93	94
HSA	96	96	97	97

Table 13–4 Experimental results of various classification algorithms on dataset 1.

Method	Precision (%)	Recall (%)	F1-Score (%)	Accuracy (%)
NN	82	80	83	84
BP	86	84	82	84
SVM	93	94	96	95
LSTM	97	98	97	98

Table 13–5 Experimental results of various optimization algorithms on dataset 2.

Method	Precision (%)	Recall (%)	F1-Score (%)	Accuracy (%)
PSO	94	93	94	93
ACO	95	94	93	95
BCO	91	94	92	92
HSA	96	98	97	97

Table 13–6   Experimental results of various classification algorithms on dataset 2.

Method	Precision (%)	Recall (%)	F1-Score (%)	Accuracy (%)
NN	89	89	87	88
BP	88	87	89	89
SVM	94	95	94	97
LSTM	98	97	98	98

Table 13–7   Experimental results of various optimization algorithms on dataset 3.

Method	Precision (%)	Recall (%)	F1-score (%)	Accuracy (%)
PSO	91	91	93	91
ACO	92	91	93	94
BCO	92	91	91	92
HSA	96	97	97	98

Table 13–8   Experimental results of various classification algorithms on dataset 3.

Method	Precision (%)	Recall (%)	F1-score (%)	Accuracy (%)
NN	82	83	85	84
BP	86	84	87	89
SVM	92	96	94	95
LSTM	97	98	98	98

Table 13–9   Comparison of the proposed model with existing models.

Method	Dataset 1	Dataset 2	Dataset 3
Kamble and Joshi [29]	83	87	81
Warner and Hirchberg [30]	72	68	71
Proposed method	98	96	97

13.4.5 Results for hate speech against immigrants and women

Table 13–7 shows experimental results obtained using four optimization algorithms in dataset 3, and the proposed method achieves best precision, recall, F1-score, and accuracy. Table 13–8 shows the experimental results obtained using four classification techniques in dataset 3, and the proposed method achieves best precision, recall, F1-score, and accuracy.

13.4.6 Comparison with existing methods

Table 13–9 shows the results of comparison of the proposed method with existing methods. The table shows that the proposed method performs better than the other methods. Fig. 13–4 displays the findings of the comparison between the proposed work and the existing approaches.

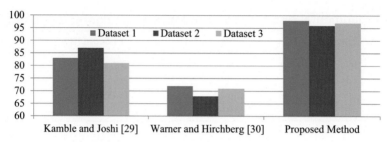

FIGURE 13–4 Comparison of the existing method with the proposed method.

13.5 Conclusion

This chapter focuses on the HSD problem, which poses a serious risk to social networks. Before they spread to other users, HS on social networks that is directed against a community or group should be stopped. The proposed work incorporates HSA for optimization. The HSA is a metaheuristic algorithm that mimics the actions a musician to produce the ideal harmony. It has been used to address a variety of optimization challenges in real-world contexts since it is easier to implement than other metaheuristics. It might achieve a balance between exploration and exploitation throughout a search. Deep Learning–based approach called LSTM is used for classification of the speech as HS or NHS. Three different optimization algorithms such as PSO, ACO, and BCO are compared with the proposed HSA. HSA achieved best performance results as it worked efficiently using the search technique. Moreover the convergence rate of HSA was high when compared with other algorithms. Three different classification algorithms such as NN, BP, and SVM are compared with the proposed LSTM. The experiments conducted show that LSTM produces best result and outperforms other classification technique. In future, we planned to conduct research by streaming all HS content from social media.

References

[1] Internet and social media users in the world. Statista, <https://www.statista.com/statistics/617136/digital-population-worldwide/>, 2022

[2] <https://www.indiatoday.in/law/supreme-court/story/supreme-court-calls-for-action-against-hate-speech-irrespective-of-religion-2288135-2022-10-21>.

[3] B. Alic, L. Gurbeta, A. Badnjević, Machine learning techniques for classification of diabetes and cardiovascular diseases, in: 2017 6th Mediterranean Conference on Embedded Computing (MECO), 2017, pp. 1–4, Available from: https://doi.org/10.1109/MECO.2017.7977152.

[4] R. Muhamedyev, K. Yakunin, S. Iskakov, S. Sainova, A. Abdilmanova, Y. Kuchin, Comparative analysis of classification algorithms, in: 2015 9th International Conference on Application of Information and Communication Technologies (AICT), 2015, pp. 96–101, Available from: https://doi.org/10.1109/ICAICT.2015.7338525.

[5] F. Ertam, G. Aydın, Data classification with deep learning using Tensorflow, in: 2017 International Conference on Computer Science and Engineering (UBMK), 2017, pp. 755−758, Available from: https://doi.org/10.1109/UBMK.2017.8093521.

[6] L. Shang, D.Y. Zhang, M. Wang, D. Wang, VulnerCheck: a content-agnostic detector for online hatred-vulnerable videos, in: 2019 IEEE International Conference on Big Data (Big Data), 2019, pp. 573−582, Available from: https://doi.org/10.1109/BigData47090.2019.9006329.

[7] S. Ghosh, A. Ekbal, P. Bhattacharyya, T. Saha, A. Kumar, S. Srivastava, SEHC: a benchmark setup to identify online hate speech in English, in: IEEE Trans. Computat. Soc. Syst., Available from: https://doi.org/10.1109/TCSS.2022.3157474.

[8] H. Watanabe, M. Bouazizi, T. Ohtsuki, "Hate speech on Twitter: a pragmatic approach to collect hateful and offensive expressions and perform hate speech detection, IEEE Access. 6 (2018) 13825−13835. Available from: https://doi.org/10.1109/ACCESS.2018.2806394.

[9] P. Sharmila, K.S.M. Anbananthen, D. Chelliah, S. Parthasarathy, S. Kannan, "PDHS: pattern-based deep hate speech detection with improved tweet representation, IEEE Access. 10 (2022) 105366−105376. Available from: https://doi.org/10.1109/ACCESS.2022.3210177.

[10] F.T. Boishakhi, P.C. Shill, M.G.R. Alam, Multi-modal hate speech detection using machine learning, in: 2021 IEEE International Conference on Big Data (Big Data), 2021, pp. 4496−4499, Available from: 10.1109/BigData52589.2021.9671955.

[11] D. Kyrollos, J. Green, MetaHate: a meta-model for hate speech detection, in: 2021 IEEE International Conference on Big Data (Big Data), Orlando, FL, 2021, pp. 2496−2502.

[12] S. Khan, et al., HCovBi-caps: hate speech detection using convolutional and bi-directional gated recurrent unit with capsule network, IEEE Access. vol. 10 (2022) 7881−7894. Available from: https://doi.org/10.1109/ACCESS.2022.3143799.

[13] P. Agrawal, H.F. Abutarboush, T. Ganesh, A.W. Mohamed, "Metaheuristic algorithms on feature selection: a survey of one decade of research (2009−2019, IEEE Access. 9 (2021) 26766−26791. Available from: https://doi.org/10.1109/ACCESS.2021.3056407.

[14] C. Baydogan, B. Alatas, Metaheuristic ant lion and moth flame optimization-based novel approach for automatic detection of hate speech in online social networks, IEEE Access. 9 (2021) 110047−110062. Available from: https://doi.org/10.1109/ACCESS.2021.3102277.

[15] S. Haseena, T. Revathi, Soft biometrics based face image retrieval using improved grey wolf optimization, IET Image Process. 14 (3) (2020) 451−461.

[16] S. Haseena, T. Revathi, Deep learning-based facial expression recognition using improved cat swarm optimization, J. Ambient. Intell. Humaniz. Comput. 12 (2) (2020) 3037−3053.

[17] S. Haseena, S. Saroja, A fuzzy approach for multi-criteria decision making in diet plan rankin system using cuckoo optimization, J. Neural Comput. Appl. 34 (16) (2022). Available from: https://doi.org/10.1007/s00521-022-07163-y. March.

[18] S. Haseena, S. Kavi Priya, S. Saroja, R. Madavan, M. Muhibbullah, U. Subramaniam, Moth flame optimization for early prediction of heart diseases. J. Comput. Math. Methods Med.

[19] S. Haseena, S. Saroja, R. Madavan, A. Karthick, B. Pant, M. Kifetew, Prediction of the age and gender based on human face images based on deep learning algorithm, Comput. Math. Methods Med. 2022 (2022) 16. Available from: https://doi.org/10.1155/2022/1413597. Article ID 1413597.

[20] S. Haseena, S. Saroja, Human centered decision making for covid-19 testing center location selection—Tamil nadu a case study, J. Comput. Math. Methods Med. (2022) 13. Available from: https://doi.org/10.1155/2022/2048294. Article ID 2048294.

[21] S. Haseena, M.. Akshaya, M.. Hemalatha, M. Manoruthra, Mining frequent item sets on large scale temporal data, in: IEEE International Conference on Electronics, Communication and Aerospace Technology, March 2018.

[22] S. Haseena, M. Bharathi, M. Lekha, M. Padmapriya, Deep learning based approach for gender classification, in: IEEE International Conference on Electronics, Communication and Aerospace Technology, March 2018

[23] X.-S. Yang, Harmony search as a metaheuristic algorithm,", in: Z.W. Geem (Ed.), Music-Inspired Harmony Search Algorithm: Theory and Applications, 191, Studies in Computational Intelligence, Springer Berlin, 2009.

[24] Joong Hoon Kim, Harmony search algorithm: a unique music-inspired algorithm, Procedia Eng. 154 (2016) 1401−1405. Available from: https://doi.org/10.1016/j.proeng.2016.07.510. ISSN 1877−7058.

[25] Soufiane Belagoune, Noureddine Bali, Azzeddine Bakdi, Bousaadia Baadji, Karim Atif, Deep learning through LSTM classification and regression for transmission line fault detection, diagnosis and location in large-scale multi-machine power systems, Measurement Volume 177 (2021) 109330. Available from: https://doi.org/10.1016/j.measurement.2021.109330. ISSN 0263−2241.

[26] Kaggle.com, Detecting insults in social commentary. <https://www.kaggle.com/c/detectinginsults-in-social-commentary/overview>, 2015 (accessed 1.12.21).

[27] T. Davidson, D. Warmsley, M. Macy, I. Weber, Automated hate speech detection and the problem of offensive language, Proc. Int. AAAI Conf. Web Social Media 11 (1) (May 2017) 1−4.

[28] V. Basile, C. Bosco, E. Fersini, D. Nozza, V. Patti, F.M.R. Pardo, et al., SemEval-2019 task 5: multilingual detection of hate speech against immigrants and women in Twitter, in: Proc. 13th Int. Workshop Semantic Eval., 2019, pp. 54−63.

[29] N. Kalchbrenner, E. Grefenstette, P. Blunsom, A convolutional neural network for modelling sentences, 2014, arXiv:1404.2188. http://arxiv.org/abs/1404.2188.

[30] W. Warner, J. Hirschberg, Detecting hate speech on the world wide Web, in: Proc. 2nd Workshop Lang. Social Media, Jun. 2012, pp. 19−26.

Index

Note: Page numbers followed by "*f*" and "*t*" refer to figures and tables, respectively.

Printed in the United States
by Baker & Taylor Publisher Services